Credit and Village Society in Fourteenth-Century England

Credit and Village Society in Fourteenth-Century England

by
Chris Briggs

A British Academy Postdoctoral Fellowship Monograph

Published for THE BRITISH ACADEMY
by OXFORD UNIVERSITY PRESS

This book has been printed digitally and produced in a standard specification in order to ensure its continuing availability

OXFORD
UNIVERSITY PRESS

Great Clarendon Street, Oxford OX2 6DP

Oxford University Press is a department of the University of Oxford.
It furthers the University's objective of excellence in research, scholarship, and education by publishing worldwide in

Oxford New York

Auckland Cape Town Dar es Salaam Hong Kong Karachi
Kuala Lumpur Madrid Melbourne Mexico City Nairobi
New Delhi Shanghai Taipei Toronto

With offices in

Argentina Austria Brazil Chile Czech Republic France Greece
Guatemala Hungary Italy Japan South Korea Poland Portugal
Singapore Switzerland Thailand Turkey Ukraine Vietnam

Oxford is a registered trade mark of Oxford University Press in the UK and in certain other countries

Published in the United States by Oxford University Press Inc., New York

Reprinted 2011

ISBN 978-0-19-726441-6

Printed and bound in Great Britain by CPI Antony Rowe, Chippenham and Eastbourne

Cover illustration: Peasant figures *c.* 1340. Stained glass detail from the Lady Chapel of Ely Cathedral. Reproduced by kind permission of the Dean and Chapter. Photograph © Keith Barley.

For Becca

Contents

Figures, maps and tables

Figures

Maps

Tables

Acknowledgements

This book has its origins in a Cambridge Ph.D. thesis, funded initially by the Arts and Humanities Research Council, and completed in 2002 during a Junior Research Fellowship at Trinity College, Cambridge (2000–4). While at Trinity I began the additional research necessary to widen the book's scope, a process that I was able to complete through the award of a British Academy Postdoctoral Fellowship in 2003. Further funding for archival work was granted from the Ellen McArthur Fund, University of Cambridge. I am most grateful to all of these institutions for their support.

For permission to reproduce published material, I would like to thank Cambridge University Press (data in Figures 6.1 to 6.6) and the Pontifical Institute of Mediaeval Studies, Toronto (Table 2.5).

I thank the archivists of all the repositories listed in my bibliography for granting me permission to use the unpublished records in their care, and for the efficient way in which they dealt with my requests. Godfrey Waller and colleagues in the Manuscripts Department of Cambridge University Library, and Caroline Dalton, formerly archivist at New College, Oxford, deserve a special mention. The good humour and all-round helpfulness of all these people helped make my frequent trips to their archives a pleasure.

I am fortunate to have been based for much of the past decade within the Cambridge Group for the History of Population and Social Structure, now located in the Department of Geography. Richard Smith, the Group's Director, has been unfailingly supportive of my work since 1997. Like all his many students, I have benefited enormously from Richard's immense generosity with his time, and with his learning. Two other friends from the Group, Leigh Shaw-Taylor and Paul Warde, have also done a great deal to broaden my horizons and stimulate my thinking. Ever since our days in the 'attic' at 27 Trumpington Street, it has been a pleasure to puzzle over the workings of past agrarian societies in their company. Also at the Group, Peter Kitson has been exceedingly generous with his technical expertise, which helped me greatly in completing Chapter 4.

I am indebted to Christopher Dyer, who kindly acted as my Academic Editor on behalf of the Academy, and provided a host of helpful comments on earlier drafts. Tracy Dennison also read the book in draft and shrewdly pointed out ways I could improve it. Phillipp Schofield first drew my attention to the fact of credit's existence in the medieval village, and in a sense this book is simply an attempt to respond to questions he has posed, both in innumerable conversations, and in his pioneering writings. Several parts of the book were first presented as seminar papers and conferences. For encouraging me to think about the wider European picture, I am especially grateful to participants at the Comparative Rural History of the North Sea Area (CORN) meeting on credit at Ghent (2003), and at the credit sessions of the European Social Science History Association conference in Berlin (2004). Philip Stickler, of the cartographic unit, Department of Geography, University of Cambridge, drew the maps. By providing practical assistance, references, ideas, or permission to cite their unpublished work, many others have helped me produce this book. I particularly wish to thank Martin Allen, Elaine Clark, James Davis, Bill Day, John Drendel, Martin Heale, Jeremy Hill, Thijs Lambrecht, John Lee, Andrew Mackersie, François Menant, Craig Muldrew, Sheilagh Ogilvie, Xavier Soldevila Temporal, and Matthew Tompkins. Needless to say, however, the author bears sole responsibility for the arguments expressed, and for any errors.

The encouragement and support of my family has been invaluable in completing this book. Life is not always simple or easy for two working parents, and during the project's final stages my partner, Rebecca Denness, had to take on a bigger share than I would have wished of the work involved in looking after our boys, Laurence and Peter. She nonetheless remained an understanding sounding board for me throughout. As a small, doubtless inadequate, gesture to show how fortunate I feel for all I have shared with Becca these past twelve years, I dedicate this book to her.

Ely
February 2008

Note on measurements, money, and the citation of manorial court rolls

The most important contemporary units of measurement used in this book are those of area and volume. The acre (ac.), equal to 0.4 hectares, comprised 4 rods (r.). One rod comprised 40 perches (p.). Readers should be aware that the acres referred to in contemporary documents and in the text are customary acres, which were not necessarily exactly equivalent to modern statute acres. The quarter (q.), equal to 2.8 hectolitres, comprised 8 bushels (b.). The monetary system of the period was based on the pound (£) which contained 20 shillings (*s.*). The shilling contained 12 pence (*d.*)

References to unpublished manorial court documents are given by repository, then roll, then membrane, then date of court session, e.g. CUL, Q 1, m.1 (12 March 1291). A few uncertain dates are given by month and year only. Many membranes contain records of the proceedings of more than one session. A 'roll' in this context typically means a collection of individual membranes stitched together at the head. Where the membranes in a roll have been numbered by a modern archivist, those numbers are used. Where they have not been numbered in this way, the first membrane in the roll as it is opened up has been treated as number 1. Usually, that first membrane is the earliest in date.

Abbreviations

BL	British Library
Court Baron	Maitland, F.W., and Baildon, W.P. (eds.), *The Court Baron: being precedents for use in seignorial and other local courts, together with select pleas from the Bishop of Ely's court of Littleport* (Selden Soc., vol. IV, London, 1890)
CRO	Cambridgeshire Record Office
CUL	Cambridge University Library
LMA	London Metropolitan Archives
NCA	Oxford, New College Archives
Q	Queens' College Archive, Cambridge University Library
TNA	The National Archives
VCH Bucks.	*The Victoria history of the county of Buckingham*, ed. W. Page (4 vols. to date; London, 1905–)
VCH Cambs.	*The Victoria history of the county of Cambridge and the Isle of Ely*, ed. L.F. Salzman et al. (10 vols., London, 1938–2002)
WAM	Westminster Abbey Muniments

1

Introduction: rural credit

'Adam Cherl acknowledges that he owes Thomas Belle four shillings and six pence for a mare that he bought from him . . .' 'Robert le Carter makes complaint against John Albyn, saying that he should render him 21 shillings and three pence that he owes him, and the aforesaid John comes and acknowledges the debt . . .' 'It appears by an inquest jury that Hugh Ryvel unjustly detains two shillings from Chilman Spilman, and therefore Chilman shall recover the said debt . . .' 'It appears by the inquest jury in which Thomas Sperner, plaintiff, and Simon Makhayt place themselves in a plea of debt that the same Simon owes Thomas 12 pence . . .'[1] Texts beginning like these survive in their thousands on the long pieces of parchment which record the proceedings of medieval England's manor courts (manorial court rolls). Manor courts were private jurisdictions held by landlords and attended by their peasant tenants and other local people, and one of their functions was to hear and settle private lawsuits, many of which concerned debts. Each of the texts above records a separate debt dispute. Almost all of the people involved in these debts and in others like them are best described as peasants. Such court roll entries thus provide a window on the credit dealings of the medieval village. They form the primary basis of this book.

Anyone who is not a specialist in the economic and social history of this period would be forgiven for expressing surprise at the idea that medieval peasants were heavily involved in credit arrangements. The idea does not fit with a received view which sees the medieval peasant as a subsistence farmer largely uninvolved in the use of money, and lacking the need or the skill to participate in sophisticated economic transactions.[2] Knowledge among students and readers of history of the extent of lending and borrowing among medieval peasants is also limited because the detailed investigation of

[1] For the Latin originals of these texts, see, respectively, the manorial court rolls of Willingham, Littleport, Balsham, and Oakington; for these sources, see below. CRO, L1/177, m.15d (24 July 1383); CRO, R 93/96, m.19d (30 July 1324); LMA, ACC/1876/MR/02/002, m.5 (6 December 1322); CUL, Q 8, m.5 (4 October 1379). The Latin form of the unusual forename 'Chilman' is 'Chilmannus'.

[2] For a survey that shows the inadequacy of such a view, see Schofield, *Peasant and community*.

the phenomenon is a relatively recent, though expanding, area of research confined to a few specialist publications. It is, of course, well known that credit was in general an important feature of the medieval economy. The aspect of medieval credit use that has probably been studied most closely and over the longest period concerns the sophisticated arrangements practised by merchants as part of the trade in bulk and high-status goods, especially that operating internationally.[3] Furthermore, credit has always cropped up in many different areas of the historical literature of the middle ages, including those relating to Jews, the parish clergy, the gentry and nobility, women, petty traders, and the finances of ecclesiastical landlords and the Crown.[4] This reflects the fact that the need to borrow from time to time was widespread throughout society. However, it is only really in the past two decades that close attention to credit in the countryside has emerged. As a result, historians of many European regions have begun to show that credit, far from being the preserve of merchants, bankers, or monarchs, was also of fundamental importance to the ordinary villagers who made up the majority of the medieval population. It is now clear that in a typical year, peasants throughout Europe might, for example, sell animals or grain for a deferred payment, borrow from a fellow to pay taxes or to fund a marriage, or lease out land to pay off an existing obligation, thereby becoming involved in extensive and complex networks of credit.

The existence of large numbers of credit relationships within villages is amply demonstrated in the case of England by the long lists of manor court debt disputes. Yet in spite of a recent growth in research on this material, this is the first book-length investigation of credit in the countryside of medieval England.[5] Rural credit is clearly a subject that demands closer attention, however, if only because the prolific evidence of indebtedness implies that credit use was in some way crucial to the functioning of the agrarian economy. A study of the middle ages also allows one to investigate the effects of credit in a largely agricultural society often characterized by widespread

[3] For example, Unwin, 'London tradesmen'; Thomas (ed.), *Calendar of plea and memoranda rolls*; Beardwood (ed.), *Statute Merchant roll*; Salzman, *English trade*, Chapters 2 and 9. Much early research on mercantile credit was inspired by Postan's seminal articles 'Credit in medieval trade' and 'Private financial instruments', first published in 1928 and 1930 respectively. More recent studies of mercantile credit include Nightingale, 'Monetary contraction and mercantile credit'; Childs, '"To oure losse and hindraunce"'; Kermode, *Medieval merchants*, Chapter 7.

[4] On Jewish finance and credit, see Stacey, 'Jewish lending', and Mundill, *England's Jewish solution*. Other works considering credit include Bowers, 'From rolls to riches'; Given-Wilson, 'Wealth and credit, public and private'; Mate, 'Indebtedness of Canterbury Cathedral Priory'; Bell et al., *English wool market*.

[5] Classic earlier works on rural credit are Clark, 'English vill' and Clark, 'Medieval debt litigation: Essex and Norfolk'. More recently, Schofield has outlined a research agenda for rural debt: Schofield, 'L'endettement'; Schofield and Mayhew (eds.), *Credit and debt*.

poverty. As such, it also has contemporary relevance, given that so many now see the provision of 'microcredit' as an effective route out of poverty and towards lasting gains in living standards for millions of people in the less developed countries of today's world.[6]

The questions addressed by this book include the most obvious ones raised by the four short texts quoted at the start: who were the people involved, the creditors and debtors; and how and why did the debts come about? The book also assesses the changing availability of village credit in its various forms; discusses the terms and conditions attached to the relevant transactions; and analyses the role of credit in relations between individuals and between families. At all times, the findings on credit are used to shed light on wider questions relating to the changing rural world of the turbulent fourteenth century.

1.1 Changing views of credit in the pre-industrial economy

By thus considering credit's availability, character, uses, and effects, this study seeks to reach an overall verdict on the strengths and weaknesses of the English rural credit market in the fourteenth century.[7] In investigating 'strengths and weaknesses', particular attention is given to the question of how far the credit market had an impact on the lives of contemporaries. Central, too, is the question of whether or not that impact was beneficial in its net effects for credit market participants. To reach a verdict on such matters, of course, some comparison with equivalent pre-industrial markets in existence in other regions and periods is required, at least in so far as the available scholarship permits. For this reason, this book makes reference to studies of early modern England, and of continental Europe (especially France and Italy) in both the medieval and early modern periods, in an effort to give greater weight to its conclusions about medieval England.

Indeed, some account of existing historical work on pre-industrial European credit in regions and periods other than that investigated here is essential for introducing the present study and setting it in context. A number of recent studies dealing with the issue are instructive, not least because they have highlighted key questions to address when assessing the strengths and weaknesses of any agrarian credit market. For example, these works have

[6] From a vast literature which debates the successes and failures of microcredit, see, for example, Morduch, 'The microfinance promise'; Morduch, 'The microfinance schism'.

[7] The term 'credit market' is shorthand here for the totality of credit transactions existing in a rural society at any one time. No real market in credit, in the strict sense of the buying and selling of transferable credit instruments, existed in the English countryside at this date.

made the case that one must try to establish the degree to which credit was accessed on an impersonal rather than just a personal basis, since credit availability clearly remained restricted when it could only be secured locally through family or friends. Where the character of the credit given is concerned, the researcher's central aims should include discovering the scale of the amounts of capital made available, and the balance between short-term and long-term credit. With respect to the uses of agrarian credit, the most crucial objective is to determine how often credit was sought only as a last resort to meet consumption needs, rather than with a eye to adding to, or investing in, existing resources. Finally, when thinking about the effects of the credit market, one must ask how far the most obvious consequences of village credit mechanisms were the dispossession of the poor and the creation or perpetuation of social inequalities, rather than the achievement of increased productivity, more intensive exchange, or even economic growth. These questions, together with related problems, are pursued in this book.

Significantly, although recent attempts by historians to find answers to such questions in relation to European credit remain fragmentary, they point to a consensus. An older historiographical tradition has been identified, which saw credit before the rise of modern financial institutions as limited in its extent, and with only a sporadic impact upon individuals. This old view has now been rejected by several authors as an inadequate account of the available evidence. Although the revisionist view is most fully articulated in a publication concerning a major city—namely *Priceless markets* (2000), in which Hoffman, Postel-Vinay, and Rosenthal investigate the ways in which massive amounts of capital were mobilized through the Paris credit market between 1660 and 1870—these scholars and others have also made similar arguments emphasizing that credit structures in various agrarian settings of early modern Europe were more extensive and efficient than was previously supposed. The revisionist note is robustly sounded, for example, in Rosenthal's study of the credit instruments used in mid-eighteenth-century Nuits St George (Burgundy). There he remarks that 'for decades historians have either ignored or bad-mouthed rural credit in pre-industrial Europe. Some have assumed that there was no rural credit worthy of study before the late nineteenth-century arrival of banks. Others have viewed debt as merely a mechanism whereby peasants lost their property.'[8] In short, most current

[8] Rosenthal, 'Rural credit markets', 288. See also Hoffman et al., *Priceless markets*, 1–3; Postel-Vinay, 'Les relations de crédit'. Sreenivasan, *Peasants of Ottobeuren*, 179–95, puts credit at centre stage as part of a challenge to prevalent views of economic change (essentially the neo-Malthusian position of a delicate balance between population and resources in a world of unchanging technology), arguing that in southern Germany, dynamic credit and land markets expanded rapidly in the later sixteenth century, allowing people to adjust to the difficulties of population pressure.

research on European pre-industrial credit adopts an 'optimistic' position, and sees lending and borrowing as an important and dynamic element of agrarian societies in the period, frequently used for innovation and investment.[9] This position is most evident in the work of early modernists, though it is easily discernible among medievalists also.[10] It contrasts with an older 'pessimistic' position, which saw little sign of credit structures, and tended to view those that did exist as merely one of several forces leading to poverty cycles and subsistence crises.

Using court litigation records and probate documents, work on England between the sixteenth and eighteenth centuries has given substantial attention to credit in the countryside as well as in towns. Broadly speaking, this work presents a picture of credit's striking impact and varied effects that sits comfortably with the positions reached in the European work just discussed. Most notably, Muldrew has revealed the extremely high number of interpersonal credit ties in existence in the later sixteenth and seventeenth centuries, and has shown that most members of society were entangled in a complex web of such obligations. In spite of profound social fears about the accumulation of such long chains of credit, and the reliance upon trust these entailed, a system of largely oral credit was crucial to the economy's successful functioning in an era of coin shortage. Indeed, this system proved instrumental in driving the growing levels of consumption that characterized the expanding economy of the long sixteenth century.[11]

Identifying the status of parties to credit transactions has played a major role in forming the view of rural credit accepted by most historians of early modern England. In no sense does the view thus arrived at regard rural borrowing as a relatively exceptional occurrence in which a poor household typically became indebted to a rich one purely to remedy temporary shortages in essential consumption items. Rather, it is recognized that most members of a community borrowed with considerable frequency, and that they did so to fund many different aspects of production and exchange. Quite substantial rural people became indebted, as is shown, for example, by work on probate accounts, which suggests that heavy borrowing was frequently a

[9] A turning point in the emergence of the revisionist view was the appearance in 1994 of a special issue of the journal *Annales* on early modern credit networks. Brennan, 'Peasants and debt', provides a summary of the revisionist view, as well as a case study which sheds doubt on some of its positions.

[10] Zerner, 'Introduction', 3; for the inadequacy of seeing rural credit in central Italy as simply a story of peasant expropriation to the benefit of city-dwellers, see Gaulin and Menant, 'Crédit rural', 66–7; Menant, 'Niveaux et réseaux', makes particularly fully the case for a 'positive' view of credit as an agent of investment and expansion; and for the period *c.*1450–1660, Poulsen, 'Rural credit and land market', 203.

[11] Muldrew, *Economy of obligation*.

characteristic of seventeenth-century yeomen of relatively high inventoried wealth. This evidence provides support for the proposition that many recurrent rural debtors were in fact borrowing to expand their farming enterprises and to maintain a relatively high standard of living, rather than to secure subsistence.[12]

It was not just borrowing that was widely practised, since an equally significant feature of such agrarian credit networks was the lack of any pronounced tendency for local credit supplies to become concentrated in the hands of a few lenders. Most people extended credit in one form or another whenever they were able to, and such activity was not confined to persons of high status or wealth. Although it has also been brought out by more recent commentators, this feature was already being stressed by Holderness in the 1970s. In contextualizing the evidence of his sample of Lincolnshire probate inventories, Holderness provided a summary view of early modern credit, writing that

> inventories and wills do indicate that money-lending was widely dispersed in English agrarian society during the early modern period and that many individuals were both debtors and creditors at the same time. The mechanism of internal credit was not controlled by a banya or village Jew nor institutionalized in a recognisable local capital or money market, since nearly everyone with surplus cash appears to have let it out at interest on a private and personal basis.[13]

Holderness also considered it reasonable

> to postulate not only that the diffusion of money-lending in English village society was significant in preventing the growth of usurious monopolies, but that the distribution of credit among the different social categories, which could, on the face of it, be seen as merely fortuitous, obeyed a clearly defined and explicable logic within a well-developed and sophisticated credit system.[14]

Holderness clearly held that an informal system in which many different members of all social groups participated from time to time in the roles of both creditor and debtor was more than capable of generating an efficient and 'productive' credit market, and subsequent commentators have agreed.[15] It must also be stressed that these key features of early modern credit networks have also been identified for the period before 1500, particularly in Clark's study of Writtle (Essex), which remains the most substantial investigation of fifteenth-century rural credit. Clark too devoted much attention to the characteristics of participants in a system of credit whose main effect,

[12] Spufford, 'Credit in rural England', 904–8; also Spufford, 'Long-term rural credit', 222–3.
[13] Holderness, 'Credit in a rural community', 108.
[14] Holderness, 'Credit in English rural society', 105.
[15] Poole, 'Debt in the Cranbrook region'; Zell, 'Credit'.

she argued, was to expedite the flow of a diverse range of goods and services, and to ensure the success of local agriculture, trades, and crafts. Like those working on later periods, Clark found an absence of specialized lenders, and a lack of hard and fast divisions separating creditors from debtors in Writtle.[16]

1.2 Credit in rural England, 1275–1400

Current historical writing concerning pre-industrial rural credit in medieval and early modern Europe, and in England from the close of the middle ages, therefore exhibits a good deal of consensus, with most commentators pointing to a role for credit in the agrarian economy that was more significant, varied, and dynamic than might be anticipated either on an a priori basis, or in the light of scholarly opinions expressed at a time prior to the commencement of systematic research on the relevant documents. How, then, does the equivalent picture for England in the late thirteenth and fourteenth centuries compare?

Little has been written about rural credit in relation either to early modern England or to continental Europe. Writings about medieval English rural credit are if anything even smaller in number. Furthermore, very little indeed has been published on the half-century that followed the Black Death of 1348–9, so that when studies of fourteenth-century or indeed medieval credit are referred to here, this means in practice those that concern the later thirteenth and earlier fourteenth century. As well as being scarce, the existing literature on medieval English credit features numerous areas where the interpretations offered are tentative simply because insufficient detailed work has been done. Any overview of this literature therefore runs the risk of imbuing it with a greater certainty and coherence than is justified. Nonetheless, it may be argued that when a comparison is made between, on the one hand, the currently available picture of village credit in medieval England and, on the other, the picture already described pertaining to a wider set of pre-industrial European societies, the contrasts are just as striking as the similarities, if not more so. Indeed, the available studies of medieval England come rather close to the older view of pre-industrial credit identified and rejected by revisionist historians of European credit. This is because they tend to depict credit as a relatively intermittent feature of the rural economy which, in so far as it

[16] Clark, 'Medieval debt litigation: Essex and Norfolk', 109–10 (creditors only had limited number of clients); Clark, 'English vill', 262–70; see also McIntosh, 'Money-lending', especially 570–1.

had any lasting impact, served largely to exacerbate pre-existing economic difficulties.

Those who have considered the English evidence of peasant indebtedness have, perhaps inevitably, typically interpreted it in terms of an account of the later thirteenth and early fourteenth century which, although much elaborated and refined in recent decades, still has its roots in seminal writings by M.M. Postan published in the 1950s and 1960s. According to this account, the six or so decades that preceded the demographic disaster of the Black Death were essentially an era of agrarian crisis, overpopulation, and generally declining rural living standards.[17] Adoption of this framework when investigating credit has led, for example, to the interpretation of sudden upturns in debt litigation visible in particularly difficult years as a further symptom of poverty and disaster, similar to others that can be traced in sources from the period. It is also implied, if rarely explicitly stated, that most peasant credit was contracted out of short-term need to buy food, or to pay basic rents and dues. Aspects of this approach gain particularly full expression in a 1997 article by Schofield which, while building on earlier work that drew a strong connection between harvest failure, crisis land sales, and social polarization, is the first study to incorporate discussion of debt into the picture, though it must be emphasized that this exploration of Hinderclay (Suffolk) in the 1280s and 1290s is concerned specifically with processes at work during a period of high grain prices and heavy taxation, and that Schofield has elsewhere given attention to the operation of credit provision in periods when such extreme conditions were absent.[18]

Several other studies that touch on rural debt see indebtedness primarily as an index of the severe poverty that affected large sections of the pre-Black Death population. For example, Razi treats evidence of activity as a debtor as characteristic of the middling peasant who 'did not do well', and evidence of activity as a creditor as characteristic of the more successful middling peasant.[19] In general, moreover, there is pessimism about the difference that credit could make to the plight of rural households. Among those few commentators who have considered the issue, the credit system of the late thirteenth and early fourteenth century is thought insufficiently developed to serve properly the needs of borrowers, because it suffered from poor organization, a shortage of lenders willing to risk their surplus cash, and a tendency for loans to be withdrawn at crisis periods when they were most needed.[20]

[17] On the early fourteenth-century 'crisis', see, generally, Campbell (ed.), *Before the Black Death*.

[18] Schofield, 'Dearth'. For a discussion not restricted to crisis periods, see Schofield, 'L'endettement'. Schofield, 'Social economy', looks at credit at Hinderclay in the context of crisis between 1300 and 1320, years which include the Great Famine of 1315–17.

[19] Razi, *Life, marriage and death*, 79.

[20] Bailey, 'Peasant welfare', 243–4; see also Dyer, *Standards*, 185–7.

Credit relationships are also generally held to have reflected and re-inforced the profound social differentiation within the peasantry that is a widely acknowledged feature of the difficulties of the decades before 1349. There is, most importantly, a tendency to note that most creditors were rich peasants, while most borrowers were poorer peasants, with relatively little overlap.[21] A similar view is traceable as an aside to Campbell's recent novel argument that the falling living standards and rural congestion of the early fourteenth century had their most important roots in the inflexible tenurial conditions on which land was held. Campbell suggests that the most characteristic type of rural indebtedness in this period involved the chronic inability of smallholders to repay their debts, including the debts such persons had contracted simply in order to acquire the tiny holdings upon which they eked out their livelihoods.[22] The Russian word *kulak* has been quite widely adopted by historians of English village society in this period to describe a wealthy peasant, and it has been found that a characteristic role of such individuals was to act as a creditor. Some of these people lent on a large scale, and apparently displayed many of the features of the specialist moneylender, or 'usurer'.[23] It is assumed that such lenders profited from their credit activities, although information on this topic is hard to gather. However, this work has placed less stress on the possibility that long-term gains in productivity or income may have accrued to the borrowers in such relationships.[24] Instead, the implication of accounts of credit relations involving 'kulaks' appears to be that they were exploitative and 'unproductive', producing a situation akin in its deleterious effects to that which appears in Marx's description of 'usurer's capital' in feudal society.[25]

[21] Schofield, 'Dearth', 13–14; for this author's subsequent position on this point, however, see Schofield, 'Credit and the peasant land market', 793–5, which presents a more complex picture, discussing contexts in which wealthy as well as poor had occasion to borrow.

[22] Campbell, 'Agrarian problem', especially pp. 53–4, 63–4.

[23] For example, Schofield describes Hinderclay peasants Robert and William, sons of Adam, as 'veritable "kulaks"' who 'used the profit from the sale of crop surpluses both to invest in land and to lend to poorer villagers': 'Dearth', 12.

[24] The finding that 'a wealthier stratum of peasants were able to exploit the indebtedness of their poorer neighbours to accumulate larger holdings in periods of food shortage' has been recently highlighted as a significant conclusion of work on thirteenth- and fourteenth-century manorial debt litigation: Dyer, *Age of transition?*, 184.

[25] 'When considered in detail, the preservation or loss of the petty producers' conditions of production depends on a thousand accidental circumstances, and each such accident or loss means impoverishment and is a point at which the parasite of usury can seize hold. The peasant only needs one of his cows to die and he is immediately unable to repeat his production on the old scale. He falls prey to usury, and once in that position he never recovers his freedom.' Marx, *Capital, Volume III*, 734. As Hoffman and his co-authors comment, elements of the 'old view' of pre-industrial credit form a traditional component of Marxist views of the pre-capitalist world, with origins in passages like that cited above. Thus the 'old view' these authors reject is to be found not only in historical work of a neo-Malthusian character.

One leaves a review of the specialist literature, therefore, with the sense that, even in the most recent writing, fourteenth-century England has been perceived as quite different from other European societies before the Industrial Revolution in terms of the availability, character, uses, and effects of rural credit. Of course, it would be naive not to expect major differences when comparing an English village's credit market in 1300 with its counterpart of some three or four centuries later, and even more naive not to anticipate differences when comparing a medieval village's credit market with that of eighteenth-century Paris. However, the differences between medieval English rural credit and early modern English and European rural credit traceable in the current literature are not restricted to the specific features that one would most expect to change over the centuries, such as, say, the average size of loans. Rather, they extend to differences in the fundamental organization and purpose of the credit market.

It is also worth reiterating that a reading of the existing rural credit literature shows contrasts between England before 1349 and the contemporary Mediterranean world, rather than just between England before 1349 and the early modern period. The contrasts within medieval studies reveal themselves in the fact that the latest work on southern Europe stresses the links between the dramatic proliferation of credit around 1300, and the commercial growth in the countryside witnessed at the same time, something which, on the whole, equivalent work on England does not do.[26] This lack of any marked tendency in the English historiography to integrate the subject of credit into discussions of rural commerce during the long thirteenth century is notable. It is also surprising, because within Europe, it is medievalists working on England who have so far done most to highlight how far the rural economy of this period was affected by developments such as the dramatic expansion in the money supply, the proliferation of chartered markets, or the growth of urban demand.[27] Arguments that stress such factors are sometimes referred to collectively as the 'commercialization thesis'. In recent debates about the early fourteenth century, such arguments have gained ground as an alternative to the 'neo-Malthusian' approach, with roots in Postan's work, in which the key to the pre-Black Death economy lies in the balance between population and a largely finite and unchanging set of economic resources. As already noted, rural credit has been considered almost exclusively in the context of harvest failure and the crisis-sensitive land market, issues which have traditionally formed key evidence to support such a neo-Malthusian

[26] Drendel, 'Le crédit'; Redon, 'Conclusions'.
[27] Britnell, *Commercialisation*; Britnell, 'Commercialisation and economic development'.

view. Rural credit has not, on the whole, featured significantly in the 'commercialization thesis'.[28]

These issues are brought out clearly in a recent essay, in which John Drendel makes a plea to historians of medieval France to look to the approaches of English historiography as a route by which French scholarship on the medieval economy might escape from the rather stagnant interpretative framework in which it has been locked since the heyday of the *Annales* historians.[29] For Drendel, credit is a key example of a topic in medieval rural history where new evidence and approaches promise to do much to demonstrate the inadequacies of the traditional interpretative framework of French historiography. Drendel claims that under the influence of French historians of a neo-Malthusian persuasion, of whom Georges Duby was the most significant, credit was traditionally seen simply as one of the means by which an impoverished peasantry fought to keep alive on ever-diminishing landholdings, typically succumbing in the process to the 'parasitical' influences of bourgeois creditor or village usurer. In other words, the demographically driven approach of the *Annales* school gave rise in the French context to one version of exactly that 'old view' of credit that Hoffman, Postel-Vinay, Rosenthal, and others have deemed inadequate, and consequently have sought to overturn. Significantly, though, when Drendel turns to work on medieval English credit, he is obliged to report a shortage of relevant research and no clearly articulated alternative approach or interpretation of rural credit to substitute for that traditionally observed by the French historians. Given the account of the historiography offered above, this should not be surprising. In fact, as already intimated here, the currently available writings on England have much in common with those older French studies the continuing dominance of which Drendel wishes to question; that is, they generally accept the idea that credit's most significant attribute is to reflect a deterioration in peasant living standards in an epoch dominated above all by agrarian crisis and population pressure.

Part of the aim of this book is to investigate these apparent contrasts between England and other parts of pre-industrial Europe. It seeks to establish whether the differences are still clear once an unprecedentedly large quantity of manorial debt litigation material has been examined. Does such an investigation show that credit structures in the medieval English countryside did indeed perform a role that was fundamentally less diverse or dynamic

[28] For example, Masschaele, *Peasants, merchants and markets*, has relatively little to say about credit, even though it otherwise stresses the extent of commercialization in the countryside. For credit and the market after *c*.1400, however, see Dyer, *Age of transition?*, 175–90.

[29] Drendel, 'Commodities, credit and land'; for similar arguments, see also Drendel, 'Le marché de la terre', 429–31.

than those identified in contemporary Europe, or in the Europe of later centuries? Or alternatively, does fourteenth-century England's apparent peculiarity with respect to rural credit actually reflect the fact that the evidence studied to date is too small in quantity and has not been interpreted properly? In what follows, it is argued that both these propositions are true to varying degrees.[30]

1.3 The evidence and its limitations

For the period before 1400, private lawsuits of debt brought before manor courts offer by far the best source of information on village credit. Indeed, serious alternatives do not exist.[31] In particular, the probate inventories and accounts used to study rural credit in early modern England do not survive in any great numbers before 1500. Nor do medievalists working on England have anything equivalent to the registers of agreements witnessed and recorded by notaries (public scribes) which are the key source for both rural and urban credit in contemporary southern Europe.[32] Fortunately, however, given our reliance on them, and in spite of the shortcomings considered below, manorial court rolls and the debt information they contain can be used to explore most of the important questions concerning rural credit.

A medieval landlord held a manor court in order to supervise the running of his manor as an economic unit, and to track the activities of his peasant tenants.[33] Although such courts existed from an earlier period and are occasionally referred to in surviving sources, the first written records of manor court proceedings, or court rolls proper, date from the 1240s. However, court rolls do not survive in substantial numbers before the final quarter of the thirteenth century. Court sessions were attended by the court suitors, the most important group of whom were the lord's villein, or customary, tenants. Villeins were typically distinguished from free tenants by the fact that they owed labour services as well as money rent for their holdings, and were subject to a wide range of other burdens arising from their unfree status and tenure, one of which was the requirement to attend their landlord's manor

[30] For preliminary observations, see Briggs, 'Creditors and debtors'; Briggs, 'Credit and the peasant household economy'.

[31] For an indication of the potential of the records of village gilds (fraternities) for the study of credit, see Dyer, *Age of transition?*, 185–6. However, the survival of such records, as well as, perhaps, the actual participation of gilds in rural credit networks, is largely limited to the period after *c.* 1400.

[32] On notarial registers, see Menant and Redon (eds.), *Notaires et crédit*; Drendel, 'Notarial practice'.

[33] Razi and Smith (eds.), *Medieval society and the manor court*.

court (suit of court).[34] However, it is also common to find some free tenants among those obliged to attend the manor court by the terms on which they held land. Court rolls also frequently mention the participation in court business of persons other than manorial tenants, including people living outside the manor. The primary reason for the manor court's existence was the protection of the lord's interest, and this was reflected in the business it conducted. However, even court roll entries generated by seigniorial prerogatives also reveal much about the identity and affairs of villagers. This is particularly true of entries concerning the transfer of tenant land. Moreover, and most significantly for this study, villagers also made use of the lord's court to protect their own private interests, most obviously by conducting their own civil lawsuits of debt-detinue, trespass, and broken agreement.[35]

It is worth outlining the machinery by which such private debt disputes were resolved in manorial jurisdictions, and by which the related court decisions were enforced.[36] Unless the plaintiff lost his case, or chose not to continue with it once begun (non-prosecution), the lord did not charge him to use the court for debt litigation. An individual began a manorial debt case by informing a court official of his wish to sue, and relating the basic details of the action. After this initial step, the court then used its powers to effect the defendant's appearance in court, so that the claim against him could be answered. The steps taken to secure the defendant's appearance involved the appointment of pledges, or individuals who guaranteed to bring the defendant to court, and, if that failed, the seizure of the defendant's livestock or other goods. The court could also amerce (fine) the defendant or the pledges if he did not turn up in court. Implementing these measures was the responsibility of the court's officials. In theory, those officials could not seize a defendant's property if it lay outside the territory under the lord's manorial jurisdiction; that is, they could not 'distrain outside the fee'. The territory in question was usually quite small, as a result of the fact that there was frequently more than one manor, and more than one manor court, within each village or parish throughout those large swathes of England where manorial structures prevailed. At every session of the manor court, a report was made on the progress of each case, and, if necessary, further orders were issued with the aim of expediting the litigation process.

[34] For a convenient summary of the obligations of villeins, see Bailey (ed.), *English manor*, 26–37.

[35] Pleas of detinue, or withholding of goods or money, are treated in this study as indistinguishable from pleas of debt, in spite of possible legal differences. Hereafter, 'debt' means cases of both debt and detinue.

[36] For the contents of this paragraph and the next, see Briggs, 'Manor court procedures'; Briggs, 'Seigniorial control'; Briggs, 'Availability of credit'. This book uses the male personal pronoun purely for stylistic reasons. Women did of course lend and borrow but, as Chapter 4 shows, the great majority of village creditors and debtors were male.

Once the defendant appeared in court, the case could be terminated in one of a number of ways. A common method was to obtain permission to seek an out-of-court settlement, called a 'licence to agree' in the records. Alternatively, a case could be 'pleaded'. In this scenario, the defendant formally answered the plaintiff's claim in court, either admitting the debt, or denying it, following which the matter was put to a jury of villagers, or (more rarely) an oath-swearing ritual ('compurgation'). If the defendant was found liable, he would be amerced by the court, and a damages payment might be awarded to the plaintiff. Following this outcome, the court would also normally make an explicit order that the defendant should repay the outstanding debt to the plaintiff. Alternatively, the defendant might be exonerated, and the plaintiff ordered to pay an amercement. Crucially, once a decision in the plaintiff's favour had been made, the court normally undertook to enforce the payment of the outstanding debt, if the defendant initially failed to pay. Like the securing of the defendant's appearance, this enforcement of debt repayment was undertaken through seizure of the movable property by the court officials. In the language of the court record, this procedure was referred to as 'levying the debt to the use of the plaintiff'.

When it worked well, the machinery described above was highly effective in helping plaintiffs to recover their debts cheaply and quickly. The manor courts' power to seize debtors' goods gave them significant sanctions against individuals who refused to answer charges in court, or failed to repay debts which were found to be outstanding. Furthermore, most manorial officials responsible for carrying out court orders had the advantage of being responsible for jurisdictions that were quite small in terms of their spatial area. This factor helped them to carry out the sanctions on debtors quickly and effectively.

The machinery of manorial debt litigation and recovery has left its legacy in the thousands of entries relating to debt plaints scattered among court roll memoranda on a wide range of subjects. The vast majority of such entries concern debts which the plaintiff was seeking to recover following non-payment, and as such they become visible in the records for the first time at this point. Unlike European notarial registers, it was not normally the function of court rolls to create a record of new credit agreements at their inception, though some of the extremely rare examples of court roll 'recognizances' that did serve this end are discussed in later chapters.

Another key feature of the court roll debt entries that make up each individual lawsuit or plaint is that they come in two basic groups with respect to the amount of social and economic data they provide.[37] The first group com-

[37] For examples, see Appendix 1.

prises those entries which do no more than indicate that a debt plaint was in progress, and state the names of plaintiff and defendant. In most such entries the detail is sparse, either because the plaint was still at a preliminary stage and the appearance of both parties in court had not yet been secured, or because a 'licence to agree' had been awarded. By contrast, the second group of entries represent occasions on which a debt case was 'pleaded'. In addition to the names of the parties and the fact of a debt dispute, entries in this second group also describe the debt claimed, and sometimes give further details about the circumstances of the debt and its repayment. Not all debt plaints reached the pleaded stage, so this second group of entries is smaller than the first. Only the second group can be used to analyse the nature and size of debt obligations.

However, entries of the first type remain extremely useful, since in spite of their sparseness of detail they do demonstrate the existence of a credit relationship and, in giving the parties' names, the identity of its participants. Except where a particular plaint ends in a 'false claim' by the plaintiff or a court decision that a debt claimed was not in fact owed, all plaints are regarded in this study as representing bona fide creditor–debtor relationships. Crucially, even though many debt entries tell us little in themselves, the court rolls frequently contain many other references to the individuals named in the debt entry, thereby allowing the researcher to reconstruct those individuals' wealth and status. Additional information about creditors and debtors identified in the court rolls is also gleaned by making links with other sources, especially surveys of tenant landholding of various kinds, and lists of those paying royal taxes.

There are, however, various problems involved in investigating the social and economic history of rural credit on the basis of manorial debt plaints. Almost all reflect the difficulties of using a legal source to shed light on everyday relationships and, more specifically, the fact that the source in question is concerned only with litigation about unpaid debts. The first problem is that even the entries in 'pleaded' cases exclude details irrelevant to the legal process. So, typically, we may be told how much a debtor owed, but remain less well informed on the historically interesting questions of when, why, and on what terms he borrowed this sum. All the information extracted from the litigation records must therefore be interpreted with great care and with an attentive eye for what may be missing.

The second problem arises in attempting to reconstruct a village's entire credit market using, as one must, only those failed credit relationships that produced debt litigation in the documented manor court. There are at least three reasons why doing so might, in theory, produce questionable conclusions. First, it is possible that the debt disputes of people living near to the manor court do not appear in that court's surviving records because they were taken to an alternative law court that enjoyed jurisdiction over debt, but does not leave records. Second, the numerical relationship between the failed credit transactions that reached the manor court and the total body of transactions extant in the locality is not obvious, nor is change over time in that relationship. Finally, it is possible that certain types of credit relationship were more likely than others to become the subject of lawsuits, with the result that documented debt is not typical of the whole. For example, there may have been a stronger propensity to sue for large debts than for small ones. Given such considerations, is there not a danger that the unavoidable reliance on manorial debt litigation might produce an unacceptably incomplete or distorted picture of a community's credit network?

There is no doubt that the inherent incompleteness of the evidence offered by debt litigation does pose a challenge to some of this book's objectives, such as the assessment of the overall size of the credit supply in the communities studied (Chapter 6), or the comparison of the characteristics of creditors with those of debtors (Chapter 4). However, by incorporating explicit assumptions about the scale and significance of the missing information, and suggesting what the implications might be if those assumptions were changed, it is possible to strengthen the conclusions reached in these and other parts of the book.

Furthermore, it is possible to move beyond speculation with respect to the scale of some of the problems just mentioned. For example, little weight should be placed on the idea of an informal village credit market that is invisible to historians because its participants never bothered to use the manor court to settle their disputes as the sums involved were too insignificant. In particular, the fact that such a large proportion of recorded debt was for small sums of less than 1*s*., with many debts of just a few pence, suggests that the amount of petty credit escaping the attention of manor court litigation machinery was negligible.[38] Also, it is important to note the existence of debtors such as John de Upstone, who in 1311 at Balsham, after admitting owing to Geoffrey le Cuppere just 8*d*., had the consequent amercement payable to the court waived because of his poverty.[39] Evidence of such debtors serves to question the notion of a hidden network of quasi-charitable lending in which debt recovery from the very poor was achieved without recourse to the manor court.

It is also possible to show that our picture of credit in a particular village is not rendered grossly unreliable by any great tendency for residents of that village to bring their debt disputes to law courts of which the records are now lost. A related research project has explored the extent to which villagers in

[38] Section 2.3.
[39] LMA, ACC/1876/MR/02/001, m.3d (1 July 1311).

the Cambridge hinterland used alternatives to their own 'home' manor courts when suing others in debt and other civil actions.[40] This suggests that before the fifteenth century, individuals rarely sued their immediate neighbours outside the 'home' manor in any alternative jurisdiction. In addition, when an individual from the manor whose rolls are being studied ('manor X') was sued by a villager from elsewhere, that creditor tended to use the court of manor X, meaning that such cases stay visible to the researcher. Only where a resident of the documented village under study acted as creditor to a borrower living elsewhere is there any great chance of that relationship escaping the historian's attention, for the creditor would most likely have conducted the associated debt plaint in the debtor's 'home' manor court.[41]

In other words, in the fourteenth century, most debt disputes that arose in a village with surviving manorial court rolls and were settled by formal legal means will be documented in those rolls. One further point must be made, however, about the documentation of debts in sources now lost. This concerns the peculiarity of Balsham, one of the Cambridgeshire villages studied in this book. Balsham was the site of an active weekly market established by a royal charter, and the court rolls make frequent reference to the market.[42] One exceptional entry of 1322 records that the steward of the manor court had assigned two men, Roger le Dene and John Rose, 'to determine all pleas and attachments in the market on each day of the market'. It notes further that the steward had given the two men a roll, so that they might 'respond from court to court' concerning all profits arising from the hearing of those pleas.[43] One cannot prove conclusively that a separate series of rolls dedicated to the recording of pleas heard on Balsham market day was kept, but if it was, it no longer survives. This raises the possibility that some disputes about debts involving Balsham villagers are now lost, and that the debt litigation that we have in the surviving manorial court roll series gives an incomplete picture of credit use in the village, because it omits transactions in the market.[44] In the chapters that follow, the Balsham data is often analysed with

[40] The main alternatives were a manor court other than one's 'home' (own lord's) court, the church courts, borough (town) courts, the courts at hundred and county level, and the royal courts of common law.

[41] Briggs, 'Seigniorial control'; Briggs, 'Travelling'.

[42] Balsham's market charter was first granted to the bishop of Ely in 1245. I intend elsewhere to publish a study of use and regulation of this market.

[43] LMA, ACC/1876/MR/02/001, m.30d (29 January 1322). A steward presided over a manor court on behalf of the lord. While he had a significant influence on the court's business and its recording, the steward was not normally directly involved in making court judgments. The steward mentioned in this entry is presumably the individual who held this particular session of the Balsham manor court, named at the head of the roll as Nicholas de Cantebrigg.

[44] None of the debt cases in the extant Balsham rolls mentions a market. For comparison, see Smith, 'Periodic market'; on market courts, see Bailey (ed.), *English manor*, 237.

the proviso that it may consistently understate the overall size of the credit transactions, and perhaps also the diversity of credit use in that village.

The final problem facing a study of rural credit based on debt litigation concerns the fact that proper interpretation of data from litigation depends upon an adequate understanding of the legal functioning of manor courts in the sphere of debt. Village credit transactions were not made in a legal vacuum. Rather, they were made with one eye on the rules and machinery of the local manor court, which for most people was the institution most likely to be used to enforce broken contracts. Hence the form of credit arrangements, with regard, for example, to the mode of security employed, was in many respects determined by the principles recognized in the court when deciding whether to uphold a plaintiff's claim. Furthermore, the readiness with which people initiated debt litigation, and perhaps also the readiness with which they entered into credit relationships, was shaped by their view of their local manor court. Where individuals were optimistic that their local court functioned in a way that would help them achieve a quick and successful outcome if a credit relationship broke down, then this may have increased their willingness to give credit, and vice versa. Work on the social and economic evidence of rural credit therefore must consider the laws and procedures of manor courts relating to debt, which were not necessarily uniform across manors.[45] Although full-scale reconstruction of those laws and procedures is not attempted in this study but is reserved for another location, questions of law and their impact inevitably occur frequently in the discussion which follows.[46]

1.4 The villages studied

As is common in investigations of medieval agrarian history, this book is an analysis and comparison of evidence from a number of local studies. These are, of course, first and foremost explorations of particular series of manorial court rolls. It is only worth attempting a systematic examination of the information on credit and credit relationships provided by a particular set of manorial court rolls if those records meet certain criteria. First, the records

[45] Briggs, 'Manor court procedures'.

[46] The main output of the research project 'Private law and medieval village society: personal actions in manor courts, *c.*1250–*c.*1350' funded by Arts and Humanities Research Council grant PID number 10197/AID number 120209, begun October 2006, is a commentary on a selection of cases, co-authored by myself and Phillipp Schofield, to be published by the Selden Society. Using evidence from more than sixty court roll series, this commentary provides a comprehensive account of the laws and procedures of manor courts in debt and covenant (broken agreements), and among many other topics will give deeper consideration to issues mentioned in this book, such as security for debts, coverture, and damages.

must contain enough examples of debt litigation to justify serious study.[47] Second, they must constitute a relatively unbroken run over a fairly extended timespan. This is necessary to allow one, for example, to track suits that continued over several court sessions, and to study fluctuations in indebtedness over time. Finally, one should ideally choose court rolls that can be supplemented with a manorial survey or equivalent document of a type that reveals the arrangement and tenants of landholdings at a particular point in time, or, failing that, with a listing of taxpayers in the village concerned. Such sources are invaluable when seeking to situate individual creditors and debtors in the village hierarchy of wealth and status.

Essentially, this means that for a successful study of rural credit, only the best surviving sets of court rolls will do. In this respect this book is like any court roll study, whatever its particular focus, in which the aim is exhaustive analysis of all relevant extant information, rather than the selection of odd examples.[48] There are not many series of court rolls which meet all the necessary criteria for the systematic study of debt material, as outlined above. However, the records of five different courts have been selected for special attention as they display many of the necessary qualities, and the book is largely based on these. Four of the courts—Balsham, Littleport, Oakington, and Willingham—were situated in Cambridgeshire, while the last of them—Great Horwood—lay in Buckinghamshire (Map 1.1). Oakington was exceptional among the five, and unusual among manorial jurisdictions more generally, in that it dealt with the affairs of more than just a single manor. Collectively, therefore, because the Oakington rolls also cover its landlord's manors at nearby Cottenham and Dry Drayton, the five courts between them shed light on seven different manors.[49] (For convenience, Oakington, Cottenham, and Drayton are sometimes referred to hereafter as the 'Crowland villages', which is a reference to the lord of these manors, Crowland Abbey). Most of the seven manors dominated the villages in which they lay, even where they did not constitute the sole manor in the parish. Therefore their court rolls effectively allow us to reconstruct and to compare the credit networks of seven different villages.[50]

[47] For variation between court roll series in quantities of litigation, see Briggs, 'Manor court procedures', 524–6.

[48] For works that discuss these general requirements, see, for example, Razi, 'Toronto school's reconstitution'; Poos et al., 'Population history'.

[49] Except where specified otherwise, the discussion in the remainder of the book concerns these seven manors and villages, and five series of court rolls.

[50] In this period, a second (undocumented) manor court was active in Great Horwood in addition to the documented Newton Longville Priory court: Briggs, 'Seigniorial control', 415. It is possible that some of Horwood's debt business was heard in this second court rather than the priory's court. Dependence on the Oakington court rolls for information about Cottenham and Dry Drayton probably means that our picture of the credit networks of the latter two places is incomplete; for details, see Section 4.2 below.

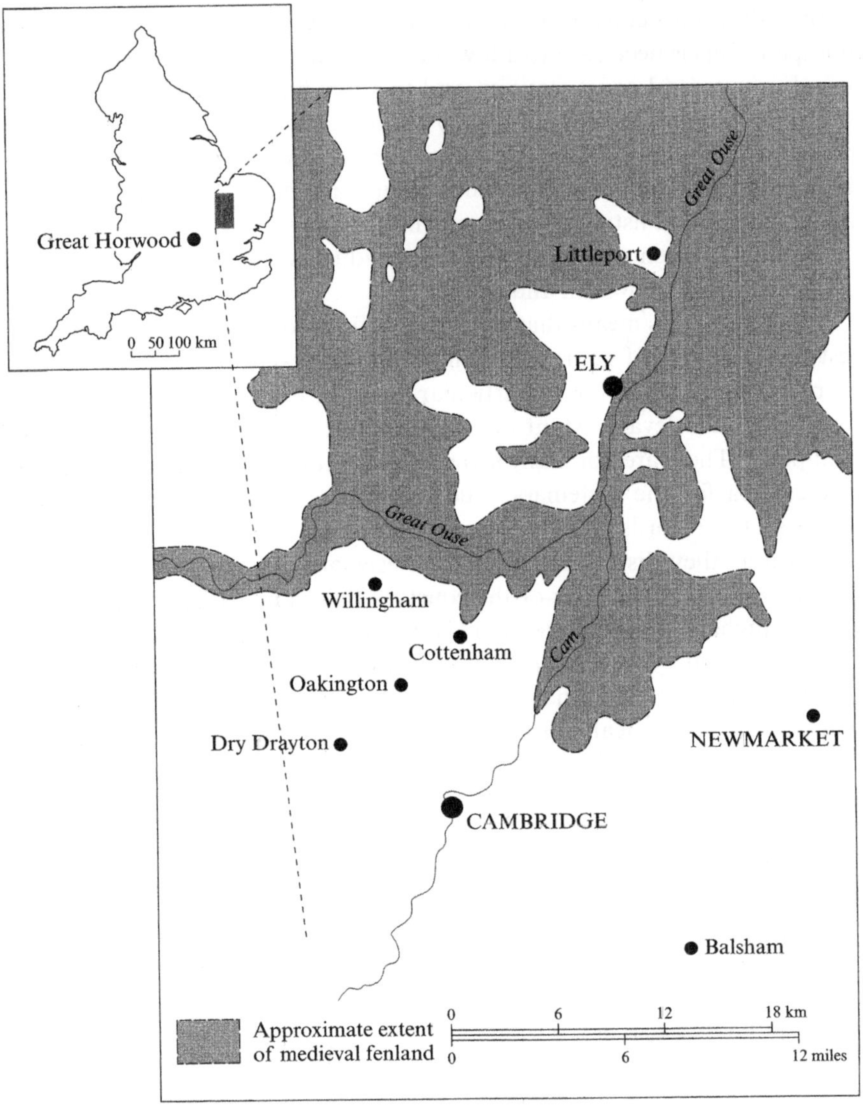

Map 1.1 Locations of the villages studied

The court roll series form two groups, the first of which comprises Oakington and Horwood, the second Balsham, Littleport, and Willingham. The difference between the groups is that the court rolls in the first have been studied more intensively than those in the second. From all five sets of rolls, every entry relating to debt litigation from specific periods has been extracted, and the key pieces of information they provide used in the analysis. However, where Oakington and Horwood are concerned, use has also been made of the large number of other entries in the court rolls that mention one or more of the parties to a debt plaint. Such entries comprise the full range typically found in the more informative court rolls, covering topics from land transfer to brewing, and they enable us to discover a good deal about the people who were involved in credit relationships, and the circumstances in which such relationships arose.[51] As a result of this relatively intensive treatment, a broader range of questions is put to the material from Oakington and Horwood than to that from the other places. Consequently, those two court roll series provide the book's core evidence, while the others are often largely supplementary; this is particularly true of Chapters 4 and 5. Yet even in the case of the less intensively studied trio of villages, some use is made of the wealth of additional information on creditors and debtors contained in the non-debt material in the court rolls.

Life in all these villages, as in England generally, altered dramatically over the fourteenth century, primarily as a consequence of the Black Death of 1348–9 and subsequent plague outbreaks. One would hardly expect the part played by credit to have stood still in the midst of later fourteenth-century developments in the peasant economy. The ratio of land to labour was transformed and a number of changes flowed from this, such as the trend towards pastoralism, and the accumulation of progressively larger landholdings. The chronological range of the documentation from the seven manors, covering both the pre- and post-Black Death periods, permits consideration in this book of the extent of such change in the role of credit. However, most attention is devoted to the five or six decades preceding the outbreak of plague. As noted above, it is this period that has been most closely scrutinized in existing characterizations of medieval English rural credit. Part of the aim in focusing on it here is to permit engagement with previous interpretations.

Investigation of the pre-plague decades is also prioritized because they are the best documented. Manor court rolls are at their fullest and most detailed on debt, as on other subjects, for the later thirteenth and earlier fourteenth century. This characteristic guided the selection of rolls for this study. It also means that most attention falls upon the earliest records in a

[51] For the method of collection and use of this additional court roll information, see Appendix 2.

series, since they are generally more informative than their later equivalents from the same series. With the exception of Willingham's, all the court rolls used begin before 1349.[52] The focus on the pre-plague period is also encouraged by the presence of useful ancillary documentation from that era comprising tenant listings of various kinds and taxation returns.[53]

It is well known that the best-preserved collections of medieval manorial records tend to be found in the archives of ecclesiastical landlords. In particular, historians of village society are best served by the archives of the richest bishoprics and monasteries, since the vast landed wealth, high regard for seigniorial rights, and institutional continuity exhibited by such lords made them unrivalled record keepers. It is not surprising, therefore, that all five sets of court rolls used here relate to manors belonging to church estates. Not all of them, it is true, were produced by greater ecclesiastical lords. A small religious house, the Cluniac priory of nearby Newton Longville, held the manor of Great Horwood at this time. Newton Longville was an alien priory, subject to the priory of St Faith, Longueville, in Normandy.[54] The lords of the other manors were the Benedictine monks of Crowland Abbey, who held Oakington, Cottenham, and Drayton; and the bishop of Ely, whose

[52] The Oakington court rolls begin in 1290 (a record of a single court session for that year) and run almost entirely unbroken into the fifteenth century apart from a gap in 1390–1: CUL, Q Boxes 3–4 (Oakington court rolls, numbers 1–10, 12). Page, *Estates*, 331–425, contains editions of a small sample of the surviving pre-1400 rolls. Other studies based on these rolls are Page, 'Customary poor law', and Ravensdale, 'Population changes'. Great Horwood's surviving rolls begin in 1302 and are studied here to 1360, whereupon they become more broken. For the year 1345 no Horwood court rolls survive: NCA, 3912–3914. These rolls are notable for their lengthy entries concerning land disputes, and for their numerous by-laws. For examples, see, respectively, Poos and Bonfield, *Select cases*, and Ault, *Open-field farming*. The first five Horwood court sessions (NCA, 3912, mm. 1–2d) have been incorrectly dated to 1289–90 and 1291–2, e.g. Poos and Bonfield, *Select cases*, 97; Ault, *Open-field farming*, 83. The court rolls of Balsham begin in 1310 and run to 1349, though there are three calendar years (1332, 1336, and 1343) in that period with no surviving rolls at all: LMA, ACC/1876/MR/02/001–011. Balsham rolls covering parts of the later fourteenth century have not been used. The main run of Littleport rolls covers only the years 1316–27, but those contain a very large quantity of debt litigation: CRO, R 93/96. For extracts from the Littleport rolls, see *Court Baron*, 107–47. The Willingham court rolls begin in 1377, and the record of at least one manor court session survives for every calendar year to 1400: CRO, L1/177–8.

[53] For the manors of Oakington and Dry Drayton (not Cottenham), rentals of 1344 give the names of tenants grouped by holding. A useful tenant list of 1346–7 relating to a small Oakington estate called the 'Picot fee', which was distinct from the village's main manor, is preserved in a later copy. There is a Great Horwood manorial extent of 1320, which describes holdings and their tenants. The Balsham rolls contain a useful tenant list of 1316. Balsham, Littleport, Oakington, Cottenham, and Drayton are covered by listings of taxpayers of the lay subsidies (royal taxes on movable goods) of 1315 and 1327. A Great Horwood return for the 1327 lay subsidy also survives. For all these sources, see Chapter 4 below, and Bibliography.

[54] Salter (ed.), *Newington Longville charters*; *VCH Bucks.*, iii, 372–4; iv, 426–7.

many manors in the eastern counties included Balsham, Littleport, and Willingham.

Heaviest use has thus traditionally been made of the manorial records produced by the great ecclesiastics, simply because these usually survive in the greatest numbers and are the most informative, and the present study conforms to this tendency. It is increasingly apparent, though, that such lords were not typical. The modal fourteenth-century estate was perhaps the couple of small manors held by a modest gentry lord, not the fifty or so large manors held by the bishop of Ely.[55] It is, then, worthwhile asking whether our dependence upon records generated mainly by a class of untypical landlords could lead to certain biases in the picture of village credit they yield.

One significant issue is that discussions based on such records are dominated by the activities of the villein or customary tenants. Nationally, customary rents and services, and therefore villein tenants, tended to form a more significant presence on large manors than on small manors. Large manors (worth £50 or more) were relatively rare, and were found mainly within the extensive estates of the greatest feudal lords, a group which included the wealthiest ecclesiastics like the bishop of Ely and the monks of Crowland.[56] Unsurprisingly, therefore, villeins were a significant presence in the tenant population of the seven manors studied here, they loom large in the manor court records, and they appear in many manorial debt cases.

However, such villeins were not necessarily typical of the majority of the English peasantry. Approximately half of the peasant population consisted of free tenants who did not share the villein's substantial disabilities of status and tenure. However, it is generally accepted that in spite of the relatively heavy burdens imposed upon the villein by lordship, the typical pre-plague villein enjoyed many economic advantages over his free counterpart. The wealthy villein, an active employer of labour and producer for the market, is a familiar figure of the period.[57] The villein's advantages mainly flowed from the fact that customary holdings tended on average to be larger than free holdings.[58] Each of the seven manors was dominated by customary tenant land divided into standardized categories of holdings which owed part of their rents as labour services. Virgates (usually 30 acres) and half-virgates, holdings large enough to require hired labour to supplement family labour, are frequently encountered in these manors. In the early fourteenth century, at least 52 per cent of the seven manors' combined customary holdings were

[55] For the Ely estate, see Miller, *Abbey and bishopric*.

[56] Campbell, 'Agrarian problem', 27–8; Campbell and Bartley, *England on the eve of the Black Death*, 83, 251–2; see also Campbell, 'A unique estate and a unique source', 23–5.

[57] For example, Raftis, *Peasant economic development*; Campbell, 'Agrarian problem', 48.

[58] Campbell, 'Agrarian problem', 34.

of 10 acres or more in extent.[59] The position of villein households occupying such holdings contrasted with that of the smallholders occupying just a few acres, many of them free tenants, who around 1300 were undoubtedly more common overall than they were in the villages studied here. Because use of a manor court for litigation was never the exclusive preserve of the villein tenants of the manor to which it was attached, a wider population of participants in the credit network does appear in our rolls. Thus we never lose sight of the credit dealings of some freeholders, smallholders, and other individuals who lived in the villages concerned, but were not tenants within the standardized customary landholding structures of the seven manors. Nonetheless, it remains true that the high-quality manorial records used here are most revealing about the credit activities of relatively wealthy villeins in possession of holdings measuring 10 acres or more, a group that formed something of an elite within English rural society as a whole.

A further feature of the high-quality manorial records of major landlords that are indispensable to village studies such as this is that they relate disproportionately to particular parts of the country, namely to lowland central and southern England, and to the eastern portion of that region in particular. The court rolls used here concern places that, by any definition, are mostly located in eastern England. However, it must be stressed that even the Cambridgeshire villages studied had more in common with villages further west than they did with many settlements in East Anglia proper, which for present purposes is defined as the counties of Norfolk, Suffolk, and Essex.

As noted already, the court rolls used here allow the study of villages whose tenant landholding and tenurial arrangements were characterized by the dominance of comparatively large villein holdings all of a standard size, such as the twenty-six Oakington 'full lands' all of 10 acres each, or the twenty-five Horwood half-virgates all of 15 acres each. In medieval England, villages with this type of landholding structure tended also to share similarities in terms of landscape, settlement patterns, the layout of fields, and agricultural practices. Concentrated within the central lowland belt of 'champion' England were nucleated villages where arable agriculture was practised in unenclosed open fields in which the tenants held scattered plots. When, as it frequently did, a village in this region contained a large manor of the kind typically held by a powerful ecclesiastical lord, that manor's tenant land was

[59] This calculation includes cottages. For landholdings at Horwood and in the Crowland villages, see Chapter 4. For the Littleport, Balsham, and Willingham villein holdings, see *VCH Cambs.*, iv, 97; vi, 130; ix, 404.

usually arranged in groups of standard villein holdings, such as virgates and half-virgates.[60] Places characterized by nucleated settlement, common open-field agriculture, and numerous customary landholdings of a standard size are often referred to as 'midland' villages. All seven villages studied in this book can be described as 'midland' villages. They all lay in the central zone of 'champion' England, although the Cambridgeshire villages can only just be regarded as lying inside this belt, and are very much at its eastern extremity.[61] All seven villages featured open fields and nucleated settlements.

The 'midland' villages that are the focus of this book contrasted with the 'East Anglian' village, examples of which were concentrated further east in Norfolk, Suffolk, and Essex. Like the villages studied here, many 'East Anglian' villages also featured unusually large manors held by the wealthiest church and lay lords. Such manors also possessed many villein tenants and tend to be well documented, and it is naturally using the records of these manors that the social and economic history of villages in this region has often been written.[62] However, rather than containing groups of holdings all of the same standard size, the large, villein-dominated manors of the 'East Anglian' village tended to feature fragmented holdings which were more numerous, smaller on average, and more varied in size than those of the typical 'midland' village. This in turn created a particular type of rural social structure that differed substantially from that of the modal 'midland' village. Moreover, the 'midland' and 'East Anglian' villages did not differ solely with respect to landholding and social structure. The landscape, settlement, and agricultural arrangements, and indeed economic life of the 'East Anglian' village tended also to contrast with that of places in the 'midland' zone, being characterized by scattered rather than nucleated settlement, complex field systems and enclosure rather than open fields, and relatively large numbers of smallholders and landless people whose livelihoods relied at least partly on wage-earning.[63]

Thus our unavoidable reliance on the best-preserved and most-informative court rolls has two main implications for the investigation of village credit

[60] The classic example is the estate of Ramsey Abbey, whose manors were concentrated in Huntingdonshire.

[61] Southern Cambridgeshire was to some extent a 'transitional zone', containing some places with 'East Anglian' features, in addition to villages of 'midland' type. For example, holdings were fragmented in the 'East Anglian' manner at Barton and Chesterton, villages which lie close to those studied here: Briggs, 'Credit and the freehold land market'; Clarke, 'Peasant society'.

[62] The estate records of the abbey of Bury St Edmunds are most notable in this regard.

[63] On differences between 'midland' and 'East Anglian' communities, see Whittle, 'Individualism and the family–land bond', 44–54; Whittle and Yates, '"*Pays réel* or *pays légal*"?'; Razi, 'Myth of the immutable English family', 15–22.

attempted in this book. First, it means that we are best informed about the substantial villein tenants. However, the freeholders and smallholders, who were perhaps more typical of the rural population as a whole, were present in each location and are not entirely hidden from view. Second, the court rolls selected for use tell us about a particular type of village located in a particular region of England, namely the 'midland' village. It is possible that this book's picture of English village credit, which is based mainly on just these seven places, may in fact be representative of 'midland' villages only. Even if this is the case, however, it should be said that such villages were not unusual, but were numerous within a broad band that ran up the centre of the country from Dorset to Northumberland. This book's focus on 'midland' villages also provides useful balance, since much, though certainly not all, of the most detailed work undertaken on medieval English village society, and on the role of credit within it, has explored 'East Anglian' communities.[64] In fact, differences between 'midland' and 'East Anglian' villages in the nature and role of credit form a central theme of the book.

Although the villages studied were 'midland' villages and shared some key basic similarities, there were of course significant local differences between them in landscape and economy. This applies particularly to the importance of pastoral versus arable agriculture, and to the extent to which residents obtained income from non-agricultural activities. Most significantly, the seven villages include one fenland parish—Littleport—in which arable cultivation was restricted to islands of high ground surrounded by more or less permanently flooded areas, as well as, in Cottenham and Willingham, two 'fen-edge' villages, where periodic inundation of a lesser magnitude affecting parts of the parishes provided common grazing of very great importance to the local economy. The other four places studied can all be described as classic 'midland' villages dominated by open-field arable cultivation, yet even within this broad categorization, each of the four had distinctive characteristics, with Balsham, for example, containing an important chalk heathland used for sheep grazing.[65]

The Cambridgeshire villages in particular were located in a region in which the infrastructure of rural commerce was relatively well developed. Several of these villages were close to the important market centre represented

[64] See, in particular, Schofield's work on Hinderclay, as well as the marked and continuing influence of studies such as Smith, 'Families and their land' (Redgrave, Suffolk), and Campbell, 'Population pressure' (Coltishall, Norfolk).

[65] For Littleport, see *VCH Cambs.*, iv, 96–8; for Balsham, see *VCH Cambs.*, vi, 127–35; for Oakington, Cottenham, and Drayton, see *VCH Cambs.*, ix, 48–63, 71–84, 192–204. On Cottenham, see also Ravensdale, *Liable*. Willingham is familiar as one of the contrasting communities in Spufford's classic work of that title: Spufford, *Contrasting communities*.

by the town of Cambridge, and although only Balsham was the site of a formally chartered weekly market active in the period under investigation, residents of most of the Cambridgeshire villages studied here had relatively easy access to such markets in nearby villages.[66] The distinctive features of the seven villages with regard to local economy and topography are taken into account as far as possible in what follows in explaining contrasting attributes in the credit market of each location.

The next chapter begins the evaluation of the strengths and weaknesses of the English rural credit system through an examination of the credit arrangements. When one compares England with other contemporary regions, do the types of credit arrangement used appear broad or narrow in range; does the quantity of credit available in individual transactions emerge as large or small; and does the set of purposes for which credit was used by borrowers appear diverse or limited? Similarly, Chapter 3 explores the possibility that medieval English rural credit networks were 'weak' relative to those of other parts of contemporary Europe, by looking at the circumstances through which lenders and borrowers made contact, and at the terms and conditions lenders imposed when they gave credit. In particular, it is asked whether lenders lent only to those about whom they had prior information. That chapter also considers the degree to which borrowers were subject to 'exploitation' as a result of conditions surrounding the duration of credit contracts, the lender's profits, and the use of security. In Chapters 4 and 5, the evaluation of strengths and weaknesses turns to the examination of the copious data on the backgrounds and relationships of creditors and debtors. Chapter 4 essentially summarizes the broad characteristics of the creditor group and debtor group in each village, asking in particular what the presence and absence of particular types of individuals (women, clergy, and outsiders) suggests about the functions or limitations of the credit market. That chapter also assesses the similarities and differences between the recorded creditors and the recorded debtors, as well as the overlaps between the two groups. In Chapter 5, attention turns to the nature and consequences of relationships between creditors and debtors. The central question in Chapters 4 and 5 asks how far the net effect of credit relations was to reinforce the emergence of a class of recurrent debtors, who, as a result of basic consumption needs, were forced to enter into repeated relationships of obligation and power with members of a separate and generally wealthier class of village creditors. Finally, Chapter 6 reconstructs changes over time in the quantity of

[66] A charter was granted in 1265 for a Cottenham market, but there is no evidence that it was active in the fourteenth century. For the density of weekly markets in southern Cambridgeshire, see Masschaele, *Peasants, merchants, and markets*, 181–5.

new credit extended. Clearly, it is difficult to describe a credit system as 'successful' if, as a consequence of disruptions and obstacles brought about by harvest failure, mortality crises, or shortages of coined money, the individuals in the best position to offer credit were in fact frequently unwilling or unable to extend it to those who sought it.

2

The forms of credit and their uses

It is difficult to think of a category of interaction or exchange in a medieval rural community which did not have at least the potential to involve credit, in the broad sense of allowing someone a benefit or granting them a service now, on the understanding that one would be able to make some claim upon that person or their family in the future. However, in spite of this potential for diversity, most credit in medieval villages throughout Europe tended to take one of a number of familiar forms. It is the aim of this chapter to discover which of these forms of transaction involving credit were in use in England in our period, and to establish which were the most important. The chapter also addresses two further, related, questions. First, what were the uses to which the credit provided in the most common arrangements was put? And second, how large were the quantities of credit extended in the villages studied, by comparison with what has been found in existing work on credit, and with what is known about the quantities of goods and sums of money involved in peasant income, expenditure, and consumption?

By evaluating just what is meant by credit in the context of the fourteenth-century village, this chapter lays an indispensable foundation for the remainder of the book. It also addresses directly the book's overall preoccupation with the strengths and weaknesses of the English rural credit system, when compared with that of other contemporary European regions. Underlying this chapter, therefore, are two alternative propositions, and the discussion which follows is in one sense an attempt to see which is best supported by the available evidence. The first proposition is that credit transactions in this period were small-scale and primarily oriented towards providing essentials on a short-term basis, thereby offering negligible longer-term benefit for the borrower, as well as scant opportunity for individuals to make a profit through lending. The second proposition is that typical borrowing in this period involved relatively large sums, and that this feature reflects the fact that transactions tended to enhance or expand not only the borrower's future income or resources, but also the lender's confidence that he was making a sensible investment in extending credit in such circumstances.

2.1 Types of credit transaction

Needless to say, investigating those propositions is in practice rather difficult, owing to the nature of the sources. The task of the scribes responsible for recording manorial debt cases was to summarize the stages in a legal process. Consequently, they usually concerned themselves only with details relevant to the progress of a particular case. In certain courts at certain periods, it is true, more particulars about the circumstances of a dispute were written down than was generally the norm. However, it remains the case that the records of debt litigation naturally tell one as much or more about the prosecution and resolution of lawsuits, as they do about the arrangements through which people got into debt.

Manorial debt pleas thus provide an incomplete picture of the forms of rural credit and their uses. Very often, even where the existence of a debt case shows that two people had been involved in a credit transaction, we nonetheless have no idea what kind of transaction it was. Thus of the 2,478 debt plaints from the five courts, no more than 1,149 (46.4 per cent) give information of any kind on the nature of the debt. Furthermore, as the subsequent discussion shows more fully, many of those 1,149 cases record only the debt itself, and nothing about the transaction that generated the debt, let alone why the transaction was entered into. One must also contend with the possibility that some debts were falsely or erroneously claimed in court. This last problem is handled by excluding from the tables in this chapter all debts, or parts of debts, which the courts decided were not in fact outstanding as the plaintiff claimed.

In spite of these problems, progress in identifying the main forms of credit is possible, provided a sufficiently large number of cases has been assembled, as it has here. First, however, an important preliminary point relevant both for this chapter and for the remainder of the book must be made. This is that virtually every individual debt recorded in the court rolls represents the outcome of a single discrete transaction between the parties; and that, furthermore, it was usual that just one debt, and hence just one transaction, was under consideration in each debt case. This needs to be stressed, since existing studies based on relatively detailed fifteenth-century court rolls have identified some cases which concerned a succession of unpaid debts arising from credit transactions between a particular pair of parties, sometimes made over a considerable period of time. In those cases, the claim or claims made by the plaintiff consisted of the balance remaining once a reckoning of the obligations between the parties had been made.[1] Clearly, if there is a significant likelihood that a simple debt claim of, say, 10*s*. in the

[1] McIntosh, *Autonomy and community*, 169–70; for Writtle examples, see Clark, 'English vill', 265, and Clark, 'Medieval debt litigation: Essex and Norfolk', 298–9.

rolls used here represents not the sum due from a unique credit transaction, but the balance of multiple outstanding debts between the parties, then this would pose considerable problems of interpretation.

Fortunately, however, the debt cases studied in this book give little sign that successive transactions between parties produced a single debt claim. One exceptional 1373 plaint involving two Drayton men does allude to such a process. In that case, Thomas Hervy acknowledged 27*s.* 7*d.* owed to Thomas Atte Pond, 'as calculated from diverse debts between them'.[2] One may add to this seven further Oakington debt cases from 1393–6 and twenty-seven Willingham cases which all refer to a single debt arising from 'certain contracts' between the parties. That phrase, however, is as likely to be a clerk's stock formula as it is proof that the settling-up of a series of obligations between two parties could result in a unique debt claim.

Some plaintiffs, to be sure, claimed more than one debt from the same defendant in a single case. In such instances, however, it remains entirely possible that each debt arose from a separate transaction between the parties. That is how such multi-claim plaints are treated in this chapter. In any case, plaints in which more than one debt was claimed are rare. Only 79 of the 1,149 cases which record debt details are in this category (6.9 per cent). If a creditor was owed more than one debt by a particular debtor, it was just as likely that he would bring a separate action for each debt. For example, in one April 1376 court, William Grey of Oakington brought two separate actions against Thomas Atte Greene of Girton. Through one of the suits William recovered 6*d.* that he had paid to the lord abbot on Thomas's behalf, while the other secured repayment of another 6*d.* owed by Thomas as part of the payment for one ox worth 12*s.*[3]

The key point then is that, normally, one debt arising from one transaction was claimed in one debt case. This is important for the analysis in this chapter. For example, establishing this point makes it possible to evaluate the size of an individual debt without worrying that it actually represents the outcome of several credit obligations. This point is also fundamental to arguments appearing later in the book.[4]

2.1.1 *Debts arising from obligations incurred involuntarily*

What, then, can one determine about the forms of credit? An initial step is to divide debts into those claimed in money and those claimed in kind (Table 2.1). The debts in money demanded the payment of actual coin, while

[2] CUL, Q 7, m.8 (9 May 1373).

[3] CUL, Q 7, m.15 (22 April 1376).

[4] See below, pp. 170–2.

Table 2.1 Debts in money and in kind in the villages studied

	Oakington, etc. 1291–1350		Oakington, etc. 1351–1400		Horwood 1302–60		Willingham 1377–1400		Littleport 1316–27		Balsham 1310–49		Total	
	No.	%	No.	%	No.	%	No.	%	No.	%	No.	%	No.	%
Money debts	163	(59.7)	127	(76.5)	64	(64.6)	282	(86.0)	180	(74.7)	60	(60.6)	876	(72.6)
Debts in kind	110	(40.3)	39	(23.5)	35	(35.4)	46	(14.0)	61	(25.3)	39	(39.4)	330	(27.4)
Total	273	(100.0)	166	(100.0)	99	(100.0)	328	(100.0)	241	(100.0)	99	(100.0)	1,206	(100.0)

Note: Where more than one debt is claimed in a case, each appears separately in the table.
Sources: CUL Q, Boxes 3–4, rolls 1–10, 12; NCA, 3912–3914; LMA, ACC/1876/MR/02/001–011; CRO, R 93/96; CRO, L1/177–8.

the debts in kind comprised demands for payment of grain, animals, and a variety of other goods. As the table shows, debts in money predominated, especially in the latter half of the century.

However, while it is easy to divide debts by the form in which they were claimed, it is harder to divide them according to the transaction type from which each arose. The reason for this is simply that the majority of debts state the sum of money or item claimed, but give no idea of the arrangement through which it came to be owed.[5] Debts in that category appear in row (h) of Table 2.2, which provides a breakdown of the reasons for debts in money, and in rows (e)–(g) and (i) of Table 2.3, which does the same for debts in kind. However, in a minority of instances, some information is provided on the arrangement or circumstances that generated the debt. Such 'known' debts appear in the remaining rows of Tables 2.2 and 2.3. It is possible to use those instances to obtain an impression of the overall range and relative significance of the different transaction types.

Not every debt case arose from a credit arrangement. There were many different ways for a villager to be 'in debt', without having entered into the outstanding obligation voluntarily and through mutual agreement with a creditor. Debts known to have arisen from such involuntary obligations on the part of a debtor appear in rows (a)–(c) of Table 2.2 and in rows (a)–(b) of Table 2.3. A debt which occurred because an executor failed to pay out a legacy, for example, clearly did not represent 'real' credit, in the sense of a voluntary arrangement made with the agreement of both parties, the most obvious example which is perhaps a loan of cash.

One could argue from the presence of debts incurred involuntarily that a significant component of manorial debt litigation had nothing to do with 'real' credit. However, it must be recognized that even when a dispute apparently revolved around an obligation that an individual had incurred unintentionally and without the agreement of a 'creditor', one cannot rule out the possibility that there was still some element of 'real' credit involved. For example, cases in which a person was in arrears for rent payable on a property leased from another villager do not explicitly show that the rent payer had been taken to court simply for missing a payment at its customary date. It is thus conceivable that in such cases the lessor may in fact have allowed a lessee a delay beyond the usual term in making a rent payment, even though in the event the rent remained unpaid in spite of that concession. In making such a concession, however, a lessor would effectively have been extending credit to the lessee. Some element of 'real' credit may also have been present in certain other debts resulting from undischarged obligations. For instance,

[5] See Appendix 1 for examples.

Table 2.2 Debts in money

Nature of debt	Oakington, etc. 1291–1350		Oakington, etc. 1351–1400		Horwood 1302–60		Willingham 1377–1400		Littleport 1316–27		Balsham 1310–49	
	No.	%	No.	%	No.	%	No.	%	No.	%	No.	%
a. Unpaid testamentary legacy	1	(0.6)	0	(0.0)	0	(0.0)	1	(0.4)	0	(0.0)	0	(0.0)
b. Other monetary obligation unmet	0	(0.0)	3	(2.4)	1	(1.6)	9	(3.2)	8	(4.4)	0	(0.0)
c. Property rent in arrears	5	(3.1)	0	(0.0)	1	(1.6)	8	(2.8)	1	(0.6)	3	(5.0)
Sub-total	6	(3.7)	3	(2.4)	2	(3.2)	18	(6.4)	9	(5.0)	3	(5.0)
d. Wages in arrears	4	(2.4)	4	(3.1)	3	(4.7)	10	(3.5)	5	(2.8)	2	(3.3)
e. In arrears for service performed	5	(3.1)	14	(11.0)	2	(3.2)	21	(7.4)	9	(5.0)	3	(5.0)
Sub-total	9	(5.5)	18	(14.2)	5	(7.8)	31	(11.0)	14	(7.8)	5	(8.3)
f. Loan	9	(5.5)	5	(3.9)	3	(4.7)	19	(6.7)	3	(1.7)	3	(5.0)
g. Deferred payment	35	(21.5)	22	(17.3)	2	(3.2)	116	(41.1)	18	(10.0)	1	(1.7)
h. Unknown reason	104	(63.8)	79	(62.2)	52	(81.3)	98	(34.8)	136	(75.6)	48	(80.0)
Total debts	163	(100.0)	127	(100.0)	64	(100.0)	282	(100.0)	180	(100.0)	60	(100.0)

Sources: See Table 2.1.

Table 2.3 Debts in kind

Nature of debt	Oakington, etc. 1291–1350		Oakington, etc. 1351–1400		Horwood 1302–60		Willingham 1377–1400		Littleport 1316–27		Balsham 1310–49	
	No.	%	No.	%	No.	%	No.	%	No.	%	No.	%
a. Unpaid testamentary legacy	1	(0.9)	0	(0.0)	0	(0.0)	0	(0.0)	0	(0.0)	0	(0.0)
b. Other obligation unmet	6	(5.5)	1	(2.6)	2	(5.7)	4	(8.7)	0	(0.0)	2	(5.1)
Sub-total	7	(6.4)	1	(2.6)	2	(5.7)	4	(8.7)	0	(0.0)	2	(5.1)
c. Grain payment in arrears for service performed	0	(0.0)	2	(5.1)	0	(0.0)	0	(0.0)	0	(0.0)	0	(0.0)
d. Grain: loan	2	(1.8)	1	(2.6)	2	(5.7)	2	(4.3)	0	(0.0)	1	(2.6)
e. Grain only	79	(71.8)	16	(41.0)	20	(57.1)	26	(56.5)	11	(18.0)	22	(56.4)
f. Animals	9	(8.2)	7	(17.9)	3	(8.6)	0	(0.0)	0	(0.0)	3	(7.7)
g. Sedge	0	(0.0)	0	(0.0)	0	(0.0)	0	(0.0)	35	(57.4)	0	(0.0)
h. Other goods: loan	0	(0.0)	0	(0.0)	0	(0.0)	5	(10.9)	0	(0.0)	0	(0.0)
i. Other goods only	13	(11.8)	12	(30.8)	8	(22.9)	9	(19.6)	15	(24.6)	11	(28.2)
Total debts	110	(100.0)	39	(100.0)	35	(100.0)	46	(100.0)	61	(100.0)	39	(100.0)

Note: Grain includes legumes (peas and beans).
Sources: See Table 2.1.

several of the debts in Table 2.2 row (b) represent the failure to render an agreed sum of compensation following damage or death caused to crops or animals. One of the more detailed debt cases of this type had its origins in an earlier unspecified trespass against William de Erheth, who acted as plaintiff in the subsequent debt action. It had been agreed following the trespass that John Porteioye, the individual who had committed it, would pay William 40*d.* in compensation, but would be allowed a delay before he was required to pay. It was John's later failure to discharge that obligation that triggered the debt case. What is notable is that, following the trespass and the recognition that compensation was due, John had been given credit of a sort. There had been no attempt, for example, to get him to discharge his obligation immediately by surrendering goods or animals to William.[6] At the same time, even if there was some element of 'real' credit present when debtors incurred obligations involuntarily, it must nonetheless be admitted that individuals obtained few if any benefits from being in debt in this way.

2.1.2 Payments in arrears: wages and services

The credit transactions proper are now considered. A significant pair of debt categories are the payments in arrears for wages and for services performed (Table 2.2 rows (d) and (e), Table 2.3 row (c)). The arrears of wages category comprises debts in cases where a wage-earner or servant claimed sums not paid by an employer. In some of these, a withheld wage is specifically mentioned. Others describe the relationship in more general terms. For instance, one of the Balsham debts in Table 2.2 row (d) was a sum of 2*s.* 9*d.* recovered by Emma Jolyf from William Kyng and owed 'for the service of Emma during autumn last past'.[7] In all, however, the basic situation was clearly that a task had been performed on the condition that payment would be made later. Many peasants in the villages studied employed labourers and servants, and transactions in which remuneration for their work was payable in arrears were certainly part of the credit economy. An important feature of these transactions, however, is that normal assumptions about the relative economic standing of creditor and debtor require re-evaluation. In such arrangements, the employee—the economically subordinate party—was the 'creditor'.

A somewhat more common source of debts than the arrears of wages was payments in arrears for services given (Table 2.2 row (e)). Unlike those dis-

[6] CRO, R 93/96, m.25 (Littleport, 1 December 1326). The defendant in the debt case was in fact John's pledge for the obligation, William Meyre.

[7] LMA, ACC/1876/MR/02/003, m.3 (8 October 1328). Debts representing wages in arrears have been noted in other court roll studies of the period; see e.g. Razi, 'Family, land and the village community', 33.

cussed in the preceding paragraph, these debts were not simply the result of labour performed on credit. Rather, they arose from transactions in which an individual had allowed his superior resources of land and property to be used to meet another's requirements, in return for later payment. Examples include debts from the hiring out of animals; from (at Littleport) the hiring out of boats; and from payments made on the debtor's behalf, such as court amercements. Also common are debts connected with ploughing, and for looking after animals (*custodia*). These two last transaction types were also numerous at Writtle. In the first, as Clark showed, individuals lacking ploughs or draught animals secured ploughing services or hired what they needed from their better-endowed neighbours, while in the second, people possessing livestock but insufficient pasture or feed with which to support them put them in the care of those who had a surplus.[8] In other words, the debts owed for services resulted when individuals lacking specific resources sought credit from those in possession of such resources.

2.1.3 Loans

Perhaps the simplest type of credit transaction was the loan. As Tables 2.2 and 2.3 show, forty-two money debts and thirteen debts in kind are known to have arisen from loans. With these debts, the relevant entry stated that the creditor had loaned (*accomodavit*) the disputed item. Alternatively, it included the terms *mutuum* or *prestitum*, or variants thereof. Further details are scant, but it appears that in a loan transaction the creditor simply conveyed to the debtor a sum of money or grain, or an animal or other item, with provision for later repayment, presumably with some extra charge added. In discussing loans, mention should also be made of the 'formal recognizances', rare court roll entries which represent not the resolution of a debt dispute, but the enrolment of a new debt at its inception as part of the court record.[9] Eight such recognizances appear in the rolls. All record the obligation to repay cash sums at specified dates, though they do not refer to the obligation by means of a term such as *mutuum*. However, the recognizances should undoubtedly be treated as cash loans additional to the forty-two revealed by litigation.

[8] Clark, 'English vill', 261–2. One Willingham debt case concerning care of animals specified that the arrangement covered the winter period: CRO, L1/177, m.34 (John Houdone v. Robert Aladene, 26 November 1389).

[9] For an example, see Appendix 1; also below, Sections 3.2.2 and 3.4.1.

2.1.4 Deferred payments

It is also known that some debts arose not from loans, but from sales made on credit. Table 2.2 row (g) contains debts from deferred payments, in which the debtor undertook to render payment later for goods received. The goods acquired through deferred payments were diverse, but grain and livestock predominated.

In some instances, then, the court record identifies the transaction that generated an unpaid debt, albeit rather vaguely. But what was the background to the remaining 517 money debts, 174 grain debts, and 125 debts of animals and other goods, where all one knows is the item claimed?[10] The circumstances behind the 517 'unknown' money debts presumably corresponded to one or other of the categories considered thus far, namely obligations largely unconnected with 'real' credit; payments for services and wages in arrears; loans; and deferred payments. However, there is no obvious way of determining the numerical significance of each category among the 'unknown' money debts.

Similarly, it seems a safe assumption that some of the 174 'unknown' grain debts arose from loans made in grain and repayable in that commodity, while some of the 125 'unknown' debts of animals and other goods undoubtedly represent straightforward loans of chattel. However, there are other credit transactions that could also have resulted in a simple debt in grain or other goods. Most important is the 'purchase price advance', in which the debtor undertook to deliver goods to the creditor at a future date in return for an immediate transfer of cash. Clark found numerous instances of the purchase price advance at Writtle, where the records tend to give relatively full details about a debt, and it has also been traced in continental European sources.[11] We should not rule out the possibility that a purchase price advance underlay some of the 'unknown' debts in kind from the villages studied here. Any evidence of the purchase price advance would be significant, since transactions of this type constituted an effective cash loan for the borrower.

It is worth trying to scrutinize closely the descriptions of debts in kind, to see whether there is any indication that they arose from purchase price advances. In parts of continental Europe, for example, it was common to find loans made upon the security of the upcoming harvest. Although a borrower was able to obtain a loan through such arrangements, the requirement that he should pledge at least part of his standing crop in advance to a lender is

[10] That is, those in Table 2.2 row (h), and Table 2.3. rows (e)–(g) and (i).
[11] Clark, 'English vill', 259; Wernham, *Salon-de-Provence*, 109–11.

usually deemed as potentially exploitative.[12] Indeed, contemporary writers on usury pinpointed lending secured on a future delivery of grain as a common mode of disguising illicit gain.[13] In theory, certainly, a creditor could have bought an agreed quantity of grain in advance at a price much lower than it was expected to fetch at the time of delivery. In doing so he would make a profit, and prevent the borrower from realizing the full value of his crop. Unfortunately, our evidence makes it virtually impossible to tell whether such transactions were in use in England. Interestingly, some of the grain debts do specify the value of the grain owed, as well as the quantity. It is conceivable that this detail was included because creditors wanted to ensure that the grain they were receiving exceeded in value the purchase price they had advanced. Unfortunately, it is difficult to move beyond speculation on this point.

To judge by their wording, just three grain debts show any real sign of resulting from a purchase price advance. The most explicit example comes from Horwood, and it does not suggest the exploitation of a poor borrower through an advance purchase of his harvest. In December 1350, one John Crofton sought from three Horwood men recovery of eight quarters and five bushels of drage, 'which they [had] sold to him'.[14] At the next court, a further debt of one quarter and five bushels of barley owed to John was acknowledged, and it was also stated that the detinue of the drage had been committed 'by the whole homage'. The large size of the debt obligation, the collective commitment to fulfil it, and the presence of a creditor otherwise unmentioned in the court rolls all suggest that this represented a major transaction in which a sizeable proportion of Horwood's grain crop had been sold in advance to a corn merchant.[15]

This transaction has few if any parallels in the records used. This fits Schofield's argument that purchase price advances are unlikely to crop up in significant numbers in court rolls, since they would perhaps typically involve the sort of grain traders or speculators not normally active within village society.[16] Explicit purchase price advances are certainly rare in the rolls used

[12] Gaulin and Menant, 'Crédit rural', 43.

[13] See below, p. 76.

[14] Drage: a mixture of spring barley and oats that was normally grown for malting.

[15] NCA, 3914, mm.52–52d (23 December 1350, 1 March 1351). This type of transaction was probably encouraged at Horwood by the unusual fact that the demesne lands there were leased to the customary tenants collectively from 1320. For the first of several such leases, see NCA, 3913, m.25 (12 May 1320); on the Horwood demesne lease and its effects, see also Ault, *Open-field husbandry*, 47, 51–2. The other likely purchase price advances are: Nicholas Schayl owed John Soper 1.5q. of wheat 'which he [had] sold to him', CUL, Q 1, m.17d (Oakington, 4 May 1303); William Ryghtso owed John Watteson 1.5q. of barley 'which he bought from him and which he ought to have delivered and did not deliver' (*que ab eo emit & que ei liberasse debuit & nondum liberauit*), CRO, L1/177, m.58d (Willingham, 19 September 1397).

[16] Schofield, 'L'endettement', 77.

here, but as the next section shows, there is reason to believe that arrangements of this type were actually more common than might appear on the surface.

Given the overall opacity of the evidence, then, is it possible to make any firm statement about the relative importance of the different credit transaction types in medieval English villages? Some attempt must be made to do so, since an assessment of the comparative strengths and weaknesses of medieval English rural credit depends in part on identification of the transactions most commonly used. In particular, it is necessary to address the contention that cash loans were rare in an English pre-Black Death system dominated by sales credit. It has been suggested that this was a weakness which meant that credit networks did little to reduce rural capital scarcity in this period.[17]

It is tempting to address the issue by dividing up the 'unknown' debts by credit transaction type according to the proportions indicated by the 'known' debts. Thus, for example, since 59 per cent of 'known' money debts from the Crowland villages before 1351 resulted from deferred payments (35 out of 59: Table 2.2), one could argue that 59 per cent of the 104 'unknown' money debts from the same places and period must similarly have arisen from deferred payments. However, this approach seems overly rigid and apt to mislead. Use of percentages in this case would imply the possibility of much greater precision than the evidence supports. For one thing, certain courts, particularly Horwood and Balsham, provide excessively small numbers of known debts. Furthermore, there is always the danger that certain courts were especially likely to record the details of particular types of credit transaction, in a fashion which changed over time.

A safer course is simply to summarize the situation as follows. Most debts were claimed in litigation as money, and this feature grew over the century. Some of these debts arose from obligations between the parties which had relatively little to do with credit in its true sense. However, the vast majority of money debts were the consequence of genuine credit transactions. These transactions fell into three main categories: work or services performed for delayed remuneration; loans; and deferred payments for goods. It is impossible to say precisely what percentage of the totality of village credit transactions belonged to each category. The distribution no doubt varied with time and place. However, a fairly safe generalization on the basis of Table 2.2 is that the deferred payment was usually the most common transaction. Delayed payments for services were next most significant, followed by deferred payments of wages, and loans.

17 Bailey, 'Peasant welfare', 243–4, followed by Kitsikopoulos, 'Standards of living', 251.

A few debts in kind were also the outcome of involuntary obligations between the parties, rather than credit proper, but their numbers were probably not significant. One is obliged to assume that the majority of the debts in grain, livestock, and other chattels arose from straightforward loans of the commodity concerned. It is rare to find explicit evidence that a debt in kind was the consequence of a purchase price advance.

This general picture of the forms of credit available in these villages and their relative importance is broadly what previous work leads one to expect.[18] In Clark's study of fifteenth-century Writtle, the 'unknown' debts that hamper work on most fourteenth-century court rolls appear to have been much less numerous. This means that less guesswork is required to establish the numerical importance of the various forms of credit at Writtle. Clark found that most known debts were claimed in money, and that approximately half of those arose from sales on credit. Somewhat less significant were debts from labour, services, and leases, which comprised some 39 per cent of the total. Just less than half of the debts in this second category arose from services performed, including ploughing, and from leases of animals. In other words, they were equivalent to the debts in row (e) of Table 2.2. The remainder comprised payments for labour and rent arrears from leases of land. Finally, loans formed just less than 10 per cent of Writtle cash debts.[19] Thus while closer inspection would doubtless identify important differences separating the commercialized vill of Writtle in the 1400s from the fourteenth-century communities studied here, the basic order of significance of the various forms of credit was the same in all places.

What is revealed by a comparison of this English picture with the situation elsewhere in Europe? The European sources also present problems when it comes to determining the credit transaction underlying a particular recorded debt. Nonetheless, the available studies do allow one to observe a pattern with respect to the types of credit transaction current in rural areas and their relative importance.[20] Debts arising from sales credit are by no means lacking in the notarial registers so far investigated.[21] However, outside England it does appear to have been most frequently the case that various types of loan in cash and grain were more common than credits given within the context of a sale. This prominence of loans may reflect the relatively significant role of specialist lenders, especially Jews, in the regions concerned.

[18] See, for example, the discussion of credit transaction types in Schofield, 'L'endettement'.
[19] Clark, 'English vill', 254.
[20] Bocchi, 'I debiti', 178–80; Wernham, *Salon-de-Provence*, 109–11; Drendel, 'Society and economy', 100, 127; Drendel, 'Le crédit', 281–2, 295–6; Furió, 'Le crédit', 426–33; Gaulin and Menant, 'Crédit rural', 40–3.
[21] See, for example, Menant, 'Notaires et crédit', 49–50.

The finding that loans were more important than sales credits in continental Europe cannot be demonstrated with quantitative certainty. However, it is well enough grounded to represent a significant contrast with the English village where, in the medieval period as well as later, sales credit, and more specifically the deferred payment, was the typical form.[22] It is also interesting that the English countryside appears to have been entirely unfamiliar with a type of credit arrangement that was increasingly important in many parts of Europe between the thirteenth and the fifteenth centuries. This was the *rente constituée*, also known as the *censal*. In this type of contract, a creditor made a one-off transfer of cash to a borrower. In return, a portion of the debtor's land was burdened with the obligation to render an annuity of money or goods to the creditor in perpetuity.[23] While not strictly speaking a loan, the purchase of a *rente* involved a transfer of capital to a borrower that was similar in character to a loan. The ubiquity of the *rente* in many parts of continental Europe, and its absence from England, therefore forms another aspect of the peculiarity of England with respect to the predominant types of credit arrangement.

Does the comparative rarity of loans illuminate an area in which the rural credit system of medieval England was weaker than its continental counterpart? Bailey's observation that in England transfers of cash via loans were less common than sales credit is borne out by the information from the rolls analysed here. He suggests that this situation could in theory exacerbate capital scarcity, and it is clear that from the borrower's point of view, a loan of cash provided the greatest possible flexibility. However, the supply of a large quantity of cash loans was not necessarily essential to allow a rural credit market to meet the demands made of it effectively. Whenever the commodities that people most wanted or needed were available for purchase or hire on credit, then it must have made as much sense to obtain them directly in this manner, as it would have done first to negotiate a loan from a separate source. Immediate access to village markets ought in theory to have given peasants the greatest chance of obtaining the goods they required in the appropriate quantities. Of the seven villages studied here, only Balsham featured an active chartered market in the period under study, though most of the other villages lay only a couple of miles from a successful weekly market.[24] Furthermore, as the following sections show, even in the absence of

[22] See Muldrew, *Economy of obligation*, 103–8, for the later continued dominance of sales credit.

[23] Duby, *Rural economy*, 254–6; Drendel, 'Commodities, credit and land', 691–2; Furió, 'Le crédit', 429; Herlihy, *Pistoia*, 137–41.

[24] As noted earlier, it is quite possible that debts from transactions in the Balsham market do not appear in the surviving rolls. Active markets close to Horwood included those at Winslow and Mursley, while residents of Willingham and the Crowland villages had convenient access to

active formal markets in most of the villages concerned, informal credit-based trade was nonetheless able to provide a wide range of commodities to borrowers, often in significant quantities.

2.2 The uses of credit

On its own, a discussion of transaction types cannot tell the full story about the comparative strengths and weaknesses of English rural credit. On the face of it, a dominant role for the cash loan might suggest a vibrant, capital-rich credit system. However, the picture would be much less positive if it turned out that all the loans actually involved small sums used exclusively to purchase essential foodstuffs. Similarly, any assessment of a village credit network dominated by sales credit, like that under discussion here, depends heavily on what was being bought, and why. To obtain a fuller picture, one is required to consider the purposes for which people took on credit.

At one extreme, it was possible to seek rural credit purely out of need. Credit of this type is referred to below as 'exigency credit'. The starkest type of exigency credit was borrowing to obtain foodstuffs which would otherwise have been entirely lacking. However, exigency credit was involved whenever a household needed to borrow simply to maintain their basic production or consumption at its earlier level, another obvious example being a loan of seedcorn. Exigency credit would usually exacerbate poverty, since a borrower who lacked essentials would not be any better off in the longer term as a result of obtaining credit, but would nonetheless face debt repayment costs in addition to pre-existing burdens. At the other extreme was 'investment credit', which was taken on not because the borrower needed simply to avoid a contraction in production or consumption. Thus borrowing to repair a plough did not constitute investment credit, if the consequence of failing to repair the plough was simply that the ability to preserve existing soil quality and yield levels was compromised. Instead, a characteristic of investment credit was that it led to the expansion of resources or an increase in the productivity of land, and was motivated by a drive to maximize income or consumption. With investment credit, the longer-term gains from borrowing are likely to have exceeded the initial costs of obtaining credit.

Loans, credit sales, and services obtained on credit could all provide either exigency credit or investment credit, and it is the aim of this section to discover where the balance lay. Of course, as already mentioned, the debt litigation evidence is hardly forthcoming on the uses of credit. Perhaps the

markets at Swavesey, Rampton, and Kingston: Reed, 'Markets and fairs'; Masschaele, *Peasants, merchants, and markets*, 181–5.

best indirect guide it provides in this area lies in the quantities of credit contracted in each transaction, which are the subject of the next section. In the present section, however, the assessment of the purposes of borrowing begins with a study of the goods and services bought on credit, or received directly as loans.

2.2.1 Services

Most of the services that were performed in return for a deferred payment appear to belong under the exigency credit heading rather than under that of investment credit. Thus an individual who could not feed all his animals in winter from his own resources, but had to buy this service on credit from another, would appear to be acting out of need. Yet even this example is not clear cut, since without fuller information it remains possible that the borrower in such an arrangement was obliged to seek this service not primarily because of the inadequacy of his pasture, but owing to some recent expansion in livestock holdings from which he stood to profit in the longer term. Other services bought on credit have a stronger flavour of investment. For example, six debts from the seven villages resulted from the hiring out of cows to the debtor.[25] The cows were probably not, strictly speaking, indispensable to the production and consumption of the borrowing household. Yet through the provision of valuable dairy products they offered a valuable boost to the diet and perhaps also to the income of that household.

2.2.2 Loans in kind

Numerous loans of grain, chattels, and animals from a range of dates probably arose from exigency credit. For example, even in the 1380s and 1390s several people acknowledged detention of brass pots and other small vessels they had presumably borrowed to service their food preparation needs.[26] There were also some loans of small pieces of equipment which were essential to cultivation, or to the processing of crops. For example, in October 1351 one Horwood man was found to have withheld one pair of traces and a collar, which one may assume he had been unable to provide for his draught animal from his own resources when ploughing or carting.[27] Another example is provided by two separate debt cases that report the detinue of

[25] CUL, Q 2, m.8d (7 December 1311), Q 4, m.15 (28 January 1348); NCA, 3914, m.60 (27 February 1354); LMA, ACC/1876/MR/02/001, m.26d (20 December 1319); CRO, R 93/96, m.1 (13 August 1316, two debts).
[26] Willingham: CRO, L1/177, mm.26 (17 March 1383: one posnet), and 58d (19 September 1397; one pot). Oakington: CUL, Q 9, m.22 (24 April 1398; pots).
[27] NCA, 3914, m.54 (13 October 1351).

winnowing equipment. These items were apparently 'fans' used for tossing the threshed grain to separate it from the husks and stalks, without which the borrowers would have been unable to carry out the processing properly.[28]

With other apparent loans of goods, however, it is not so obvious that the underlying transaction was driven by a borrower's need to procure essentials. A good example is provided by the thirty-five debts of sedge which were claimed at Littleport. Sedge (*Claudium mariscus*) is a plant with long, tough leaves, which were used extensively as a thatching material.[29] It was one of the natural products exploited by inhabitants of fen villages like Littleport in order to supplement the agriculture of the small 'island' zone upon which each settlement lay.[30] The harvesting and sale of sedge in the fen was highly regulated in Littleport and in other locations where it occurred. At Littleport, the right to cut sedge was restricted to those with common rights, which meant the tenants. All tenants, from holders of full lands to cottagers, were allowed to cut 6,000 sedge (a 'hundred' of sedge consisted of 120 bunches) in the year.[31]

What were the circumstances behind the thirty-five debts in sedge? The cases concerned simply state the quantity of sedge owed, plus, in some instances, its value.[32] One possibility is that quantities of sedge were loaned by those with a surplus to those who had no right to collect it, so that the latter could use it to thatch their buildings. Yet this seems improbable. Even cottagers had the right to cut a large quantity of sedge annually, and it is unlikely that there were many Littleport households lacking access to their own sedge. Further, if it really was the case that sedge was loaned to households enjoying no right to collect their own supplies, it would have made no sense to demand repayment of the loan in the form of sedge.

To obtain a more convincing explanation for these numerous debts in sedge, it must be recognized that this and other fen products were valuable commodities, and that the demand for them outside the locations in which they were found was undoubtedly high. This is revealed, for example, by one formal recognizance of 1322, in which John Fox junior of Littleport bound himself to pay to Walter Clerk of Ely '200 sedge, or 30*s*.' The loan that John was agreeing to repay in this entry had almost certainly been made in cash. However, the fact that repayment in sedge was acceptable suggests the value

[28] Horwood: NCA, 3914, m.8d (2 November 1328; *vanna*); Balsham: LMA, ACC/1876/MR/02/004, m.1d (14 December 1330; *pannus ventator*).

[29] Rowell, 'Sedge'.

[30] See e.g. Darby, *Medieval fenland*, 22–38.

[31] CRO, R 93/96, m.20d (27 June 1325) (*Court Baron*, 143). For the 'hundred', see Rowell, 'Sedge', 144.

[32] Care has been taken to exclude cases which allege that sedge had been 'carried away', since these should be regarded as trespass rather than debt actions.

of that commodity in the nearby town.[33] Given sedge's considerable market value, an alternative explanation for these thirty-five debts is that most of them do not represent loans of sedge, but arose instead from purchase price advances. In other words, villagers with surplus sedge sold it to others in return for an advance payment. Of three debt cases which give the value per hundred of the detained sedge, two state that 500 sedge were worth 7*s.*, while a third mentions an obligation of half a hundred of sedge priced at 6*s.* More than three-quarters of the sedge debts which give the quantities detained specify 500 sedge or more. This indicates that the typical effective loan received by a person selling sedge on credit could amount to at least several shillings. Occasional trespass cases support the hypothesis that sedge was bought via the purchase price advance. For example, in 1324 John Mounfort complained that John Fox junior had delivered to him 1,000 sedge of worse quality than he had bought from him.[34]

Assuming that the Littleport sedge debts did indeed arise from purchase price advances, who was buying this commodity on credit? As already mentioned, the most profitable market undoubtedly lay outside the vill. However, previous studies of fen villages stress that one important element of the regulation of sedge use was the prohibition on selling it outside the community. For example, at nearby Downham there were 185 instances of the amercement of villagers for selling sedge outside the vill.[35] Yet it is undoubtedly wrong to assume that the by-laws on sedge did much to prevent the inhabitants of fen villages from selling their sedge in external markets. The large number of presentments from Downham simply shows that the ban on selling sedge to outsiders was worth flouting. At Littleport, selling to outsiders was not in itself prohibited by the fullest by-laws concerning sedge. Rather, their requirement was that all sales of sedge, including sales to outsiders, should be made with seigniorial licence.[36] Presentments for selling sedge outside the community 'against the ordinance' were much rarer at Littleport than at Downham. This was apparently because the option of obtaining a licence to make such a sale was available at Littleport, but not at Downham. At any rate, the fact that Littleport residents did sell sedge directly to outsiders on credit is shown by a debt case of 1316, in which Adam Cornewale admitted owing Nicholas Niker of Ely 2,000 sedge.[37] Most of the remaining debts in sedge were owed to Littleport residents, or at least to persons not

[33] CRO, R 93/96, m.16 (9 December 1322).

[34] CRO, R 93/96, m.21 (18 October 1324) (*Court Baron*, 138–9).

[35] Coleman, *Downham-in-the-Isle*, 21. The Downham court rolls cover the period 1310–77.

[36] CRO, R 93/96, mm.20d (27 June 1325), and 23 (11 December 1325) (*Court Baron*, 143, 145). For evidence that Littleport residents were selling sedge to strangers in the early thirteenth century, see Darby, *Medieval fenland*, 34.

[37] CRO, R 93/96, m.1 (13 August 1316).

explicitly stated to have been non-resident. It is possible that some of the people to whom sedge was owed were engaged in buying up large quantities to sell on elsewhere. Whatever the case, it is almost certain that the Littleport sedge debts represent not loans, as might at first appear, but purchase price advances. As such, the typical credit arrangement concerning sedge was not the transfer of a scarce resource to a household in need, but a sale by a 'borrower' who exchanged his rights over a natural product for a substantial advance of cash.

Some clues to the possible stimuli behind a credit transaction may also be obtained by looking at the types of grain owed in debts (Table 2.4). Wheat and barley were the grains most commonly detained. There is no explicit indication of the uses made of wheat or barley obtained via a loan. It could therefore have been used as seed, or processed to make bread or ale for consumption or for sale. In the Crowland villages before 1351, peas and beans were also owed with some frequency. Any loans of this poorer quality foodstuff are probably indicative of exigency credit.

More interesting are the numerous pre-1351 debts from the Crowland villages of malt for brewing.[38] For these villages, records survive of eighteen apparent loans of malt, plus five quantities of malt obtained by deferred payment. Fifteen of these twenty-three debts were owed by Oakington residents. There are indications that later medieval Oakington specialized in malt production. For example, the information on tithe grain contained in the reeves' accounts shows that from the early fourteenth century onwards, the major share of the grain received from land other than the demesne was drage. Wheat and other crops apart from peas were present in small amounts only.[39] Further evidence on Oakington malt-making is provided by an exceptional but revealing agreement enrolled in September 1337. It records that William Wright of Oakington acknowledged receipt of 20 quarters of drage from Thomas Wych of Cambridge 'to make malt thereof', to be delivered to Thomas the following Easter, for which work William would receive 4*d.* per quarter.[40] This entry raises many questions. It is interesting to speculate, for example, about whether Thomas had bought this drage within the village.

[38] For additional comments, see Briggs, 'Credit and the peasant household economy', 243.

[39] *VCH Cambs.*, ix, 201–2; Page, *Estates*, Appendix II (see also review of Page, *Estates*, by R.V. Lennard, in *Economic History*, 3 (1934–7), 130–5). Alex Sapoznik is currently carrying out systematic analysis of the tithes recorded in the Oakington accounts as part of a doctoral research project.

[40] CUL, Q 3, m.25 (30 September 1337): *Willelmus le Wryghte venit hic in curia et recognouit se recepisse de Thoma Wych' de Cantebrigg' viginti quarteria drageti ad braseum inde faciendum, solvendo eidem Thome ad festum Pasche nunc proxime sequentem per plegium Willelmi Katelyne, et dictus Thomas persoluet eidem Willelmo stipendium pro factura brasei predicti videlicet pro quolibet quarterio iiii.d.*

Table 2.4 Types of grain owed in debts

Grain	Oakington, etc. 1291–1350		Oakington, etc. 1351–1400		Horwood 1302–60	Willingham 1377–1400		Littleport 1316–27		Balsham 1310–49
	Loans/ debt in grain	Bought in deferred payment	Loans/ debt in grain	Bought in deferred payment	Loans/ debt in grain	Loans/ debt in grain	Bought in deferred payment	Loans/ debt in grain	Bought in deferred payment	Loans/ debt in grain
Wheat	14	1	3	0	10	3	2	3	0	4
Barley	18	2	0	0	5	15	2	5	0	10
Drage	12	1	2	0	3	0	1	0	0	1
Malt	18	5	1	1	0	5	7	0	2	2
Peas/beans	14	1	5	0	0	2	2	3	0	4
Oats	1	0	0	0	3	0	1	0	0	0
Maslin	2	0	2	1	1	0	0	0	0	1
Rye	0	0	0	0	0	1	1	0	0	1
Unspecified grain	2	2	4	1	0	2	0	0	0	0
Total	81	12	17	3	22	28	16	11	2	23

Sources: See Table 2.1.

What does seem clear, however, is that William would not have been able to make or fulfil such a contract without having sufficient specialized facilities of his own for malt-making.

The presence of malt debts implies that the specialist village producers of malt made surpluses for exchange. Yet what exactly was the character and objective of the Oakington credit transactions involving malt? One possibility is that these debts represent loans of malt made by maltster households to households that specialized in brewing for sale. Yet at Oakington, few households brewed commercially. Between 1320 and 1345, the median number of Oakington individuals amerced for brewing or selling against the assize was just three, compared with seventeen at Horwood in roughly the same period.[41] If households received loans of malt, therefore, it is likely that they did so in order to brew for their own domestic consumption. Any loans of this nature cannot necessarily be described as exigency credit, however. The median volume of malt owed in the eighteen debts from the Crowland villages was one quarter. Since a quarter of malt could produce approximately 50–75 gallons of ale, individuals taking on a loan of malt of this size would have enjoyed the potential to consume ale at a period when ale consumption was not generally frequent in peasant households.[42]

However, as with the Littleport sedge debts, it is difficult to accept that the Oakington malt debts really were loans repayable in the same commodity in which they had been advanced. If Oakington households had to borrow malt for brewing because they did not produce their own malt, then it is hard to see how they could be expected to pay back their malt loans in that commodity. It is more likely that the simple Oakington debts in malt, like the Littleport sedge debts, actually arose from purchase price advances. This possibility is also suggested by the analogy of certain debts in grains other than malt, which are comprehensible only if they are considered as the outcome of a purchase price advance. For example, Thomas Wych, the Cambridge man who made the 1337 contract with an Oakington maltster, also claimed substantial quantities of barley and wheat from two Oakington men in separate plaints of 1338 and 1346.[43] What was almost certainly happening here was that the Oakington men had failed to deliver grain which they had promised to supply to Wych in return for an advance payment. That scenario is much more plausible than the alternative: that an urban resident, not known to have had any land in the village, was lending grain to substantial cultivators.

If the suggestion that the Oakington simple malt debts should be regarded

[41] Briggs, 'Rural credit', 175.

[42] Stone, 'Consumption of field crops', 16; Dyer, *Standards*, 152, 157.

[43] CUL, Q 3, m.28 (16 March 1338, 4q. barley); Q 4, m.9 (11 October 1346, 2q. 1b. of wheat, 2 q. barley).

as the outcome of purchase price advances is correct, then one must regard the malt sellers as the 'borrowers' in such transactions. These individuals would have received an advance payment for malt to be delivered later. Since they were apparently making malt and selling their surpluses for profit, the credit the sellers received through such transactions is unlikely to have been contracted for reasons of exigency.

2.2.3 Cash loans

The purposes for which individuals borrowed cash can only be guessed at using the information in the debt plaints. However, the circumstances of debtors, as revealed by the full range of entries in the court rolls, can sometimes provide an indication of the reasons for taking cash loans.

One important question that may be tackled concerns the extent to which individuals borrowed cash in order to finance land purchases. The use of credit to buy land is one of the three key interactions between the credit market and the villein land market considered in this book.[44] In order to enter into possession of a holding, the new tenant of a villein property was required to render both an entry fine, payable to the lord, and, in many *inter vivos* transfers, a purchase price, payable to the seller. Very often, entry fines could involve hefty sums of cash. For example, when in 1292 William son of Hervy Cosin succeeded to his father's holding in Oakington, he gave 6 marks (£4) as a fine.[45] Although rarely recorded, the typical purchase price in the early fourteenth century is unlikely to have been significantly less per acre than the entry fine.[46] What role did credit play in facilitating such payments?

Some decades ago, Postan pointed to this puzzle of how thirteenth-century villagers were able to find, without much apparent delay, the large sums demanded as entry fines. The answer, he suggested, lay in the role of substantial villagers who acted as creditors, thereby allowing buyers to acquire the necessary sums.[47] Very few, if any, entries in the court rolls studied here, or in any other series, will provide an explicit statement proving that land purchases were financed through borrowing. Nonetheless, Postan's hypothesis can be investigated by looking at the debt litigation histories of individuals who obtained customary land. If one can show that a large proportion of known debtors had recently entered land, then this might provide evidence, albeit circumstantial, that the acquisition of a holding was a major reason for seeking credit.

[44] For the others, see below, pp. 82–92, 156–69.

[45] CUL, Q 1, m.2 (1 August 1292). On the rates of entry fines, see Dyer, 'Seigniorial profits'.

[46] Campbell, 'Agrarian problem', 52; Dyer, 'Seigniorial profits', 235.

[47] Postan, 'Medieval agrarian society', 627.

To explore this possibility, attention is restricted to the three Crowland manors and Great Horwood.[48] These manors were of the 'midland' type, in that their villein holdings comprised standard units—virgates, half-virgates, cottages, and so on—maintained in an unfragmented state.[49] The majority of transfers of villein property in these manors involved entire holdings, rather than odd acres. A large number of people known to have borrowed are also recorded in the court rolls as entering a property. Yet how likely is it that the borrowing was linked to the land acquisition?

To establish a more secure answer, attention was concentrated on those buyers of land who also appeared as debtor in a debt case that began in the year of their purchase, or in the five years following it. For such people, it could reasonably be assumed that the debt case might have arisen because the money they had borrowed to buy land had not been paid back in its entirety.

In the Crowland villages, there were fifty-one debtors in this category. However, when one looks more closely, it is unlikely that all of these people were borrowing cash to buy property. If a buyer of land is subsequently stated to have owed a sum of money, it is possible that the debt arose from a loan, even if the word *mutuum*, or similar, is not actually used. However, nine of the fifty-one persons who acquired land and then crop up as debtors have recorded debts in grain and goods only. Therefore, it cannot be argued that those people borrowed cash to acquire property. A further nine individuals apparently had nothing to borrow for: they acquired properties for which the entry fine was waived, and because none of these acquisitions was an *inter vivos* transfer, there can have been no purchase price. Such acquisitions were particularly common after the Black Death. We are therefore left with just thirty-three debtors—less than 10 per cent of the total number of debtors—who may conceivably have taken loans in an effort to pay an entry fine, or to find a purchase price.[50] Thirteen of these bought properties after 1350, when the need to go into debt to finance land purchase was perhaps not as great as previously, as a result of a substantial fall in the level of entry fines, if not necessarily in the price of land.[51] Furthermore, it should not be assumed that all of the thirty-three indebted land buyers were hitherto landless individuals making their first purchase through acquisition of a holding previously in possession of another family. In eleven instances, in fact, either the 'buyer' obtained the property from a family member, usually as an inheritance, or, less commonly, he already held some property at the point when the purchase under scrutiny was made. Before 1351, only twelve apparently landless indi-

[48] For the Crowland manors, only the period 1291–1380 is considered.

[49] See Chapter 1.

[50] There was a total of 345 debtors in 1291–1380.

[51] For land prices in the fifteenth century, see Dyer, *Age of transition?*, 182–3.

viduals took land formerly belonging to another family, and can be shown to have been in debt shortly thereafter; the equivalent figure for the period after 1350 is ten. On these 'midland' manors, therefore, there is little sign that the cash loan served to any great extent as a means by which an individual entered the ranks of the landholding peasantry.

A similar picture emerges from Horwood. There, nineteen buyers of land crop up in a debt case either in the year of their purchase, or within the five years following. However, seven of these people owed debts in kind only, or entered a vacant holding without paying a fine. Most of the remaining twelve debtors either were related to the previous holder of the land, and received it as an inheritance, or were adding the property to an existing holding.[52] Just five apparently landless persons appeared in debt cases after acquiring holdings previously occupied by other families.

A closer look at the debtors who acquired land from non-kin, and their case histories, shows that a few people almost certainly went into debt in order to gain a property. The prime example is William Fraunce, who in 1303 paid an entry fine of 46*s*. 8*d*. for permission to enter a vacant virgate in Dry Drayton. The nature of at least some of the host of debts later owed by William and recorded in subsequent litigation is such that one may be confident that they represent the legacy of the loan or loans he took to obtain this holding.[53] In other cases, however, it appears fairly unlikely that an individual contracted a loan to pay an entry fine or purchase price, even where that individual can be found in debt shortly after acquiring land. For example, in 1329 Thomas Hervy entered a vacant holding, again a virgate in Drayton, this time together with its accompanying messuage. Some years later, in 1334, Thomas admitted owing Robert Gilberd 18*s*. One might reasonably surmise that this sum was part of a loan taken in order to buy the land. However, the entry fine in 1329 was only 2*s*., and since Thomas entered a vacant holding, no purchase price can have been involved.[54]

As in some parts of southern Europe, then, there is little sign that loans were made to finance land purchases in these villages, and therefore we must revise upwards our estimate of the reliance placed on savings when entering holdings.[55] Why are the signs of this use of credit so scanty? In the absence of a separate, exhaustive study of the movement of land in each village, conclusions must be cautious. It does seem likely, however, that before the

[52] There was a total of 103 debtors in 1302–60.

[53] For Fraunce, see Briggs, 'Creditors and debtors', and below, pp. 153–5.

[54] CUL, Q 3, mm.12d (12 December 1329), and 24d (20 July 1334; Gilberd v. Hervy).

[55] On the limited use of loans to buy land in Trets (Provence), see Drendel, 'Le marché', 434; for a somewhat different picture from Valencia, however, see Furió and Mira Jodar, 'Le marché', 592–610.

Black Death, there were in each village few opportunities for an individual from outside the established landholding families to obtain a property. Vacant niches in the landholding structure were rare, which is why, for example, men paid such high fines to marry widows with their land on the Crowland manors.[56] Since few people had the chance to acquire a vacant holding, or to buy one in an *inter vivos* transfer, there were few loans made to fund such purposes. Furthermore, it seems likely that few creditors would have been willing or able to lend the sums involved in making such purchases. Perhaps, therefore, the purchases tended to be made only by those in possession of substantial savings. Many, if not most, of the pre-plague transfers were inheritances, and here no purchase price was required, which meant the necessity of taking a loan was less. After the Black Death, entry fines were lower, which may help to explain why evidence of borrowing to secure land is limited for that period also.

It is likely that future research will indicate that, in East Anglia, much more credit was contracted with the aim of acquiring property than was the case in villages with a 'midland' landholding structure, such as those under investigation here. In Norfolk and Suffolk, fragmentation of holdings meant opportunities to buy land were simply more numerous than they were in the midlands. Similarly, given the smaller parcels of land involved in sales in those counties, the purchase prices and entry fines would typically have been smaller in absolute terms, if not in per acre terms. In other words, the fines and prices were small enough to be within the range capable of being advanced by local creditors. As a result, there was simply greater scope in that region for a loan to be driven by the wish to obtain land. It is in East Anglia proper, and not in the villages in the midland zone, that one is most likely to encounter the scenario of a landless individual acquiring a small parcel of land and becoming heavily indebted through this process.[57]

2.2.4 *Deferred payments*

A wide range of items, from straw and pieces of leather, to medicine and arrows, were bought with provision for a delay in payment. Many of the commodities bought were destined for immediate consumption, and their purchase thus represents exigency credit. Several debts, for example, were owed for ale and victuals purchased by deferred payment.[58]

[56] Ravensdale, 'Population changes'; Briggs, 'Empowered or marginalized?', 42 n. 41. These fines to marry widows are included in the present investigation of the use of credit to buy land.

[57] As is envisaged in Campbell's model of the early fourteenth century: Campbell, 'Agrarian problem'.

[58] E.g. CUL, Q 4, m.1 (9 December 1344; 22*d.* for ale), Q 6, m.15 (20 November 1367; 3¼*d.* for victuals); CRO, L1/177, m.23 (13 March 1385; 2*s.* 2*d.* for wood and victuals), m.36d (28 September 1390; 3*s.* 1*d.* for ale).

Many other debts, however, are not so obviously the outcome of exigency credit transactions. Sometimes, the quantities purchased were just too large for immediate consumption by the borrower. For example, the 20*s*. worth of fish bought by William Burghard of Willingham for a deferred payment are unlikely to have been entirely for William's domestic consumption.[59] Similarly, Amicia Sebely of Oakington is unlikely to have intended to wear each of the thirty-two pairs of gloves which she had bought for a deferred payment prior to her marriage.[60] It seems much more likely that both William and Amicia bought goods using this credit mechanism with the intention of selling them on to others.

In other cases, the commodities bought suggest transactions as likely to have been driven by investment credit as exigency credit, if not more so. For example, the purchase of a boat would have allowed enhanced scope for the marketing of produce, and thus had the potential to raise future income.[61] However, it was purchases of livestock via deferred payments that were most likely to function as investment credit. Debts for oxen, horses, and cattle are all mentioned in considerable numbers, and there are also scattered references to money owed for sheep and pigs purchased. Of course, it may be that all the livestock obtained via deferred payments were bought simply as replacements. If so, then the transactions concerned cannot really be regarded as investment credit. On the other hand, any purchases of animals additional to those already held had the potential to improve a villager's access to draught power, to boost the quantities of manure available as fertilizer, or to increase the role of meat in the household's diet.

Willingham provides the strongest evidence that deferred payments for livestock were not normally exigency credit transactions. Of the 116 Willingham deferred payment debts (Table 2.2 row (g)), 56 were owed for animals bought, and 22 of those were for young steers (*boviculi*). The Willingham debts for livestock purchases are a reminder that the focus of the village economy lay in the large and frequently flooded common fen pasture and the extensive grazing it provided.[62] A number of by-laws and presentments recorded in the court rolls suggest that for Willingham residents, a

[59] CRO, L1/177, m.57 (28 March 1397). In 1381, John Pelle admitted owing John Cherl 2*d*. for six fish. If one assumes that John owed the full purchase price for these six, and that William Burghard bought the same species, then the latter's 20*s*. would have bought some 720 fish.

[60] CUL, Q 4, m.5d (14 January 1346; John Noteman v. John Sebely senior and his wife Amicia). Another possibility is that the gloves were purchased for distribution to friends at Amicia's wedding; see Laslett, *World we have lost*, 103, for this custom in the seventeenth century.

[61] CRO, R 93/96, m.4 (27 July 1317; 8*s*. for one boat).

[62] Spufford, *Contrasting communities*, 129–34.

typical transaction was to purchase from a non-resident cattle drover beasts for fattening, which would later be sold for meat to butchers originating both inside and outside the village.[63] Deferred payments for steers arose in both types of sale.

The purchase of outsiders' animals on credit is suggested, for example, by a presentment of June 1386, which reported that fourteen Willingham residents had bought steers from drovers using tallies and grazed them in Middlefen (a large section of common pasture) before they had paid for them, in prejudice of the lord and in contravention of an earlier by-law of March 1384.[64] The court rolls show the grazing of livestock before they had been paid for in full to be a matter of frequent seigniorial and communal concern.[65] The apparent reason for this was that the practice exacerbated the general problems of policing the commons to prevent fraudulent overstocking. An important basis for that policing was that villagers should only put their own animals on the common. This, in turn, meant a ban on agistment, which was the practice whereby a villager looked after and grazed animals belonging to others, especially outsiders, in return for payment.[66] Some of those taking in animals in this way apparently tried to avoid being accused of agistment by making a token payment for the agisted animals to their owner. The objective was to convince the officials supervising the common that the animals were actually the property of the villager grazing them.[67] The oft-repeated requirement that livestock could only be grazed when they had been paid for in full, which is interpreted here as revealing that animals were frequently bought on credit, was thus a consequence of the general attempt to

[63] For a contemporary description of this practice of purchase, fattening, and later resale at seventeenth-century Stretham, a nearby fen-edge village, albeit without reference to credit, see Cunningham (ed.), *Common rights*, 288.

[64] CRO, L1/177, m.26d (22 June 1386). The tally was an accounting device consisting of a wooden stick split into two. One part would be kept by each of the parties to a transaction, and the tally could be produced as evidence of a debt. For the 1384 by-law, see CRO, L1/177, m.19d (21 March 1384).

[65] For further entries concerned with punishment of villagers who grazed animals 'before making satisfaction' (i.e. full payment) for them, see CRO, L1/177, m.53d (1 March 1396); CRO, L1/178, mm.9–20 (1 July 1405), 22d–23 (11 March 1406), and 25–25d (22 November 1406).

[66] For explicit references to agistment and its punishment at Willingham, see, for example, CRO, L1/178, mm.25–25d (22 November 1406); L1/179, m.7 (20 March 1426).

[67] For example, the by-law of 1384 makes provision to deal with any person 'who buys beasts from any man with one penny "under colour" [i.e. in pretence that they are his own] and shall not satisfy the vendor for the aforesaid beasts' (CRO, L1/177, m.19d (21 March 1384)), while in 1431 five men were presented for having beasts bought from outsiders and 'going "under colour" of their own property', for which they had given to the outsiders '12*d.* per head, as gain' (CRO, L1/179, m.20 (17 September 1431)). For the practice of 'colouring' foreign beasts by including them with one's own flock, see Ravensdale, *Liable*, 73.

eradicate the disguising of agistment. In other words, the village authorities wanted livestock to be paid for outright, since only then could they be sure about how many of their own animals each person had on the common. Of course, it is possible that the measures taken against agistment and the devices for disguising it had the effect of reducing the incentive to buy beasts on credit from non-residents. However, the credit purchase of livestock from apparently non-resident cattle dealers did happen, as is shown by the presence among the creditors of four individuals described as 'drover', either by surname or by occupational descriptor.[68] Furthermore, Willingham's machinery of commons management did little to restrict people's freedom to sell animals on credit once they had been fattened. Numerous by-laws and presentments concern the issue of 'foreign butchers' being led to view beasts grazing in the fen.[69] If nothing else, these almost certainly demonstrate that butchers came into the parish to buy livestock. The potential importance of butchers as purchasers of animals via deferred payments is further indicated by the presence among the debtors of six individuals described as 'butcher', either by surname or by occupational descriptor.[70]

An examination of the goods borrowed and bought on credit shows that village credit served a wide variety of purposes. Exigency credit and investment credit co-existed. At one extreme, villagers borrowed small items like cooking vessels that were essential for food preparation. At the other, they bought beef animals which they intended to sell for a profit after fattening. In the next section, this impression of striking variety in the uses of credit is subjected to closer scrutiny by looking at the amount of credit given in a transaction.

[68] Hugh Drover, CRO, L1/177, m.17 (20 January 1384, one action); John Ropere Drovere, CRO, L1/177, m.54 (17 May 1396, two actions), CRO, L1/178, m.3d (26 July 1400, three actions); Thomas Sperman Drovere, CRO, L1/177, m.18d (20 January 1384, one action); and Hugh Taillour Drovere, CRO, L1/177, m.30 (16 September 1387, five actions).

[69] See, for example, CRO, L1/177, m.61d (18 March 1398). The concern was not that butchers should be kept out entirely, but that the viewing of animals should take place only with the assent of their owners, or under the supervision of the fen reeves. The aim was clearly to prevent fraudulent sale of another's beasts.

[70] John Bocher of Willingham was the most prolific debtor in the rolls, appearing in sixty actions in this role between 1383 and 1400; John Bocher of Swavesey, CRO, L1/177, mm.31d (9 June 1388), and 41 (11 December 1391); John Bocher of 'Wersle' (unidentified), CRO, L1/177, m.42d (3 July 1392); Richard Bocher, CRO, L1/177, mm.17d (4 December 1383), 23 (13 March 1385), 35–6 (27 July 1390, four actions), and 48 (16 December 1394, two actions); John Maign' bocher, CRO, L1/177, m.32 (3 December 1387); Richard Smyth bocher, CRO, L1/177, mm.23d (13 July 1385), and 25 (13 December 1385).

2.3 The size of debts

In determining whether credit was sought for reasons of exigency or for investment, an obvious question to ask is, how much credit did a lender give? A relatively large debt arising from a loan, for example, might signify that the loan had been taken for more than just essentials. A lender would be unlikely to extend a big loan to someone who was struggling to support his household. Equally, a borrower who was unable to maintain his existing level of production and consumption would probably not have wished to add to his problems by taking a loan larger than the minimum sufficient to meet his immediate needs. However, if both lender and borrower were confident that taking a loan was likely to have a positive net impact upon the borrower's future income, then a relatively generous extension of credit would probably be forthcoming. The larger the loan, of course, the greater the number of uses to which it could be put. A loan of 10*s*. would have given a borrower a much better chance of, say, investing in the purchase of an additional plough beast than a loan of 10*d*. would. These points about the size of loans in money and kind also apply to the level of credit allowed in deferred payments. The greater the purchase price, or proportion of the purchase price that a seller would permit to be deferred, the more likely it is that the debt was contracted with productive intentions. The importance of the evidence on the size of credits is thus obvious, and this section accordingly examines the size of debts in money and grain.[71]

Debt litigation evidence must be used with caution when investigating the size of credits. A sum of money or volume of grain mentioned in a debt case could, in theory, represent just part of the debt originally contracted. Collectively, the courts provide numerous cases in which a creditor attempted to recover more than was eventually allowed by the court. For example, in 1397 at Willingham, John Watteson junior recovered a debt of 17*d*. from Thomas Tredgold, but the jury adjudicating the case also amerced John for claiming from Thomas a further 2*s*. 6*d*. that was not in fact due to him.[72] One plausible interpretation of this and similar cases is that although part of the original debt had been paid off by the time the case came to court, the creditor still attempted to recover the entirety of the original debt. Many debts must have been partially paid off by the time they came to court. Where the creditor did not attempt to recover the part which had already been repaid, as well as the part still outstanding, there is no reason why the court record should mention the fact that a debt claimed and recovered represented just a

[71] Unfortunately, there are not enough published data available on continental European rural debt sizes to permit a comparison with the English material.
[72] CRO, L1/177, m.58 (27 June 1397).

part of the obligation originally contracted. If widespread, this factor could lead to underestimation of the amount of credit given. On the other hand, any sum claimed and recovered would presumably have included the principal plus any additional amount charged as interest. This factor, by contrast, would lead us to overestimate the credit received by the borrower. Thus while evidence derived from debt disputes provides a guide to the amount lent in village credit transactions, it does not always do so in a straightforward way.

A final factor worth mentioning is the 40-shilling jurisdictional limit, which required that debt claims of 40 shillings or more had to be sued in the king's courts, while lesser claims were reserved for the manorial and other local courts.[73] In theory, this rule removes debts of 40 shillings and above from the manorial evidence. However, as Table 2.5 shows, the 40-shilling rule was not stringently enforced in each of the five courts.[74] Furthermore, as the table shows, debts of more than 20*s*. were relatively rare, so it is unlikely that many large debts would be missing from the manorial evidence even where the 40-shilling rule was strictly observed.

Table 2.5 shows the percentages of debts falling within various size ranges in the villages studied here. Also included, for comparison, is equivalent information from investigations of other rural courts. The table shows that in the seven villages, most debts involved sums of 5*s*. and below. Debts in this bracket comprised a minimum of 68.2 per cent of all money debts (Horwood), and up 81.6 per cent (Balsham).

The majority of village credit, therefore, involved sums of 5*s*. or less. Median money debts could be as low as just 14¾ *d*., as at Balsham, and the highest median money debt, which is found in the Crowland villages between 1291 and 1350, was just 3*s*. Existing work has regarded debts of this magnitude as 'small'.[75] Of course, credits of just 2–3*s*. will inevitably attract the description small when viewed alongside sums of 20*s*. and more that were occasionally recovered in debt actions. But were the sub-5*s*. credits also small in an absolute sense, that is, in relation to other aspects of peasant income and expenditure?

In many ways, the answer is yes. To give some impression of the comparative size of these credits, attention may be given to grain prices and rents. The Crowland account rolls show that, locally, the average prices per quarter for wheat and barley between 1290 and 1322 were, respectively, 5*s*. 1*d*. and

[73] Briggs, 'Seigniorial control', 417, and references therein.

[74] Some of the debts of more than 40*s*. in Table 2.5 are recorded in formal recognizances, not litigation.

[75] Dyer, *Standards*, 179; Schofield has described debts of 2*s*. and less as small, debts of 6*s*.–12*s*. as medium-sized, and those of more than about 20*s*. as large: Schofield, 'Social economy', 54–5; Schofield, 'Access', 117–18; Schofield, 'Peasants and contract'.

Table 2.5 Percentages of money debts falling within various size ranges

Seven villages

	Size of debt						
	≤1*s.*	1*s.* 1*d.*–2*s.*	2*s.* 1*d.*–5*s.*	5*s.* 1*d.*–10*s.*	10*s.* 1*d.*–20*s.*	20*s.* 1*d.*–40*s.*	>40*s.*
Oakington, Cottenham, and Dry Drayton, 1291–1350 (N=162)	25.9	14.8	30.2	11.7	11.7	3.7	1.9
Oakington, Cottenham, and Dry Drayton, 1351–1400 (N=124)	30.6	26.6	23.4	13.7	4.0	1.6	0.0
Great Horwood 1302–60 (N=63)	31.7	14.3	22.2	15.9	14.3	1.6	0.0
Willingham 1377–1400 (N=272)	23.5	20.6	27.9	14.7	9.2	3.3	0.7
Littleport 1316–27 (N=172)	25.0	20.3	29.1	13.4	7.0	3.5	1.7
Balsham 1310–49 (N=60)	41.6	21.7	18.3	15.0	3.3	0.0	0.0

Castle Acre and Fulmodestone, Norfolk

	Size of debt			
	3*d.*–4*s.* 11*d.*	5*s.*–10*s.*	11*s.*–20*s.*	21*s.*–39*s.* 11*d.*
1270–1310 ('113 pleas')	48	22	15	15
1338–1356 ('41 pleas')	49	34	5	12
1377–1409 ('84 pleas')	48	31	14	7

Writtle, Essex, 1382–1490

	Size of debt				
	1*d.*–5*s.*	6*s.*–10*s.*	11*s.*–20*s.*	21*s.*–40*s.*	41*s.*–£10
Loans (104)	57	21	11	7	4
All pleas (889)	46	27	14	9	4

Note: Data on the seven villages exclude money debts from rows (a) and (b) in Table 2.2.
Sources: See Table 2.1; Clark, 'English vill', 263; Clark, 'Medieval debt litigation: Essex and Norfolk', 203.

just over 4*s*. 2*d*.[76] In the Crowland villages, a money loan of median size would therefore not have been sufficient to purchase a quarter of wheat or barley at this mean price, though it would have been just enough to buy a quarter of wheat in the very cheapest years, such as 1318–19. The money element of the annual rent of the standard villein tenements at Horwood and the Crowland manors varied from holding to holding within each group, with a maximum of 6*s*. 3½*d*. for an Oakington 10-acre 'full land', 11*s*. 5¾*d*. for a Drayton 30-acre virgate, and 4*s*. 8*d*. for a Horwood virgate.[77] Clearly, any tenant who needed to seek credit to pay the entire money rent for any of those holdings would not be able to do so with a single loan of median size.

It must also be acknowledged that Table 2.5 contains many very small obligations that were almost certainly the outcome of consumption credit. Some 10.7 per cent of all money debts were for sums of 5*d*. or less. An important aspect of the presence of numerous debts of just a couple of pence is that it indicates that little petty credit escaped the court record. Yet the presence of such small debts also provides a guide to the uses of credit. At Balsham in particular, the picture is dominated by small debts which are most likely to have been contracted out of need, and there is little sign of the larger debts that may reflect the use of credit for investment. That said, one must bear in mind the possibility that debts contracted in Balsham's weekly market were recorded only in a separate, lost series of rolls.[78] If we could prove that this happened, it might show that we are receiving a misleading picture of the size of Balsham debts. For example, it is not unreasonable to imagine that the Balsham villagers' credit purchases of expensive investment items like livestock mainly happened on market day. If so, our reliance on records that do not include debts incurred in the market would lead to an underestimation of the average amount of credit extended to Balsham residents.

In any case, it would be a mistake to write off all village credit as small scale. Debts of 10*s*. and more certainly involved what by contemporary standards were large sums of money. One should therefore not disregard the fact that debts greater than 10*s*. comprise more than 10 per cent of all money debts in three of the series of court records, all of which concern the pre-1351 period. To be sure, and unsurprisingly, that proportion is substantially less than has been found in studies of late medieval urban debts.[79] The courts of

[76] Price data are not available for all years; see Chapter 6.

[77] All these holdings also owed labour services.

[78] See Chapter 1.

[79] Kowaleski, *Exeter*, 203 (42 per cent of all debts in 1378–88 of more than 5*s*.); Britnell, *Growth and decline*, 108 (65.4 per cent of debts in 1387/8 and 79.5 per cent of debts in 1398/9 of 5*s*. or more); Postles, 'Loughborough', 19 (47 per cent of debts of 5*s*. or more). See also Dyer, 'Small towns', 524.

Castle Acre and Writtle studied by Clark also yielded a greater proportion of debts of more than 10*s*. than did those of the seven villages (see Table 2.5). However, it is perhaps surprising that this contrast is not more marked, given the unusually diversified and vibrant economy of Writtle, and the fact that the Castle Acre records relate to an honorial court that heard debt pleas, many of them mercantile in nature, originating in commercial centres all over Norfolk.

One must also consider the possibility that one individual could contract separate debts simultaneously from more than one creditor.[80] If there was a ceiling on the amount of credit that a single lender would give, such a mode of operating would perhaps have been a necessity. If one accepts the notion that credit could be sought from more than one source at the same time, then the median debt sizes cited above no longer look quite so small. For example, with respect to the rents cited above, two loans of 3*s*. would cover the greater part of the Oakington cash rent and the whole of the Horwood rent. It also needs to be recognized that borrowers would make purchases partly in cash and partly on credit. That this happened is shown by numerous deferred payments from Willingham, in which the creditor recovered, for example, '18*d*. remaining from the purchase of steers'. The debt outstanding represented the balance that had not been paid immediately in cash. The fact that the median money debt was only 3*s*. or less in the courts studied here need not be regarded as such an obstacle to the acquisition of important resources, once one recognizes that many borrowers had cash reserves that they were able to put towards their purchases.

Table 2.6 shows the size of debts in wheat and barley. In what follows, it is assumed that these debts arose from grain loans. However, as the discussion in the previous section showed, one cannot rule out the alternative possibility that some simple grain debts actually represent the grain that ought to have been delivered in return for a purchase price advance.

Is it possible to infer from the average quantities of wheat and barley owed whether the grain was borrowed for immediate consumption in the household, for processing and sale, or for seed? The wheat debts were small in terms of the median quantities owed. Any household borrowing wheat for consumption would not have been able to eat wheaten bread every day if they possessed it only in these quantities. However, the borrowing of wheat, which tended to be used for loaves of higher quality than those typically consumed in the pre-plague peasant diet, is in itself interesting. If an individual simply wanted to keep himself and his family alive, he would more likely have chosen to borrow and repay a lower value grain.

The median volume of barley owed varied considerably. At Balsham, creditors recovered just 1.5 bushels on average, whereas at Willingham later

[80] Dyer, *Standards*, 180.

Table 2.6 The size of wheat and barley debts (in bushels)

Place and grain	Debts	Mean volume	Standard deviation	Median volume
Oakington, etc., 1291–1350				
Wheat	14	5.2	4.2	4.0
Barley	17	11.2	11.1	8.0
Horwood				
Wheat	10	2.6	3.4	2.0
Barley	5	5.5	2.4	4.3
Willingham				
Barley	15	11.2	9.0	10.0
Balsham				
Barley	10	4.1	5.0	1.5

Note: Includes loans and 'apparent loans' only. Debts only included where at least five debts giving volumes in the category are extant.
Sources: CUL, Q Boxes 3–4 rolls 1–5, 12; NCA, 3912–3914; LMA, ACC/1876/MR/02/001–011; CRO, L1/177–8.

in the century the median barley debt was 10 bushels. This suggests a real temporal contrast in the uses of credit.[81] The small average amounts of grain borrowed at Balsham suggest the possibility that creditors were unwilling to lend more because the grain was destined to be used up in immediate consumption. It is significant in this connection that seven of the ten Balsham debts in Table 2.6 date from between 1310 and 1322, the period in the century in which the need to borrow basic foodstuffs was most acute. At Willingham, by contrast, the median barley debt was much larger. A barley loan of 10 bushels would perhaps have supplied about three-quarters of the grain component of one adult's annual diet.[82] No doubt Willingham lenders could loan more grain because they had greater surpluses than did the Balsham lenders earlier in the century. However, one must also consider the possibility that the amount of grain loaned reflects the uses to which it was going to be put. Willingham borrowers in the last quarter of the century may have been in a better position than their pre-plague counterparts to put the grain they borrowed to productive uses, for example by processing it and selling it as bread or ale, or by using it to sow additional acres.[83]

[81] We must bear in mind the real possibility that larger debts in grain were incurred in Balsham market for which the evidence is now lost.
[82] Dyer, *Standards*, 152–3.
[83] At an average seeding rate, the 10 b. of the median Willingham barley debt would have allowed the borrower to sow some 3.3 acres.

2.4 Conclusion: the varied functions of credit

To establish what sorts of credit transactions were used by English villagers, and to discover why credit was sought, we have no choice but to make inferences on the basis of those disputed debts that were the subject of manor court litigation. It was never the intention of the manor court scribes to give a full account of the transaction underlying each debt, or to explain why a debtor had contracted credit. In spite of these uncertainties thrown up by the sources, however, this chapter has largely confirmed what previous historians have found or suspected when they have sought to identify the types of credit transaction most commonly in use. This is that most credit was extended within the context of a transaction such as a sale or an agreement to perform a task or service for another person. Straightforward loans of money are not a particularly prominent feature of the evidence from the seven villages. Thus whenever this book makes reference hereafter to individuals lending or borrowing, those phrases must be taken to indicate not only the contracting of loans, but also the rather more common practice of giving or receiving a commodity or service on the basis that payment would be made later.

As a result of this characteristic, the medieval English countryside presents something of a contrast to the contemporary European rural scene, where money loans and advances of cash made in *rente* contracts were as widespread as sales credits, if not more so. It might be thought that the relative scarcity of cash loans in England signifies a weakness of rural credit in that country by comparison with parts of southern Europe. However, it is by no means obvious that loans were rare in England purely because would-be lenders were unwilling or unable to offer them. An equally plausible explanation for the muted profile of the cash loan in England is that the credit system functioned quite well without many loans. There would have been relatively little need for loans if without them villagers could still acquire on credit the commodities they wished to buy. To be sure, cash loans were undoubtedly very useful for a range of purposes. Had cash loans been more readily available, for example, more landless families might have sought them in their efforts to buy a holding than appear to have done so in practice. However, as argued above, it was the shortage of opportunities in the villages under investigation, as much as the issue of credit availability, that prevented more of the landless from borrowing to acquire land.

An examination of the commodities named as debts, and of the size of debts, suggests that individuals had a wide range of reasons for contracting credit. Alongside numerous debts arising from transactions in which borrowers evidently sought short-term credit purely to cover their basic needs, are references to commodities purchased on credit or borrowed which could well have been deployed in a quest to maximize the longer-term income or consumption levels of the borrower. It is virtually impossible to give a quantitative answer to the question of whether most village credit was exigency credit or investment credit. As a final point, however, it is worth stressing the way in which certain important debts in kind—the Littleport sedge debts, and the Oakington malt debts—look, on closer investigation, ever more likely to have resulted from investment credit than from exigency credit. The discussion of the sedge and malt obligations presented above suggests that the transaction underlying many such debts was probably a purchase price advance, made in return for a later delivery of the goods, rather than a loan in kind. Far from being the recipient of a small loan in kind made to tide him over a temporary shortfall, the 'borrower' in these transactions appears instead to have received a cash loan on the strength of his future ability to provide the lender with substantial quantities of a highly saleable commodity.

3

The formation of credit relationships

On 26 July 1322, Hugh in Angulo ('at the corner') attended the manor court of Balsham to answer Stephen Carpenter of the nearby village of West Wratting in a plea of debt. The court record states that on 'a certain day', Stephen had lent 20*s.* to Richard Schimming, to be repaid in instalments at the feast of the Purification of the Virgin (2 February) and at Easter, which in 1322 fell on 11 April. Hugh had acted as pledge, or personal surety, to secure the debt. The record states, however, that when Stephen came to collect his money, neither Richard nor Hugh would offer repayment. Instead, the 20*s.* was detained, for which reason Stephen now sued for repayment, and for damages of 6*s.* 8*d.* In court, Hugh acknowledged that he had acted as pledge and had failed to render 10*s.* of the 20*s.*, but objected that the other half of the debt had already been repaid, a claim which was then accepted by Stephen. The court concluded that Stephen should recover the outstanding 10*s.* with damages of 2*s.*, and that both men should be amerced (fined), Stephen for making a 'false plaint', and Hugh for unjust detention of 10*s.*[1]

This case has been described in full because it touches on many of the themes of this chapter, which is concerned with the means by which lenders and borrowers came together, and the terms and conditions of their agreements. Although the detail given in this debt plea is relatively rich, it raises as many questions as it answers. For instance, it might conceivably have been the case that Stephen and Richard, who lived in different villages, did not already know about each other before this loan was made. If so, by what route did Stephen, as would-be lender, come to contract with Richard, as would-be borrower? What were the duties and responsibilities of Hugh as pledge, how was he selected, and what induced him to serve? If, as appears to have been the case, land was not used as collateral, why was this? Did the damages payment claimed and awarded function as a kind of interest payment that was in some way linked to the size of the debt, and did parties perhaps agree at the outset about the imposition of such penalties in case of non-payment? Apart from the damages, was any other provision made for gain or profit to the lender? More generally, how common among all credit transactions were the

[1] LMA, ACC/1876/MR/02/001, m.31d.

various features present in this particular transaction, especially the fixed repayment dates and the use of pledges rather than land as security?

Investigating the techniques borrowers used for identifying and selecting likely lenders, and vice versa, and establishing the terms and conditions on which credit was extended, is vital for assessing the strengths and weaknesses of English rural credit. Where potential lenders had difficulties in discovering potential borrowers and assessing their circumstances, and where the generally observed terms and conditions of lending were such as to act as a disincentive to the formation of contracts, relatively little wealth is likely to have been mobilized in the countryside in the form of credit.

3.1 Information and intermediation

How did an individual with spare cash to lend, or goods that he was prepared to sell for a deferred payment, find a suitable borrower or buyer to whom he would be willing to extend credit? The first requirement was that the lender should know of the existence of a person wishing to receive credit, and be in a position to make contact with that person. The second requirement was that the lender should know enough about the credit history and likely fortunes of the potential client to be satisfied that any debt would be repaid. In a society like fourteenth-century England, it is likely that most suitable borrowers fulfilling these requirements would be people living in the lender's own village about whom he had personal knowledge. In intra-community contracts of this type, the problems of 'asymmetric information' were minor. The lender could make an assessment based on personal knowledge of whether the potential borrower would try to get away without repaying, or was likely to experience circumstances leading to default. In such circumstances, in other words, the dangers of moral hazard and adverse selection would not form much of a disincentive to lending.

Seeking out suitable borrowers with whom the lender was not already familiar through daily contacts—which essentially meant looking outside one's own village community—might involve greater obstacles. It might be costly to search out such people, and in lending to them adverse selection and moral hazard would loom larger. Yet the likelihood is that a credit market which was not restricted to pre-existing personal, intra-village contacts would have had greater strengths, especially from the point of view of borrowers, than one that was. The quantity of credit, and the diversity of credit arrangements available at any one time, would have been larger if previously unknown lenders were encouraged routinely to enter a village's credit networks.[2]

[2] See generally, Schofield, 'Access'.

The potential advantages to be gained from this largely explain why historical studies of European credit have laid such great stress on the role of intermediaries.[3] Figures such as notaries are regarded as crucial links between lenders and borrowers who might not otherwise find out about one another. Intermediaries had information about individuals who wished to lend and about trustworthy borrowers, and brought them together. Intermediaries facilitated loans and reduced the risks involved. In the case of notaries, the incentive to do this came from the financial gains arising from charging fees to register contracts. The most powerful case for the importance of intermediaries in the mobilization of capital has been made in relation to the notaries of eighteenth-century Paris, yet in the same period other figures played the part of intermediary in other contexts with similar effects, as is shown, for example, by the clerks of seigniorial courts in rural Flanders studied by Lambrecht.[4]

Debt litigation material provides no direct evidence of any clearly identifiable group of intermediaries operating in the medieval English rural credit market. One obvious candidate for the role of intermediary was simply not present in the fourteenth-century English village: the notary. Although notaries public are documented in England for the fourteenth century, the work of these figures was emphatically not the same as that of those notaries who, by the later thirteenth century, were authenticating vast numbers of everyday private credit acts of peasants as well as townsmen in Roman law areas of southern Europe. Did the absence in England of figures like the notary lead to a chronic shortage of information, with potential lenders' savings lying idle because they could not identify and contact borrowers to whom they could extend credit with confidence?

The first point to make is that if the role of intermediaries was indeed relatively muted in the medieval English countryside, then this may represent a particularly marked contrast with later centuries, rather than with contemporary Europe. There is as yet no agreement regarding the suggestion that notaries channelled information between lenders and borrowers on any significant scale in the small towns and villages in southern Europe in the fourteenth century. Furió has expressed support for the general idea that the Valencian notary played a crucial role not only in registration, but also as intermediary and broker in the credit market.[5] Yet others have expressed scepticism on this matter, Drendel, in particular, arguing that much credit

[3] Hoffman et al., *Priceless markets*; Engerman et al. (eds.), *Finance, intermediaries and economic development*. For many of the issues discussed in this chapter, see also Guinnane, 'Cooperatives'.
[4] Lambrecht, 'Money lending in rural Flanders'.
[5] Furió, 'Le crédit', 432.

registered by local notaries in Trets in Provence involved parties between whom connections were already well established.[6]

Second, and more important, as is shown in Chapter 4, it is not the case that rural English creditors and debtors were invariably drawn from the same community. True, the rolls studied here do not contain a massive number of non-resident lenders and borrowers identifiable by a domicile noted in the record. However, it is likely that numerous individuals who were not explicitly recorded as non-resident nonetheless lived outside the seven villages.[7] People who did not live and work alongside one another lent and borrowed from one another. This is not entirely surprising. The degree of geographical mobility present in English rural society at this period was probably sufficiently high to allow would-be lenders to hear about borrowers through third parties encountered in everyday contexts. Presumably, too, weekly village markets provided an important point of contact for hitherto unconnected individuals, and, although we are rarely told of the setting for a transaction, it is here that many of the credit sales documented in debt litigation may have taken place. Even in the absence of intermediaries, therefore, credit was clearly mobilized across the boundaries of communities. We can only really speculate about how contact was made between lenders and borrowers who did not already know each other. What is clearer, however, is how lenders in this situation reassured themselves that they would be able to get a stranger to repay. As is argued later in this chapter, this was achieved largely through the system of pledges, or personal sureties.

3.2 The loan term

Among the more important conditions of any credit agreement is the repayment term. On this issue, as with so many other aspects of the nature and purpose of medieval peasant credit, the information in the manorial debt litigation is scanty and hard to interpret. However, provided enough debt cases are surveyed, some conclusions about the loan term may be reached. The first issue addressed here is whether a date or dates for discharging the debt was always set when money was lent or a deferred payment agreed. And second, what was the usual duration of credit agreements?

[6] Drendel, 'Le crédit', 291–3.

[7] Section 4.3.3 below.

3.2.1 Fixed-term or open-ended credit?

Existing work on fifteenth-century court rolls has noted the existence of contracts in which repayment was made 'on demand' at the creditor's request, rather than on a prearranged date. This was a natural arrangement where an ongoing series of reciprocal dealings between two individuals was anticipated. In her study of Havering (Essex), McIntosh suggested that it was possible for two individuals to extend such open-ended credit repeatedly to one another. Over time, such obligations would more or less cancel each other out, and recourse to court for collection of the balance might be required only rarely.[8] Clark also stresses the significance of 'on demand' credit in fifteenth-century Writtle. In general, Clark found considerable evidence of 'reciprocal indebtedness' at Writtle, with credit passing back and forth between pairs of individuals.[9] However, in her discussion of 'on demand' credit, she argues that lending without a fixed repayment date could also engender patron–client relations. The creditor concerned would 'exploit' a personally beholden debtor during the period in which a loan remained uncollected, principally by ensuring that he would remain a loyal customer of the creditor when obtaining goods and services.[10] 'On demand' credit also occurred elsewhere in Europe; for example, 12 per cent of loans in early fourteenth-century Trets were of this type.[11]

If we assume that, in litigation entries, fixed repayment and 'on demand' terms are equally likely to be mentioned, then it is clear that the fixed repayment date was much the more common arrangement in the villages studied. Sixty-six debt cases from the five courts mention a specific lapsed repayment date or dates. There are also a further five cases which state that repayment had been due either 'on a certain day' or 'at a certain term now past'.[12] By contrast, just a single debt action uses the 'on demand' form. This is an Oakington case, begun in 1350, in which John Dayt successfully claimed he had not been repaid one and a half quarters of drage priced 7*s.* lent to Geoffrey King, and payable 'when he [John] shall request it'.[13]

This preference for prearranged repayment days revealed by the fourteenth-century evidence investigated here thus marks a contrast with the picture

[8] McIntosh, *Autonomy and community*, 169.

[9] See Section 5.5 below.

[10] Clark, 'English vill', 265; Clark, 'Medieval debt litigation: Essex and Norfolk', 164–6.

[11] Drendel, 'Le crédit', 303; for notarial acts with 'on demand' repayment terms, see Reyerson and Salata (eds.), *Medieval notaries*, 46, 54.

[12] See, too, the Willingham case which, although the roll is damaged, apparently states that 33*s.* owed for purchase of steers (*boviculorum*) ought to have been paid 'on Monday after the feast of St Laurence in the 11th year of the reign of King Richard II when it shall be requested': CRO, L1/177, m.47 (15 July 1394).

[13] CUL, Q 5, m.5d (28 October 1350).

available from those fifteenth-century localities studied to date. The preference for fixed dates is suggestive of a tendency, already noted in Chapter 2, to treat each credit arrangement as a self-contained entity. The typical rural credit transaction studied here was not normally an open-ended arrangement, settlement of which was seen as dependent on a string of future deals anticipated between the same parties. One can make the argument that credit transactions with repayment terms agreed 'up front' gave less potential for exploitation of the debtor, since they reduced the likelihood of default, and hence of penalties for late repayment coming into effect. Drendel raises this possibility through his interpretation of 'on demand' credit transactions as attempts by Christian creditors to secure gain for themselves while avoiding accusations of usury.[14] The imposition of financial penalties following a delay in payment was viewed by medieval canonists as an acceptable compensation for a lender. As we shall see below, the most convincing explanation for the damages payments often awarded to creditors in English manorial courts is indeed that they represented compensation of this type. If a debtor knew exactly when a debt was to become due, he could plan for that date as far as his resources would allow. By contrast, in suddenly presenting an unprepared borrower with an 'on demand' request for repayment at short notice, a lender stood a good chance that the debtor would not have the wherewithal to pay him back, and hence incur a further penalty destined for the creditor's pocket, which in the English context meant a damages payment. In fourteenth-century England, with 'on demand' credit a rarity, few debtors would have been hit by unexpected requests for repayment at difficult times of the year.

There are of course alternative interpretations of the proportions of credit transactions with fixed and open repayment dates, few if any of which are susceptible to empirical investigation. It is possible to argue, for instance, that 'on demand' credit tended not to increase default and the exactions upon debtors, but rather to reduce those features, by allowing creditors to wait before seeking repayment until those who owed them money enjoyed good financial circumstances. On balance, it is probably safest simply to observe that the prevalence of fixed dates of repayment shown by the fourteenth-century evidence probably reflects a credit market in which terms were usually set out relatively fully at the outset, as they would have to be where persons were involved who did not necessarily know each other well, and could not count on the building up of future obligations in the course of everyday contacts which could be 'set off' against the debt. In other words, the prevalence of fixed repayment dates is more compatible with a system of

[14] Drendel, 'Le crédit', 303.

rural credit which enjoyed some success in overcoming the problems of asymmetric information, than it is with one confined to actors prepared to transact only on the basis of long-established intra-village relationships.

3.2.2 Duration of credit agreements

Over what period of time was money lent, or credit on a sale extended? Few debt entries in our records provide both the date of credit extension and the date or dates at which repayment fell due. In total there are just thirteen cases from the five courts that yield this information.[15] These cases give a median repayment term of sixty-one days. These thirteen loan terms ranged from a single day, as in a Balsham case of October 1346 in which 15*d.* lent on the 'Wednesday after Hokeday' (26 April) was to be repaid on 'the Thursday next following', up to one year, as in the Oakington case in which 20*s.* lent at Michaelmas (29 September) 1352 was to be repaid on the same feast one year later.[16]

A tiny number of debt entries in the case study rolls, the formal recognizances, represent not the resolution of a debt dispute, but the enrolment of a new debt at its inception as part of the court record.[17] They name the creditor and debtor, and state the sum lent, the date or dates for repayment, and the consequences of non-payment. There are eight in total from the five courts. The formal recognizances are considered further below in the discussion of security and written instruments (section 3.4.1). Here, however, it is necessary to note that eight of the thirteen cases that constitute our evidence on loan terms are in fact the formal recognizances. The credit transactions described in the formal recognizances often involved unusually large cash loans. Because the recognizances clearly represent the bigger loans of village society, one might suppose that the lenders involved allowed longer delays in repayment than was the case where, say, the purchase price of a small quantity of grain was in question. Since we are so dependent on the formal recognizances for our information about the loan term, we must ask how typical they are of the totality of credit transactions.

Unfortunately, the five contentious debt plaints that indicate the loan term offer markedly contrasting figures and no clear picture. They comprise the two terms of one day and one year described above, plus terms of four and thirteen days in plaints from Willingham, and a further term of one year

[15] In Chapter 6 below, the evidence from these cases and from those sixty-six cases that state the repayment date is combined to provide the estimate of the time interval between credit extension and the first appearance in court of the related debt case.

[16] 'Hokeday' was the second Tuesday after Easter, i.e. 25 April in 1346. LMA, ACC/1876/MR/02/010, m.2 (8 October 1346); CUL, Q 6, m.13 (23 January 1367).

[17] Section 2.1.3 above; Appendix 1.

from Oakington. Few of the formal recognizances suggest terms of just a few days. The shortest term indicated by the eight recognizances is 20 days, the longest 228 days. The loan terms in eleven further formal recognizances collected in research for this book ranged from 28 days to 794 days.[18] The five main series of rolls investigated simply do not provide enough detail on dates for one to be certain whether reliance on the potentially exceptional recognizances leads to an overestimate of the loan term that would have been specified in the generality of transactions. However, to gain some further information on this matter it is possible to turn to the fourteenth-century court records of West Halton (Lincolnshire), where there is an unusually high level of detail regarding dates in entries that record contentious litigation (see Table 3.1).[19] The table shows that while five creditors required repayment after two weeks or less, the remainder allowed terms in excess of 120 days. At West Halton, then, median loan terms in transactions formed without a recognizance were often no shorter than among those enrolled as a recognizance in the five courts.

Table 3.1 Length of loan term in credit arrangements at West Halton, Lincolnshire

Debt	Credit extension date	Repayment date	Date of lawsuit	Loan term (days)
29*s*.	2 Dec 1311	29 Sep 1312	14 Jul 1315	296
6 q. malt, price 5*s*. 6*d*. per q.	20 Jan 1314	1 Aug 1314	17 Mar 1315	192
13*d*. outstanding from 4*s*. for 1 q. malt	23 May 1314	29 Sep 1314	4 Aug 1315	129
4*s*. 2*d*. for 1 q. rye	1 June 1310	14 June 1310	8 Oct 1313	13
25*s*. for 5 q. barley	25 Mar 1314	29 Sep 1314	21 Oct 1314	188
16*s*. for 2 q. barley	15 Sep 1315	29 Sep 1315	16 Jan 1319	14
2 q. barley	1 July 1318	15 July 1318	16 Jan 1319	14
2 b. wheat	29 Sep 1333	4 Oct 1333	5 Sep 1334	5
46*s*. 8*d*.	4 Oct 1332	24 June 1333	17 Jan 1334	264
20*s*. for wheat, barley, and hemp	29 Sep 1333	27 March 1334	28 May 1337	179
4*s*. 6*d*. for malt	5 May 1334	15 May 1334	16 Apr 1337	10

Note: All pre-1350 debt claims stating dates of credit extension and repayment date are included, except where the court decided that the debt was not owed as claimed, i.e. verdict in defendant's favour.
Source: WAM 14544–14552.

18 Recognizances from: Framlingham (Suffolk), 21 October 1346 (Cambridge, Pembroke College Archives, A1); Blickling (Norfolk), 1 August 1319, 5 May 1320, 2 June 1321, and 14 March 1324 (Norfolk Record Office, NRS 10115 2F6); Meldreth (Cambridgeshire), 22 October 1321 (LMA, HO1/ST/E/079/006, m.1); Bottisham (Cambridgeshire), 26 July 1343 (TNA, SC 2/155/49, m.25d); and Swaffham Prior (Cambridgeshire, four recognizances), all 15 January 1337 (CUL, EDC 7/13/5). Where repayment was required in instalments, the latest date is used.
19 WAM 14544–14552.

To summarize: the meagre evidence suggests that in English villages credit could be given for a few days, or for any period up to a year, yet terms in excess of a year were exceptional. The median was some two months. On the face of it, by later standards this was short-term credit. For a borrower, short-term lending was disadvantageous in that it was not conducive to investment in long-term projects. Also, short-term lending presumably limited the amount people could borrow as they had less time to pay off the debt. Yet just how short were loan terms in the fourteenth-century English countryside compared with those in observation elsewhere in the middle ages?

The answer is that very little comparable medieval credit was extended for periods in excess of one year in the first instance. For one community in eastern England in the following century, McIntosh found that debts were repayable at terms ranging from a few days to a few months.[20] Even in a somewhat more elevated sector of the early fourteenth-century credit market—that represented by the Statute Merchant certificates of debts owed to English parochial clergy—credit was given for just five months on average.[21] The notarial records of the medium-sized town of Salon-de-Provence, which contain credit transactions involving both rural and urban residents, indicate that between 1391 and 1405 repayment was required within six months in 59 per cent of cases and within one year in 95 per cent of cases.[22] At Trets in Provence in the first half of the century, most credit was extended for terms ranging from three to eleven months.[23]

Thus, if credit in our selection of English villages was short term by later standards, the same can be said of other parts of contemporary rural Europe. Of course, it might be misleading to focus solely on the initial loan term given, as de facto terms could clearly be longer. In Provence, when a debt became due it was frequently the case that parties returned to the notary to record an extension or renewal of a loan.[24] We should not assume that similar opportunities for obtaining repayment extension were unavailable in fourteenth-century England. For example, the extremely numerous 'licences to agree' granted by manor courts to debt disputants were almost certainly the precursor to many extra-curial renegotiations of the terms of existing

[20] McIntosh, *Autonomy and community*, 166–8. Clark provides no data on the loan term, but confines her attention to the time period between credit extension and the day of pleading in the manor court, which is documented for 265 Writtle debts: Clark, 'Medieval debt litigation: Essex and Norfolk', 166–7; Clark, 'English vill', 251–2.

[21] Nightingale, 'English parochial clergy', 97. The recognizances that record the large-scale moneylending of several king's clerks indicate an average repayment term of roughly six months: Pugh, 'Some mediaeval moneylenders', 278.

[22] Wernham, *Salon-de-Provence*, 158–61.

[23] Drendel, 'Society and economy', 117.

[24] Drendel, 'Society and economy', 119–22; see also Soldevila Temporal, 'Credit'.

overdue debts, the effects of which were to allow debtors more time. This surmise is made on the basis of those occasional notices of a 'licence to agree' which also record the new conditions for repayment, such as the Littleport example dated 1 December 1326 in which Richard Abbot agreed to repay Thomas Tame the chaplain 2*s*. 6*d*., with half to be rendered at Christmas and half at the feast of the Annunciation of the Virgin next following (that is, 25 March 1327).[25] Thus while the typical English credit transaction had the formal repayment terms appropriate to an agreement that might take place between strangers, there was, if both parties were amenable, always scope for extension of the effective loan term.

3.3 Interest and usury

The usury laws of the medieval church forbade Christians from making a loan with the expectation of receiving anything back beyond the principal. Yet the extensive writings of the medieval canonists, with their lengthy discussions and condemnations of the many ways in which usury could be hidden, themselves reveal better than anything the reality that lending for gain was an everyday occurrence throughout European society. Historians have naturally assumed that the kinds of credit dealings that generated debt plaints in English manor courts involved some degree of profit to the lender.[26] However, they have largely been unable to detect the mechanisms by which this was achieved.

In particular, references to the charging of interest are almost entirely lacking, a silence that is also encountered in European evidence of rural lending among Christians.[27] As many authors have remarked, this silence is not surprising if, as seems likely, contemporaries did not wish to draw attention to activities that may have attracted the charge of usury. In the Mediterranean world of notarial registration, credit agreements could easily be framed to allow for the repayment of a sum of money or quantity of goods larger than that lent without the need to mention this fact in the original act. Similarly in England, where contracts were usually oral, the agreement could easily be couched in terms that would make any reference to gain avoidable in the event of the dispute coming before the manor court. Such precautions made sense in the rural English context where both the manor

[25] This case was in progress by 30 April 1326 and appears in the records of three separate court sessions: CRO, R 93/96, mm.23d, 24, and 25 (30 April, 28 August, and 1 December 1326).
[26] For example, Bailey, 'Peasant welfare', 243.
[27] For example, Redon, 'Conclusions', 344–5; Drendel, 'Society and economy', 101.

courts, mainly by means of the 'view of frankpledge', and the church courts had the power to punish infringements of the usury ban.[28]

Examples of the punishment of usury in church and manor courts are known to be rare. The five court roll series under examination here yield only two instances of condemnation for usury. The earliest in date was made in a Balsham court session of May 1317, and records that John Crane lent Thomas Pistor 10*s*. and that 'for the aforesaid 10*s*. the same John had bread, ale, and money to the value of 8*d*. for three weeks in the name of usury'.[29] The other reference, from Oakington, begins as a fairly standard debt plaint of 1347, in which Henry Makhayt of Cottenham was found to owe Henry Tankret junior 2*s*. 3*d*. However, much more unusually, the record then goes on to note that Henry Tankret is amerced for lending the aforesaid sum to Makhayt 'usuriously'.[30] Prosecutions of usury in manor courts other than the five that are the focus here are equally hard to find, though a couple of reasonably well-known examples exist in the Wakefield (Yorkshire) court rolls of 1315–17, and an isolated presentment of 1325 in the rolls of Meldreth (Cambridgeshire) simply notes that 'Agnes Bateman is a common usurer', and records her 12*d*. amercement.[31] One should not conclude from this small haul that lending for profit was rare. Numerous usury prosecutions are not to be expected if, as already suggested, most people took the precaution of framing their agreements in a form not publicly recognizable as usurious.[32] Also, it is probable that in the manor courts, as in the church courts, the instances of usury formally punished probably represent only those deemed especially egregious by the leading villagers responsible for reporting them to each jurisdiction. In particular, 'excessive' gain in dearth periods may have been especially prone to attract attention. There is a hint of this, for example, in the Balsham presentment cited above, which appears at the height of the Great Famine of 1315–17.[33]

[28] Helmholz, 'Usury and the English church courts'; for usury as an article of the view of frankpledge, see Bailey (ed.), *English manor*, 225.

[29] LMA, ACC/1876/MR/02/001, m.15d (10 May 1317): *Item presentant quod Johannes Crane accomodauit Thome Pistore x.s. & pro predictis x.s. idem Johannes habuit nomine userie pro tribus septimanas ut in pane & cervisia & denariis ad valentiam viii.d.*

[30] CUL, Q 4, m.16 (7 November 1347): *Henricus Tankret junior in misericordia quia recognouit se quod prestitit Henrico Makhayt predictum debitum sub usura etc.*

[31] Lister (ed.), *Court rolls*, 156, 159; see also Seabourne, *Royal regulation of loans and sales*, 181. Meldreth: LMA, HO1/ST/E/079/005, m.1 (17 October 1325).

[32] Medieval writers on usury also appear to have been doubtful as to whether some of the ways of extending credit common in the English village—especially sales credits—were usurious at all: Wood, *Medieval economic thought*, 176–7.

[33] On this point it is interesting to note the presence of two prosecutions for usury in a rare record of ecclesiastical jusrisdiction at parish level, also from 1317: Tringham, 'Parochial visitation of Tarvin', 212, 214.

Until sound evidence to the contrary emerges, therefore, it must be assumed that most creditors made provision for profit in some form, although just how they did it is hard to tease out of the court roll evidence. The subject cannot be ignored, however, since understanding the manner and level of lender's profit built into rural credit arrangements is crucial for any estimate of, first, the extent to which borrowers were 'exploited', and second, the degree of incentive offered by the credit market to the would-be money-lender, or seller of goods on credit. Therefore this section briefly considers the main possibilities for gain, with the exception of the 'gage of land', various aspects of which are treated more fully later in the chapter.

It is easy to imagine how gain could be disguised in each of the main types of credit transaction practised in English villages. In a loan of cash, for example, the amount to be repaid could, as already intimated, simply be greater than that lent, but we cannot know for sure whether this occurred, since the court roll only ever tells us the sum owed. Just one exceptional entry—a Littleport recognizance involving an unusually large debt—gives a hint of the underlying arrangement, in noting that at Christmas and Easter next following the lender, John Fox, should be repaid '£4 6*s*. 8*d*., with one mark [13*s*. 4*d*.] of his damages contained in the said £4 6*s*. 8*d*.'[34] As is discussed further below, the wording of court rolls occasionally gives hints that for contemporaries 'damages' was synonymous with gain or interest, and that certainly seems to be the case in this Littleport example.

As with cash, in a loan of grain, a return for the lender could be secured simply by requiring that the volume repaid should exceed that lent. As Chapter 2 showed, it is possible that some of the debts claimed as a simple quantity of grain may well have arisen not from a loan in that commodity, but from a cash advance of the purchase price. Both the loan made and repayable in grain, and the purchase price advance for grain gave ample scope for making a profit as a result of price changes over the course of the year. For example, a loan of a quarter of barley made in the autumn and repayable in early summer would have yielded a profit owing to a probable rise in price over that period. Alternatively, as mooted in Chapter 2, a lender could have made an advanced purchase at a price lower than the grain would be expected to fetch at the time of its delivery. In a minority of debt cases, the inclusion of the value as well as the quantity of the grain claimed, as in the form 'one quarter of barley priced 4*s*.', hints at credit arrangements designed to profit from changes over time in the price of grain. It may be, for example, that some creditors stressed the market price of the grain claimed as well as the volume because they wanted to ensure that what they received was of suffi-

[34] CRO, R 93/96, m.10 (24 October 1320).

ciently high quality, and therefore value. Unfortunately, however, in seeking to reconstruct the ways in which credit arrangements specifying repayment in grain may have been designed to yield profits consequent upon price change over the agricultural year, we are rather too reliant upon guesswork.

Finally, in a deferred payment on a sale, the sum to be paid by the debtor at the due date could simply be set slightly higher than the price of the article sold at the time of the transaction. The difficulty of checking this hypothesis using the available data, however, can be illustrated by looking at four different Willingham debts from between 1378 and 1384, in which sums of 7*s.*, 8*s.*, 8*s.* 4*d.*, and 13*s.* were claimed, in all cases as the deferred purchase price of one cow.[35] Even if we assume that the full purchase price was owed in each case, one cannot tell whether the amounts claimed varied because a different premium was added as profit in each instance, rather than as a result of real differences in the value of the animals.

It is thus frustratingly difficult to move beyond speculation about how lenders made their profits. But, assuming that some or all of the mechanisms presented above were indeed practised, it should be pointed out that they all had disadvantages for the lender. Most importantly, the possibility of gain depended on repayment being effected successfully at the end of the term, since these methods gave no obvious scope for securing income from interest during the term.

The final step in this section is to consider the possibility that the damages payments mentioned in the debt litigation entries functioned as a form of interest, a possibility that has been raised by at least one historian.[36] Damages payments were frequently claimed by debt plaintiffs, and paid by debtor to creditor once awarded by the manor court. As noted above, canonical theory on usury allowed that a penalty in favour of the lender was legitimate compensation in the event of a delay in payment.[37] The manorial damages payments should certainly be seen in the context of that provision. Occasional manor court roll entries suggest that some contemporaries certainly thought of the function of damages in terms of their role in providing a legitimate return on a creditor's loan.[38] An entry from the Cambridgeshire village of Bottisham, for example, records a plaint in which the debtor acknowledged an outstanding obligation, whereupon it was ordered by the court that 'the 29*s.* of principal and 12*d.* of damages' should be levied to the use of the creditor, Thomas Gerard.[39] However, although damages payments clearly

[35] Respectively, CRO, L1/177, mm. 13 (22 September 1382, two actions), 20d (6 September 1384), and 2–2d (4 May 1378).

[36] Bailey, 'Peasant welfare', 243.

[37] McLaughlin, 'Teaching of the canonists', 139–43; Wood, *Medieval economic thought*, 188–90.

[38] For the sole such entry from the five courts, see the Littleport example cited earlier.

[39] TNA, SC 2/155/52, m.8 (11 October 1371).

represented a useful windfall for many creditors, and an unwelcome additional burden to many debtors, it is clear that damages did not operate as a mechanism through which the profits to be made in the medieval English rural credit market were routinely or systematically secured.

For one thing, while the bigger debts tended to be accompanied by the biggest damages claims, there was no obvious relationship between the principal debt sought in litigation and the amount of damages claimed, of a kind that would suggest a generally accepted 'sliding scale' of damages payable according to the monetary size of the debt. At Oakington, for example, damages of 4*d.* were claimed in separate plaints by creditors seeking the recovery of debts of 6*d.*, 11*d.*, and 24*d.* respectively.[40] Very frequently, the court revised down the creditor's damages claim and awarded a much lower sum, and the creditor seemingly had little control over the final amount received. Furthermore, assuming that the court roll always mentions damages when they were claimed or awarded, it is clear that many creditors did not actually seek damages. Table 3.2 shows the total of cases in the five courts in which at least one debt was successfully recovered by a plaintiff, and indicates the proportion of such cases also featuring a claim or award of damages. It shows that damages were sought or received in addition to the principal debt in a little over 54 per cent of cases. Even at Willingham, where damages were most consistently mentioned, creditors 'remitted' the damages awarded to them by the court in 79 of the 261 cases in Table 3.2. Creditors did not always exact damages, either through leniency towards their debtors or, perhaps more likely, because they had made adequate alternative provision for gain. Most crucially, damages were never a guaranteed form of profit to a lender, because

Table 3.2 Debt cases in which damages were claimed and/or awarded

Court	Cases in which at least one debt recovered (A)	Cases in A in which damages awarded/claimed (B)	B as percentage of A
Littleport	225	50	22.2
Balsham	90	43	47.8
Willingham	315	261	82.9
Oakington	396	222	56.1
Great Horwood	91	31	34.1
Total	1117	607	54.3

Note: Excludes debt cases ending in 'false claim', or complete exoneration of defendant.
Sources: See Table 2.1.

40 CUL, Q 5, m.13 (Admund v. Goldyng, and Hervy v. Wryth, 23 January 1354); Q7, m.15 (Grey v. Atte Grene, 22 April 1376).

receiving a damages payment depended on the debtor making default and the case coming to court. In providing for their own advantage when forming credit relationships, therefore, creditors placed most reliance on one or other of the strategies which—albeit with an inevitable degree of speculation—were outlined in the earlier portion of this section.

3.4 Security for credit

When forming credit relationships, what measures did lenders have at their disposal to reduce the likelihood of default, or at least to minimize its impact on themselves? How successful and widespread were such measures, in comparison with those employed in other times and places in pre-industrial Europe? Obtaining security for a debt involved at least two key aspects: first, that of proving that an obligation had in fact been contracted and was still outstanding; and second, the right and power to seize the borrower's property as compensation for non-fulfilment. Both these aspects crop up in the following discussion of the primary means of protection against default practised in the medieval English countryside. The question of whether collateral, typically land, was required or available in an agrarian credit market is important, since it is usually held that the ready use of collateral reduces the problems of 'asymmetric information' and, more specifically, perhaps stimulates contracting between individuals from different communities in the manner stressed at the start of this chapter.[41] Also, it is probable that, given lenders' attitudes to risk, the more effective the various security measures used are, the larger the overall quantity of credit available at any one time is likely to be, and the larger the size of individual credits.

3.4.1 Written instruments

In the European regions where Roman law prevailed, everyday private transactions, including credit transactions, were routinely given written form via notarial acts. Kept in massive quantities, these acts, when copied into the notaries' registers, functioned as an indisputable authentication of each contract which could be produced as proof in the event of any allegation of its non-fulfilment. Large swathes of rural southern Europe, therefore, were part of a culture of record use in which creditors protected themselves through writing as a matter of course. Not surprisingly, strong claims have been made for the critical role of the notarial system in promoting the effective func-

[41] For a discussion, see Udry, 'Credit markets', 252–61.

tioning, extension, and development of the rural credit market in these regions.[42]

England, by contrast, was the 'land of the sealed document', where individual charters validated by the private seals of contracting parties, rather than notarial acts authenticated and maintained by an officially sanctioned third party, were the mode of proof of private transactions.[43] Numerous types of sealed deed were used to record credit agreements, notably the bond.[44] Such instruments are ubiquitous in some forms of evidence on credit such as early modern probate documents, or cases concerning high-status debts heard in the medieval courts of common law.[45] The medieval manorial sources, however, rarely mention written instruments of debt. Almost certainly, the reason for this is that manor courts did not have the power to consider the sealed writing, or 'specialty', as a means of proof in a debt case. In effect, the manor court could only be used to enforce oral agreements.[46] If writings could not be used to prove that a debt was outstanding in what was 'court of first resort' for most English village creditors, then it probably follows that such writings were rarely used by them to record a debt and its terms and conditions. Further, if we assume that a contract made in a purely oral manner offered a lender less security than one recorded in writing, we arrive at one of the major questions addressed by this section: did the less extensive use of written evidence make English lenders worse off than their continental counterparts in terms of security, and if so, did this act to impede the growth of the English credit market by comparison with that in southern European areas of notarial culture?

A fuller answer to this question must be deferred until the section's conclusion, since it demands that the other forms of security be explored first. At this point, though, it is necessary to note that the use of writing as proof of a debt was not entirely absent from the manorial scene. Reference has already been made to the formal recognizances, which represent the registration of a new debt agreement on the court roll. The formal recognizances collected in research for this book, which all date from between 1319 and 1346, vary in their wording. However, the type probably most advantageous to the lender from the point of view of security provided that, in the case of non-payment, the bailiff of the lordship would cause the outstanding sum to be levied from the debtor's goods and chattels; that is, property would be

[42] Furió, 'Crédit, endettement et justice'.
[43] Clanchy, *From memory to written Record*, 298–9. For the limited role of notaries in recording private acts in England, see Cheney, *Notaries public*, 50–71; Finucane, 'Two notaries'.
[44] Postan, 'Private financial instruments', 29–34.
[45] Spufford, 'Long-term rural credit', 217; Poole, 'Debt in the Cranbrook region'; Palmer, *English law*, 69–72.
[46] Beckerman, 'Customary law', 224–6; Schofield, 'L'endettement', 81.

seized. Eleven of the nineteen recognizances have this key clause. At present it is not clear exactly how the bailiff's involvement was triggered, since no further reference can be found to any of the debts described in the recognizances. Apparently, though, the village creditors who arranged the enrolment of these instruments obtained a proof of their debtors' obligations and guarantee of automatic assistance in recovery in case of default, which in form and effects was close to that enjoyed by the predominantly mercantile lenders who used the debt registration system created by the statutes of Acton Burnell (1283) and Merchants (1285).[47] In essence, the manorial recognizances were modelled on the instruments used by that system. The remaining eight recognizances do not provide for the automatic seizure of movables, but make other provisions, usually the appointment of pledges who guaranteed to repay the debt in the event of default by the principal debtor.

Why are the formal recognizances so rare? As already mentioned, they record some of the largest debts encountered in court rolls. Among the fifteen recognizances for debts in money the smallest is for a sum of 5*s.*, which is some way above the average for all money debts (see section 2.3), and there are eight debts of 20*s.* or more in recognizances, including two massive Littleport debts of £4 6*s.* 8*d.* (mentioned above) and 11 marks sterling (£7 6*s.* 8*d.*). One potential explanation for the rarity of recognizances could be that the alternative modes of security considered in the next two sections normally sufficed for creditors, and that it was only worth requesting the court to enter a recognizance when the debt was sufficiently large to justify the trouble. On the other hand, it did not necessarily cost anything to enrol a recognizance; no charge to the creditor is recorded in the nineteen examples collected here. Thus it is perhaps surprising that more creditors did not take advantage of this form of protection. After all, even though a creditor could use the ordinary manorial debt litigation procedures in order to secure the same official powers of levying debts from a non-paying debtor as could be obtained through a recognizance, doing so was not automatic as it was in the case of the recognizance, since it required a court judgment in the plaintiff's favour.[48]

A further and important explanation for the rarity of recognizances in manorial court rolls lies in the background, experiences, and even culture of the lenders who typically procured them. The creditors most likely to request that a formal recognizance should be entered on the manorial court roll

[47] Postan, 'Private financial instruments', 35–40; McNall, 'The business of statutory debt registries'. The Statute Merchant certificates generated by this system have been used in various studies by Nightingale.

[48] Briggs, 'Manor court procedures', 548–50.

would have been those who knew about such instruments from institutional and legal contexts outside the village. In this connection, it is notable that in eight of the nineteen recognizances, the lender was a member of the parochial clergy. The parish clergy produced some significant operators in credit markets existing at regional as well as at village level, and many rectors, parsons, vicars, and chaplains used the system of Statute Merchant recognizances.[49] The rarity of formal recognizances in the manorial documentation perhaps reflects the fact that few within village society were sufficiently conversant with these instruments to request their use. Within the small group who did know about recognizances from their wider experiences, and valued the security they gave, parish clergy were probably numerically significant.

3.4.2 Land

Medieval and early modern lenders in England and elsewhere in Europe often required that collateral in the form of land or other real property be given by the borrower as security for a loan. The employment of land as collateral was just one of the various and intricate ways in which the transfer of land and the provision of credit were interconnected in village societies more generally.[50] In addition to the use of land as security, there were at least two other contexts in which credit and the land market interlocked, namely the purchase of land on credit and the use of land sales or transfers as a means of repaying existing debts. Both are considered elsewhere in this book. The subject of the present section is the transfer of land from debtor to creditor at the outset of a credit relationship, and as a condition of credit extension. The aim of this was to confer rights over some part of a debtor's property to his lender, which the latter could subsequently exploit to recover a debt in the event of non-payment. Although the literature on rural credit is not replete with discussions of the details of arrangements of this kind, they were clearly widespread, and examples can be found in contexts ranging from thirteenth-century France to seventeenth-century Yorkshire, albeit with a good deal of variation with respect to the precise form taken.[51] How common were they in fourteenth-century English villages?

In England, the main way of using land to secure a credit arrangement in this period was the mortgage. The common law mortgage of freehold land had a fairly straightforward form. A property was conveyed by borrower to lender, which would later be reconveyed back to the borrower if he repaid the

[49] Nightingale, 'English parochial clergy'.

[50] Béaur, 'Foncier et crédit'; Furió and Mira Jodar, 'Le marché'.

[51] Gaulin and Menant, 'Crédit rural', 40–4; Beck, 'Historiographie', 124–5; Pelaquier, 'Les mutations foncières', 143; Kew, 'Mortgages'; French and Hoyle, 'Slaidburn', 369–75 (for mortgages).

debt on or before a specified date. However, if the borrower did not make such repayments successfully, the lender would then either acquire, or continue to enjoy, permanent ownership of the land.[52] Mortgages containing these same key elements could also be made with villein or customary landed property, which is the kind of property to which attention is restricted in this section, since only customary, and not free land transfers can be fully examined using manorial court rolls.[53] Scholars have spotted examples of mortgages of customary land in manorial court rolls. However, they are rare, and are most likely to be found after 1400. This chronology is suggested by their unusual prominence in Whittle's evidence for her study of Norfolk in the years 1440–1580, and the fact that four of the five mortgages of customary land included in Poos and Bonfield's collection of property law cases date from between 1385 and 1573.[54]

No mortgages of land have been traced in the five fourteenth-century court roll series that form the core of the evidence here, nor in any of the pre-1350 court roll series searched in the wider trawl undertaken for this book.[55] This evidence appears to speak for a negligible role for the employment of land as security in English village credit. In part, of course, the lack of written reference to mortgages in the manorial court rolls is simply another aspect of the overwhelmingly oral quality of rural credit. Since the terms of credit agreements were rarely written down at their inception, it is no surprise to find little reference to the part played by collateral in such agreements. Is it then possible that provision for the use of real property as security was nonetheless made in the purely oral contracts favoured by English peasants?

As evidence against this suggestion, it should be noted that it is not just the recording of new agreements involving the conveyance of land with conditions dependent upon debt repayment that is rare in manorial court rolls. In fact, direct references to land pledged as security hardly ever crop up in any area of manor court business, even in likely areas such as disputes over the rights to real property. Nonetheless, it is worthwhile pushing the available evidence harder in an effort to determine whether the almost complete absence of the employment of land as security is as real as it appears.

[52] Brand, 'Aspects of the law of debt', 31; Barton, 'The common law mortgage'.
[53] For a preliminary study of credit and the freehold peasant land market, based on charters, see Briggs, 'Credit and the freehold land market'.
[54] Whittle, *Agrarian capitalism*, 116–19; Poos and Bonfield (eds.), *Select cases*, clxiii–clxvii. For a largely fruitless search for clear examples of mortgages in the Wisbech (Cambridgeshire) court rolls 1327–77, see Parkin, 'Courts and the community', 216–18.
[55] A formal recognizance dated 1320 from Blickling, one of the nineteen discussed in the previous section, includes the appointment of pledges to guarantee the repayment of the principal debt, plus a mortgage of 1r. 15p. of the debtor's land to the use of one of the pledges, to be held by the pledge and his heirs if the debtor shall fail to make payment.

For this purpose, temporary subletting is examined. Inter-peasant leases of customary land are recorded in large numbers in many manorial court rolls. The entries recording these transactions contain no direct statement that the lease was connected to a debt. Nonetheless, some historians have advanced the possibility that many leases were not 'husbandmen's leases' used to redistribute land for cultivation, but were instead motivated by the aim of securing credit.[56]

The suggestion seems reasonable, given that the mortgage proper, discussed a moment ago, itself sometimes took the form of a conditional lease or demise for a set period of time, which would become permanent only in the event of non-payment. Contemporary texts on usury such as confessors' manuals and the writings of canonists confirm that the lease, or 'gage of land', was a widespread method of securing a loan, and of allowing the creditor to make an illegal usurious profit.[57] The typical scenario described in those sources involved a borrower immediately transferring his land in a lease for a term, in return for a loan from the lessee. During the loan term, the lender took the profits from the land but did not subtract them from the original debt. In this way, he obtained a gain beyond the principal. The fact that the gage of land was known to be a standard device for disguising illicit gain illuminates the possibility that some inter-peasant leases in court rolls might relate to the inception of credit arrangements, even though they do not explicitly say so. In order to avoid accusations of usury, peasants may have wanted to omit phrases establishing a clear link between the lease and a credit deal, when having their leases recorded in the court rolls. In short, the peasant lease market is an obvious place to look for transactions that performed a function similar to the formally enrolled mortgages, while leaving their terms and conditions unrecorded.

Table 3.3 shows the numbers of inter-peasant leases for terms of years of portions of customary standard holdings recorded in the Oakington and Horwood court rolls before 1351. Not all series of court rolls contain leases like these, and some feature only a handful. Court records of 'midland' manors and villages, where the tenant land was held in relatively large, unfragmented standard holdings, are more likely to contain them than those of 'East Anglian' manors, in which former standard holdings had long fragmented into small pieces. The four manors covered by the Oakington and Horwood rolls were of the 'midland' type. Most of the permanent transfers of land on these manors were of entire standard holdings. Many transfers of

[56] Brooke and Postan (eds.), *Carte nativorum*, lvii–lviii; Harvey, *Westminster Abbey*, 317; Schofield, 'L'endettement', 83–4; Schofield, 'Manorial court rolls', 241.

[57] McLaughlin, 'Teaching of the canonists', 112–15; Haren, *Sin and society*, 164–6.

Table 3.3 Inter-peasant leases, Oakington (with Cottenham and Dry Drayton) and Great Horwood

	Leases	Leases with lord's licence	Leases without lord's licence	Not known whether licensed
Oakington, Cottenham and Dry Drayton, 1291–1350	262	120	121	21
Great Horwood, 1302–1350	164	69	95	0

Sources: CUL, Q Boxes 3–4 rolls 1–5, 12; NCA, 3912–3914.

these standard holdings were inheritances passing between kin, rather than *inter vivos* sales between non-kin.

The temporary subletting of small parcels of customary holdings, where the modal area leased was around half an acre (Table 3.4), was distinct from the permanent alienation of entire holdings.[58] A typical subletting entry is: 'John Kylle demised to John Lomb by lord's licence half an acre lying upon Metelond [a furlong, or subdivision, of the open field] for two croppings, namely from the feast of Michaelmas last past for the two years next following, fine 4*d*.'[59] The detail is minimal. We are not told how the land was going to be worked or who was going to receive the proceeds during the term, nor the rental arrangements. Leases required seigniorial licence, for which a small payment (fine) was made. Subletting initially carried out without licence was reported to the court (Table 3.3), but one cannot know how consistently such illicit transfers were reported. One reason for the varying incidence of leases in different sets of court rolls was that some lords allowed short leases of a year or two without licence, while others did not. Leases for a term too short to require a licence do not appear in the records. At Oakington, Cottenham, and Drayton, and at Horwood, the length of most leases was fixed by the agricultural year, as they are given in numbers of 'croppings'. Here, even leases of one 'cropping' or year required seigniorial licence, and the vast majority of leases lasted for two 'croppings' or years, or less (Table 3.5). Local variations in the demise permissible without licence perhaps had some influence on any employment of leases to secure debts, because pledging of land in this way would perhaps have been more attractive if there was no seigniorial charge on it.[60]

Is it possible that a borrower sometimes granted a lease to a creditor at the same time as receiving an (unrecorded) loan from him, and that the lease served as security? As the example lease in the previous paragraph shows,

[58] Not all leases give the area of the land transferred.

[59] CUL, Q 3, m.1d (21 January 1325).

[60] Harvey, *Westminster Abbey*, 321

Table 3.4 Area of land leased in inter-peasant leases (ac.), Oakington (with Cottenham and Dry Drayton) and Great Horwood

	Leases	Leases giving area	Mean (acres)	Median (acres)	Mode (acres)
Oakington, Cottenham and Dry Drayton, 1291–1350	262	209[a]	1.03	0.75	0.50
Great Horwood, 1302–1350	164	153	0.98	0.50	0.50

Note: [a]In thirty-seven instances the area leased is given in selions. The records suggest one selion covered approximately 1r.
Sources: See Table 3.3.

Table 3.5 Length of term of inter-peasant leases, Oakington (with Cottenham and Dry Drayton) and Great Horwood

	Length of term ('croppings'/years)					
	1	2	3	4	5–10	Total
Oakington, Cottenham and Dry Drayton, 1291–1350						
Leases giving term in 'croppings'	63	33	3	13	0	112
Leases giving term in years	1	10	14	4	9	38
Great Horwood, 1302–50						
Leases giving term in 'croppings'	11	81	0	5	1	98
Leases giving term in years	5	1	1	1	3	11

Note: Length of term is not known for all leases. A lease of one 'cropping' (*vestura*) presumably allowed the lessee to crop the land once, two 'croppings' allowed him to take two crops etc.
Sources: See Table 3.3.

there is no information about what happened to the land at the end of the term. There is no suggestion that it would pass permanently to the lender in the event of non-payment, as it would in the mortgage proper. However, even without such a condition, a lease could still conceivably have acted as security, because if the debtor did not repay, the creditor could recover what was owed to him out of the income from the leased land.[61] Furthermore,

[61] Brand, 'Aspects of the law of debt', 30, describes an arrangement common in the later twelfth century in which land was 'gaged' to the creditor as security until the debt was paid off, but which involved no permanent transfer to the creditor.

separately from its functions as security, any lease made in favour of a creditor as a condition of a loan could potentially have served as a means of profit for the lender, as the contemporary writings on usury were at pains to point out. Even if a lender took the crops of just a single year from the borrower's land in addition to the principal, a useful profit could still have been made on a credit arrangement accompanied by a lease.

Unfortunately, however, even if we concentrate just on the lease's possible role as security, we are uncomfortably reliant upon unproved suppositions. There is no way of obtaining a reliable estimate of what proportion—if any—of the leases were actually gages of land made at the beginning of a loan. However, some progress can be made by examining the chronological incidence of leases (Figures 3.1 and 3.2).[62]

At Horwood, and at Oakington at least before 1337–8, there is a pattern of numerous years with few or no leases, punctuated by years in which leasing was much more common. Some of these years of above-average leasing activity are well-known 'crisis years' of dearth and high prices, heavy taxation, or a combination of the two. For instance, an active lease market is documented for 1295–6, 1321–2, 1330–1, and 1331–2. An obvious response to this evidence is to say that if there was a connection between the leasing of land and the credit market, it was simply that peasants sublet their land to raise money to repay debts once they became overdue in years when they were in difficulties, and not that land was leased as security at the start of credit relationships.

This argument is perfectly plausible, and probably explains the motivation behind many short-term leases. However, if we look more closely at exactly which years before 1351 saw the greatest leasing activity, and which saw little, it appears we cannot entirely dismiss the idea that some leases were functioning as security. For instance, in Chapter 6 it is argued from the litigation evidence that some new credit continued to be extended at Horwood even in the dearth year 1321–2. It is therefore striking that 1321–2 saw the greatest total of Horwood leases. Some of these leases may have accompanied new loans, the high incidence of leases in that year being a sign that creditors were demanding an unusual degree of security as a condition for extending credit in such unpropitious circumstances. Similarly, the Oakington shift from the year 1337–8 to a relatively high annual total of new

62 Figures 3.1 and 3.2 use the Michaelmas (29 September) to Michaelmas accounting year; 1300 is the year 1299–1300. By contrast, Briggs, 'Creditors and debtors', and Briggs, 'Manor court procedures' use the calendar year beginning 1 January when presenting data on annual totals of debt plaints. Half the 'unknown' actions—i.e. those with insufficient details to determine whether they are debt or trespass, and which could be debt—are entered in Figures 3.1 and 3.2 as 0.5 actions. All actions (debt and 'unknown') terminated as 'false claim' or 'false plaint', or with the defendant's complete exoneration, are excluded from Figures 3.1 and 3.2.

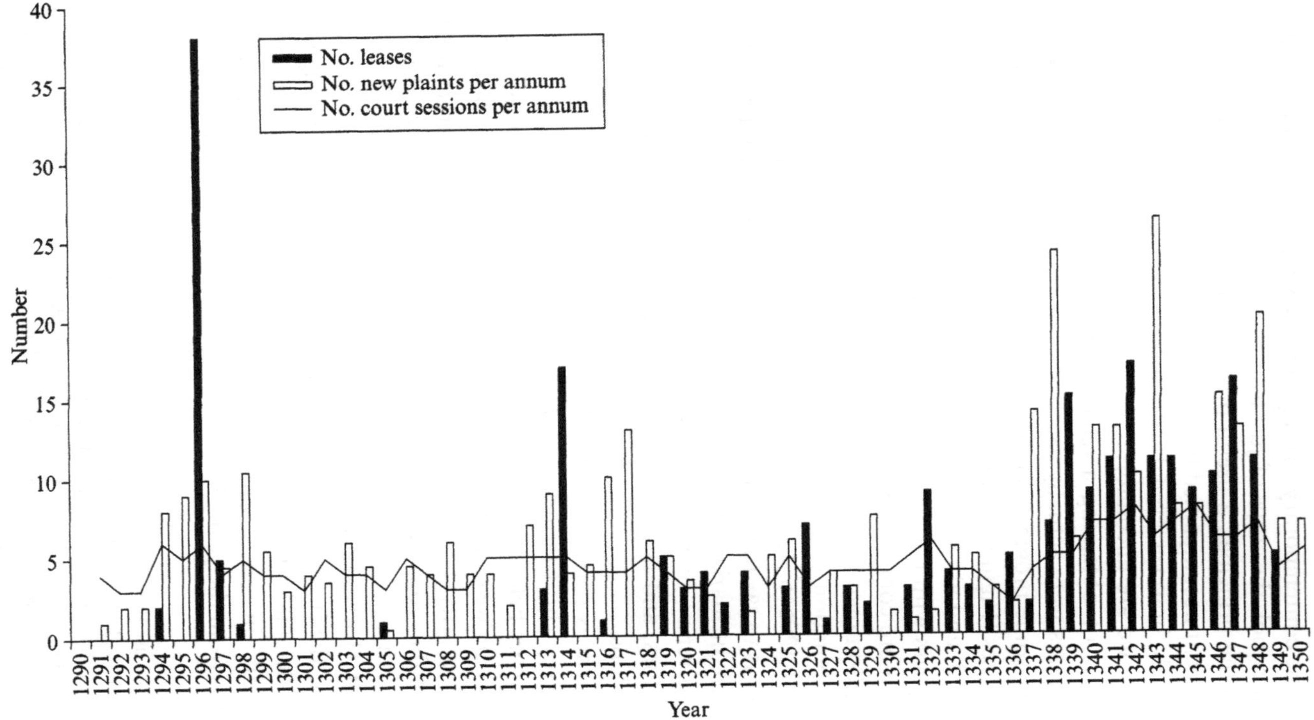

Figure 3.1 New debt plaints and inter-peasant leases per annum, Oakington (with Cottenham and Dry Drayton), 1291–1350

Notes: Includes half 'unknown' actions, excludes 'false claims', etc. 1300 = harvest year 1299–1300.
Source: CUL, Q Boxes 3–4, rolls 1–5 and 12.

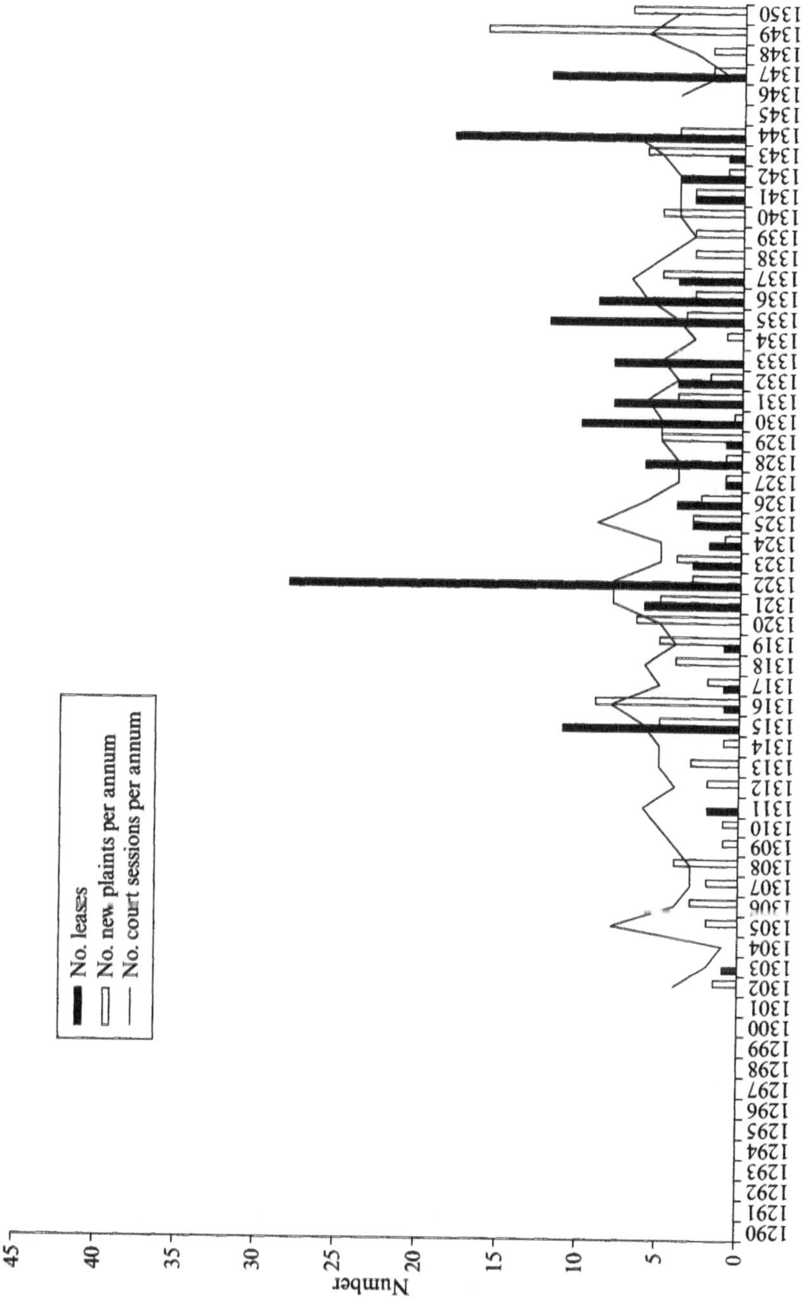

Figure 3.2 New debt plaints and inter-peasant leases per annum, Great Horwood, 1302–1350

Notes: Includes half 'unknown' actions, excludes 'false claims', etc. 1300 = harvest year 1299–1300.
Source: NCA, 3912–3914.

leases throughout the following decade is compatible with the claim in Chapter 6 that the period from 1337 to the Black Death saw a relatively healthy credit supply on the Crowland manors. Many leases on the Crowland manors between 1337 and 1349 may thus have represented the collateral that creditors demanded in order to extend credit, rather than simply being a device for generating liquidity in order to meet outstanding obligations.

Leases thus tend to crop up mostly in those years which Chapter 6 argues saw a maintenance of credit availability in spite of conditions of dearth or heavy fiscal exactions. This, in turn, leads to the argument that some leases may indeed have been requested as security. The only instance that does not fit with this argument is the period 1329–31 at Horwood, years in which leases were relatively numerous but credit supplies, in so far as one can tell from the litigation pattern, broke down.[63] On the other hand, further support for the argument comes from the evidence of those years which had very few or no leases. It is particularly striking that leasing was so rare at both Oakington and Horwood in the famine years 1315–16 and 1316–17. One possible explanation for this, of course, is that subletting was not reported in court at this time because people were turning a blind eye to illegal, unlicensed leases out of consideration for the desperation of individuals. Nonetheless, if leases were solely a way of raising money to repay debts, one might expect more of them in 1315–17, given the severity of the conditions. The rarity of leases in those years is even more surprising in the light of those studies of 'East Anglian' manors which have repeatedly shown that the sale of small pieces of land peaked in 1315–17.[64] These sales are usually seen as the equivalent of the short-term leases of small plots of 'midland' manors, and, like them, are often interpreted in terms of the sellers' short-term need for cash to repay debts and buy food. A possible solution to the conundrum of the rarity of Oakington and Horwood leases in 1315–17 may lie in the evidence, presented in Chapter 6, that credit was largely withdrawn in the midst of the famine conditions. If, as is being currently suggested, a certain number of leases were made at the outset of credit transactions as a form of security, then we would not expect to encounter many leases in the record for years when lending was in abeyance.

If some leases were used for security, as well as to generate cash for debt repayment in difficult years, this would also help to explain why leases crop up in some numbers on occasions when short-term crisis was absent. At Horwood such years include 1314–15, 1334–5, and 1343–4, while at Oakington they include 1313–14 and 1325–6. Of course, the predicaments of particular individuals often explain unusual patterns. For example, six of the

[63] See Chapter 6, p. 190 below.
[64] Campbell, 'Population pressure', 114; Clarke, 'Peasant society', 105–43.

seventeen leases of 1313–14 on the Crowland manors were all made by John Wilwes (Willows) of Oakington, who leased a total of more than nine acres to six different lessees in September 1314.[65] Yet even without John's leases, the total in that year would still have formed a marked contrast to the almost complete lack of leasing since 1300. One of several possible explanations for this is that lenders in 1313–14 were demanding increasing security in the form of leases.

A conclusive verdict on the functions of subletting is unlikely to be easily reached. In any case, the functions of a lease, and the motivations behind it, undoubtedly varied from one instance to another. What does seem clear is that subletting was connected with indebtedness in some shape or form. As will be seen later, when the focus returns to subletting and the relationships it entailed, most leases were made by people known from the litigation evidence to have been debtors, while known creditors loomed large among those to whom land was demised.[66]

The pledging of land as security for credit in these villages is hard to demonstrate conclusively, and even when one adopts assumptions that are most favourable to the idea that it did happen, one cannot reasonably claim that it was present in more than a small minority of credit transactions. 'Real' mortgages of customary land, in which the creditor was explicitly granted title to the debtor's land in the case of non-payment, are not extant at all in these rolls. Some short-term leases of tenant land may have been designed to allow a creditor/lessee to take the proceeds of a half acre or so in the event of non-payment, or even in addition to the principal loaned, but there is no evidence that the land leased would do anything other than return to the debtor/lessor at the end of the term of the lease. Furthermore, and crucially, even if we accept the argument that some leases were connected to new extensions of credit, it is clear that they were only sporadically so employed. This is because the debt litigation evidence reveals such a large number of failed credit relationships for which there is no corresponding lease in the court rolls.[67]

Future court roll research might conceivably show that the wider incidence of 'real' mortgages of peasant customary land was greater than that revealed by the sample of manors studied here. In particular, mortgages were perhaps more likely to occur in 'East Anglian' manors than in 'midland' manors, since the small parcels of land most appropriate for mortgaging were readily available for permanent transfer in the typical 'East Anglian' manor. In 'midland' manors, by contrast, alienations of land rarely involved any

[65] CUL, Q 2, m.10 (28 September 1314).
[66] Section 5.2.
[67] See Table 5.2.

parcel smaller than the entire standard holding, and for obvious reasons few peasants are likely to have wished to risk the loss of their entire landholdings by mortgaging them. Future research might also uncover more conclusive evidence than that presented here for the hypothesis that some short-term leases acted as security for debts. For the moment, however, one must conclude that the use of land as security was a relatively unusual feature of the landscape of English rural credit. It was certainly more unusual there than elsewhere in Europe, where devices such as the *prêt sur gage* and the *rente constituée* were frequently employed by borrowers to raise loans on the security of their holdings.[68]

3.4.3 Personal sureties

The final way of securing a debt was the use of a personal surety, or pledge. Sureties or cosigners—persons produced to guarantee the payment of a debt on behalf of a principal debtor—are a widespread feature of credit institutions both past and present. The previous two sections suggested that written instruments and landed collateral played a relatively muted role as security in the English village. The system of personal sureties, however, was much more important in this respect, as argued here. The evidence suggests that by requiring a borrower to produce personal sureties at the time of lending, a village creditor gained access to a fairly effective means both of providing later verification that a debt was outstanding, and of ensuring that he had alternative means of recovering the money or goods owed.

Because the system of pledges operated in a world of largely oral credit, evidence of it surfaces only occasionally in the written record.[69] In 98 of the 2,478 debt cases begun in the five courts, it is stated that the defendant or, more rarely, the plaintiff in the case was not the principal creditor or debtor, but a pledge who had stood surety for the principal creditor or debtor.[70] In the most common scenario, the court roll tells us only that the plaintiff was

68 For the *prêt sur gage*, see Gaulin and Menant, 'Crédit rural', 40–1; Berthe, 'Marché', 301–2; for the *rente constituée*, see Section 2.1.4 above. Perhaps, technically speaking, the establishment of a *rente* upon a property did not equate to a loan upon security as defined in this chapter, because the property was not conveyed to the creditor with the aim that it should be used by him to recover the principal in the event of non-payment. However, the *rente* does represent an institutionalized mechanism for raising a loan on the strength of real property of a kind that was rare in England.

69 Personal pledging was of course an institution of larger importance in medieval village society, with a range of uses. Most importantly, pledges were used to guarantee the performance of orders made by the manor court. See, for example, Pimsler, 'Solidarity in the medieval village?'; Postles, 'Personal pledging'.

70 In thirty-four Oakington, six Horwood, six Balsham, twenty-three Littleport, and twenty-nine Willingham cases.

suing the defendant for a debt owed 'as pledge' of a third individual.[71] In a much less common situation, the plaintiff had 'acquitted' the defendant by paying off the latter's creditor, and was now suing for compensation.

Beyond this, one must rely on a few scraps of further direct information, plus a good deal of informed guesswork, to reconstruct the system of pledging that operated within rural credit networks. Most probably, when a credit contract was formed, both parties would produce pledges to witness the act and, in the case of the debtors' pledges, personally guarantee repayment. If a creditor subsequently needed to claim an unpaid debt in the manor court, his own pledges could presumably be brought forward to testify that the contract had been made as alleged. It is probably their testimony that is being referred to when, in the court roll's recurrent phrase, the plaintiff 'produced suit' to support his claim.[72] If a case was put to a manorial jury, and its members had to find proof regarding the status of a debt, the most reasonable course open to the jurors, given the inadmissibility of written instruments as proof, was to ask the debtor/defendant's pledges to swear as to whether the debt had been incurred as claimed, and whether, as far as they knew, it was still outstanding. The information yielded by such questions put by the jury, or on its behalf, probably lie behind the dozens of terse verdicts in the form 'the said Robert does/does not owe the said debt' that pepper medieval court rolls. Also, it was perhaps, one might guess, the debtors' pledges who were given the role of 'oath-helpers' when a debtor chose to defend himself by compurgation, and the oathswearing ritual it involved.[73] For the testimony of pledges to have been useful and reliable as proof, there must also have been some mechanism whereby the creditor would inform the pledges of both parties when a debt had been successfully repaid. This would have notified all pledges that further claims on the debtor were now relinquished.

A system of using personal sureties to secure debts such as this could not have worked without the manor courts. For a lender, it would not have been worthwhile requiring that a borrower appoint pledges if there had not existed a 'neutral' institution like the manor court which could require a pledge to testify publicly as to the truth of a lenders's claim, and use that testimony to give an enforceable legal decision that was binding on all parties. Just as crucially, without harnessing the authority of the manor courts by bringing an action against a pledge, a creditor would have had little or no leverage over the property of his debtor's pledges. The corollary of this close interdependence between the court machinery and the system of securing credit primarily

[71] See Appendix 1 for an example. In such cases, the debtor is also often said to owe the debt *ex plegiagio*.

[72] For 'producing suit', see Beckerman, 'Customary law', 15–16.

[73] On compurgation, see Beckerman, 'Procedural innovation', 203–7.

by using personal sureties was that the use of sureties would only have worked well from the creditor's point of view if the available local manor court were relatively speedy, cheap, and effective to use. It was, of course, almost certainly not the case that all manor courts were equal in this regard.[74]

The manor courts had a central role, therefore, in the operation of the system of pledging for debts. Through the manor court, creditors could use a debtor's pledges to secure debt repayment, either by obtaining supporting proof of a claim from their testimony, or by raising a repayment from the pledge's own property. A crucial consequence of this was that a creditor did not necessarily need to know a borrower, or his circumstances, in order to be confident about extending credit to him. If a debtor defaulted, a pledge could end up being pursued in court for the principal's debts, so a debtor especially prone to default is likely to have had a hard time finding pledges. Thus, simply by being able to produce the required pledges, a borrower could demonstrate that he was a person of good credit, known as someone who usually repaid his debts. The system also worked well because it offered incentives to the pledge. We cannot rule out the possibility that pledges were paid for standing surety for debts, though there is no obvious way to investigate this empirically. Yet even if they were not paid for their services, an individual who guaranteed the debts of a creditworthy borrower would presumably be able to call on that borrower to perform an equivalent service in return at a future date. This was potentially vaulable.

Furthermore, the use of pledges could help overcome the problems of 'asymmetric information' in lending between people from different localities, not previously known to one another. A number of cases in the court rolls reveal the use of pledges in credit relationships involving lenders and borrowers from different settlements. For instance, at Littleport in 1317 John Albyn accepted that he owed Robert le Charet' 13*s*. 4*d*. as pledge of Michael, vicar of Milton, who presumably resided in the latter village.[75] Almost certainly, both John and Robert lived in Littleport.[76] This is significant in a number of respects. John may have been especially acceptable as a debtor's pledge from the point of view of Robert, the lender, because he knew that he would certainly be able to get John to give testimony or answer a personal action in court at Littleport in the event of non-payment by Michael. By virtue of his residence in Littleport, John dwelt within the area of the bishop of Ely's manorial jurisdiction in Littleport, and thus could be compelled to answer a charge in that court by seizure of property. Also, if we assume that John would not have acted as pledge for Michael if he had not known him per-

[74] Briggs, 'Manor court procedures'.

[75] CRO, R 93/96, m.4 (27 July 1317).

[76] They both appear on the lay subsidy list of 1315 and feature very frequently in the court rolls.

sonally, and that John knew Robert because they both lived in the same village, then we might also speculate that John, by knowing both creditor and debtor, had perhaps played some role in bringing them together, perhaps functioning thereby as a kind of intermediary, as well as a surety.

A slightly different example of a lender and a borrower from different villages coming together in a credit relationship involving a surety is provided by a case at Willingham of November 1397. In this, John Reder of the nearby village of Haddenham successfully sued Walter Schetere for a debt of 4*s*. that he owed as pledge of Nicholas Soutere. As far as one can tell, both Walter and Nicholas lived in Willingham. Here, then, the debtor's pledge lived locally to the principal debtor. In accepting Walter as his borrower's pledge, John presumably knew enough about him to be sure that, should it become necessary, it would be possible to secure Walter's appearance, either as a witness or a defendant, using the machinery of a convenient manor court.[77] In short, the issues of adverse selection or moral hazard—of a debtor disappearing without paying back a debt—were greatly lessened by having the bargain witnessed by a third party who could be compelled by a manor court to give truthful testimony about a debt, or indeed to render the debt on the principal's behalf.

Personal sureties, then, were almost certainly used on a greater scale than either written instruments or land to secure debts in the English village context. We do not know what proportion of all credit transactions were secured by pledges as witnesses and sureties. Most of the time, the pledges were never sued in the manor court in order to recover a debt, so their involvement tends to remain invisible. Furthermore, the role of pledges as witnesses in jury process can at present really only be inferred, not demonstrated. Presumably pledges were more likely to be demanded in connection with relatively large debts. However, there are cases of pledges answering claims for debts of just a few pence, so it is clear that the use of pledges was not confined to the upper echelons of the village credit market.[78]

3.5 Conclusion: an effective system of oral credit transactions

The steps by which credit contracts were formed, and the terms and conditions imposed when they were created, loom large in the assessment of the overall strengths and weaknesses of the English rural credit market. Three

[77] For this possible use of local witnesses or pledges to inform jury decisions, see Phillips, 'Collaboration and litigation', 230–1.

[78] For instance, at Littleport pledges owed debts on behalf of principal debtors of sums of 8*d*., 10*d*., and 12*d*., while at Willingham the smallest sums owed by pledges were 8*d*. and 16*d*.

questions in particular require attention as part of this assessment. The first concerns the quantity of credit extended in fourteenth-century English villages, in terms of both its overall value and the average size of individual credits. Did the way medieval English credit contracts were formed, and the character of the terms imposed, lead to quantities of credit that were high or low compared with those in other comparable agrarian societies? The second question concerns the expropriation and exploitation of debtors, either by punishingly high levels of interest, or by the loss of land and other property pledged in connection with debts. Were the terms observed in English village credit bad or good for borrowers, compared with elsewhere in Europe? Finally, how far were credit contracts formed in a manner, and according to terms and conditions, that tended to promote the efficient mobilization of capital, including its mobilization between communities as well as within them?

These are not easy questions to answer, and our comparisons with other medieval and early modern agrarian credit markets are crude at best. On some matters, however, it is possible to point to some important areas of similarity and contrast, and to state their possible implications for the three questions outlined above.

First, it is clear that most English rural credit was extended on a short-term basis, occasionally for more than six months but hardly ever for more than a year. This factor obviously implies some major weaknesses, most obviously in terms of the limits upon the amount of credit that could be made available on such a short-term basis. However, rural England may not have been alone in this regard. The categories of credit transaction most closely comparable to those prevailing in rural England—the simple loans and sales credits—were, as far as one can tell, made with similar short terms in other parts of Europe. Most medieval credit was short term in the countryside.[79]

The significance of the predominance of fixed repayment dates in the fourteenth-century English village credit studied here is hard to assess, but such arrangements may have been less exploitative of the debtor than 'on demand' repayment conditions, which may perhaps have tended—and may even have been intended—to take a debtor by surprise and trigger default.

The effects of interest arrangements on the amount of lending and the fortunes of borrowers cannot really be assessed or compared, owing to lack of adequate evidence for both England and continental Europe. Where the evidence is better is in the matter of security. It is a commonplace of the wider literature on agrarian credit that the inability to provide collateral leads to an inflated 'risk premium' being imposed by lenders on repayments, and to

[79] This statement excludes the purchase of *rentes*, since the annuities payable by the debtor on a *rente* contract were often perpetual.

the perpetuation of an informal, almost entirely localized credit system.[80] Compared with contemporary southern Europe, land appears to have been little used as collateral in the English village, though there are some hints that some inter-peasant subletting represented the pledging of odd acres as security. What were the effects of the fourteenth-century English village's relative reluctance or inability to use customary land as collateral?

The most common form of credit in medieval English villages was credit extended in the context of a sale, rather than the more versatile simple loan of cash or grain.[81] Since, in the broader medieval context, collateral was normally used for securing loans only, not sales credits, it could be argued that the relative shortage of loans in England was due to the highly constrained employment of land as security. That said, the causation could just as easily work the other way round, and the striking dominance of sales credit in England and the relative scarcity of loans might explain why little collateral was used there.

The position with respect to land as collateral also has implications for the experiences of borrowers. A limited requirement for land as security might lead one to think that people without land could easily borrow in England, or that foreclosure and the loss of land gaged as security was not a problem that greatly afflicted the English medieval borrower. However, it should be mentioned that creditors did make claims on the land of their borrowers even if it was not pledged at the outset of a relationship, since the sale and especially leasing of land was such a common way of raising the wherewithal to repay a debt. As is observed later, in one way or another the possession of land was a key factor shaping one's ability to obtain credit.[82]

If the limited role for land as security in the English rural credit system represents a weakness, this was compensated for by its alternative method of securing credit, the network of personal sureties.[83] However, the employment of sureties—which was, however, not exclusive to English credit contracts, but is also found in other parts of Europe—formed part of an English world of predominantly oral village credit, which is in striking contrast to the world of closer ties between writing and rural credit found in the southern European areas of notarial culture. Does the English dependence on oral contracts, which was absent in southern Europe, imply a comparative weakness in the way that English village credit relationships were formed, and their terms and conditions enforced? It seems at first glance plausible to

80 See, for example, Bottomley, 'Interest rate determination'.

81 Section 2.1.4.

82 Chapters 4 and 5.

83 Other studies suggestive of the potential importance of systems of personal sureties to the development of credit include Kowaleski, *Exeter*, 208–9.

suggest that in southern Europe credit must, other things being equal, have been available in greater quantities, and mobilized more efficiently across greater distances, than it was in comparable parts of the English countryside. This happened, one could claim, because southern European credit acts were authenticated in written records which underpinned the process of repayment, and greatly eased and simplified it.

Such an argument raises many complex issues. One important point to make in response is that historians are far from agreed that all southern European village credit contracts were recorded in a notarial act.[84] In other words, a substantial proportion of credit in that region may actually have been based on oral contracts like those used in England. One must also stress that to work effectively from a creditor's point of view, a method of security had to provide some mechanism which allowed the creditor to seize the debtor's property in lieu of repayment, or to have it seized on his behalf. This mechanism would ideally be put into effect by some recognized public authority or institution. It is true that English rural credit contracts and their terms and conditions were almost entirely oral matters, and that, when dispute occurred, the room for debate, uncertainty, and even deception about who owed what to whom was undoubtedly greater than it must have been in parts of Europe when a written act could be produced. However, when claims that a debt was owed were upheld in the English village by the manor court, the crucial factor was that the power of the manor court could be harnessed in order to enforce the claim, by seizing the debtor's goods as repayment of a debt, or it could be at least in those particular manor courts that were functioning efficiently as institutions of debt recovery.[85]

By contrast, although the notarial system's great strength lay in the written authentication of obligations, there is little to suggest that it was as powerful in enforcing them. Particularly in southern France, the notarial system in the countryside does not appear to have been connected closely to a system of courts that had the machinery to execute the claims of creditors against non-paying debtors quickly and efficiently.[86] It is true that a significant characteristic of rural credit in the lands of the crown of Aragon—in Valencia and Catalonia—is that the powers of authentication offered by a system of debt registration were coupled with the powers of enforcement provided by a system of village and town courts, all of which were able to seize

[84] Menant, 'Notaires et crédit', 44–7; Drendel, 'Le crédit', 291. Menant, personal communication.

[85] On enforcement, see Briggs, 'Manor court procedures', 548–50.

[86] For references to courts, see Gaulin and Menant, 'Crédit rural', 46–7; Drendel, 'Le crédit', 293. The example of Marseille shows that notaries and courts certainly co-existed in large towns: see Smail, 'Notaries, courts, and the legal culture', which demonstrates the necessity of a court system for enforcing debts created by notarial acts, and explores the functioning of this 'symbiotic relationship' in Marseille.

the goods of non-paying debtors. Lenders in Valencia thus to some extent had the best of both worlds, enjoying the benefits of widespread employment of written debt registration in conjunction with a local court network.[87]

Even in the Valencian case, however, it is uncertain whether the system for proving that debts were owed, and for enforcing their repayment, was as effective as the English one in making non-paying rural debtors meet their obligations.[88] With respect to the speed of court decisions, for example, it is notable that at Oakington before 1351, eight out of ten debt plaints were terminated in just a single manor court session. Between four and five sessions per annum were held on average, so justice there was clearly rapid; most creditors who secured an enforceable court decision in their favour did so within three months of the debt plaint's initiation.[89] Unfortunately, the current state of research makes it impossible to demonstrate conclusively that English manor courts reached decisions in debt litigation more quickly than equivalent institutions elsewhere in Europe. New, genuinely comparative research is also required in order to explore other aspects of the effectiveness of rural courts in enforcing private debt repayment, such as the frequency with which debtors actually discharged their obligations once the court had ordered them to do so.[90] Yet these uncertainties do not prevent one at least raising the distinct possibility that the presence of the manor courts bestowed special advantages upon the credit markets of the English countryside that were not shared by other regions of rural Europe. The manor courts enforced even oral peasant debt contracts effectively and, as a consequence, encouraged the formation of new credit ties.[91]

[87] Furió, 'Crédit, endettement et justice', esp. 37–8.

[88] Most of the Valencian evidence comes from the later fourteenth and fifteenth centuries. It is not clear that these systems of debt registration and enforcement were as well developed in the thirteenth and earlier fourteenth centuries as they became later.

[89] Briggs, 'Manor court procedures', 529, 540.

[90] On this issue, see Furió, 'Crédit, endettement et justice', 47.

[91] For evidence that England's manor courts had no real continental equivalent in terms of their extensive use of writing to record proceedings, their competence over civil matters, and the small (and therefore relatively controllable) territories under their jurisdiction, see Razi and Smith, 'Origins of the English manorial court rolls', 36.

4

Creditors and debtors

So far this book has considered credit transactions largely in isolation from the people who performed them. In this chapter and the next, by contrast, these people take centre stage. The basic questions of the present chapter are quite simple: who were the creditors and debtors in fourteenth-century English villages? How numerous were they? How distinct were the creditors and the debtors as groups? What were the overall traits of credit network participants, and did the creditors and debtors differ in their traits when considered as groups? Once some answers to these questions have been produced, it will then be possible to go on in Chapter 5 to enquire into the nature of the relationships between the individuals whose characteristics Chapter 4 has established.

Chapters 4 and 5 combine two approaches to the study of villagers. The first approach is to seek reliable generalizations about individuals in the aggregate. In this case these are all the creditors and debtors of a particular village, or even the whole body of such people under scrutiny, which means some 1,780 different persons from the seven villages. Clearly, however, generalizations about such a large number of people are dangerous. This accounts for the second approach, which is to use the riches of the court rolls to add qualification and nuance to the generalizations. This is achieved by reconstructing the experiences of creditors and debtors who were particularly significant, typical, or just as importantly, untypical.

The evidence on creditors and debtors and their relationships in this chapter and the next is vital to this book's wider task, which is to assess the overall strengths and weaknesses of medieval English rural credit. In other words, this evidence will help us to determine how far credit was, on the one hand, an intermittent feature of village life which served only to exacerbate poverty and economic and social divides, rather than the alternative, a positive and efficiently organized feature of the local economy which assisted both consumption and investment. To do this one must first return to the currently available view of English rural credit in this period, outlined in Chapter 1. What picture do the studies underlying that view provide on the matter of the identity and characteristics of creditors and debtors? It is essential to sketch this picture in brief, as the rest of this chapter is designed, in part, to explore the key issues it identifies, and indeed to test the picture itself using the large body of data on lenders and borrowers at our disposal.

As stressed at the start of this book, all those who have written about creditors and debtors in late thirteenth- and fourteenth-century English villages either have been primarily concerned with other, albeit connected, issues, or have been offering preliminary statements about a topic where little close research has been undertaken. For this reason, it is wise to regard the findings of these studies as provisional. On the other hand, all this work takes much the same line, which suggests there is basic agreement about the characteristics of typical credit network participants. Almost all the work in question focuses on the six or seven decades preceding the Black Death. Its wider concern is typically with the various forces producing agrarian 'crisis' in that period—especially overpopulation, harvest failure, and heavy state fiscal demands—and their impact upon highly socially stratified peasant communities. This is the context in which the characterization of typical creditors and debtors has taken place. Two main points emerge. First, creditors tended to be richer than debtors. The creditors came primarily from the richer sections of village society, the debtors from the poorer. The commentators in question are generally doubtful that debtors could normally be found among the very poorest, though Campbell's model of the early fourteenth century assumes that those with little land gained access to additional land through taking credit from richer villagers. The second point to come through most strongly from these studies is that creditors and debtors tended not to overlap very much as groups. An individual was usually a lender or a borrower, but not both.[1]

According to this view, therefore, the credit market typically involved the village rich lending to those poorer than themselves, and there was minimal overlap between the two basic groups of creditors and debtors. Although the studies just mentioned rarely say so explicitly, such a credit market was probably one in which weaknesses were more marked than strengths. If most debtors came from the poorer elements of rural society, then this would suggest either that most borrowing was for consumption and not investment, or that borrowing was itself part of what made one poor. Also, the absence of significant numbers of people who both lent and borrowed ('creditor-debtors') points to a credit market in which the supply of credit was determined by the

[1] Razi, *Life, marriage and death*, 76–88; Razi, 'Family, land and the village community', 11; Schofield, 'Dearth', 13–16; Schofield, 'L'endettement', 90–1; Schofield, 'Access', 115–20; Campbell, 'Agrarian problem', 52–3. See also references on relations between creditors and debtors, below, pp. 149–51. Schofield, 'Social economy', implies that the poorest villagers were excluded from access to credit in the decade 1311–20, but the study provides little specific information on the characteristics of lenders and borrowers. Schofield also explores contexts in which richer peasants became borrowers: 'Credit and the peasant land market', 793–5.

attitudes of a potentially small group of habitual and dominant lenders, rather than involving a more efficient scenario in which all members of the community might potentially extend credit whenever they were in a position to do so. But how far are these two key propositions—that the creditors were usually richer than the debtors, and that creditor-debtors were rare—supported by the evidence collected for this study?

Scrutiny of these propositions dominates much of the discussion that follows in this chapter, while their implications for the nature of credit relationships are tackled in the next. Like the studies just discussed, this chapter concentrates on the pre-plague decades, not only because that period is so critical in our understanding of rural credit, but also because comparative evidence is available from a greater number of our villages for the pre-plague period than it is for the decades after 1349. However, that later period is not ignored, and an effort is made to see how far the composition of the creditor and debtor groups changed once the crisis conditions of the earlier fourteenth century had passed. The aim here is not only to build on and test the picture that emerges from existing studies on England, but also to make comparison with equivalent work on other parts of Europe. Available village credit research typically shows differences between England and elsewhere in terms of the identity of those who belonged to credit networks, such as in the extent of the presence of urban lenders in rural settings. These issues, too, therefore shape the choice of material examined below.

4.1 Litigation evidence and the identification of creditors and debtors

To begin with, however, some words are needed on the obstacles to this chapter posed by our evidence, and on ways of overcoming them. It has been necessary several times to repeat the point that the information available from court roll debt cases is not a complete record of village credit, nor is it even necessarily a representative sample of it. Instead, it tells us only about debt relationships of a kind that broke down and ended up as litigation in the manor court. Those relationships, and the people in them, may not be typical of the whole. Where the identification of creditors and debtors in particular is concerned, this reliance on litigation and court rolls throws up at least three problems.

First, there may have been village creditors and debtors about whom we know nothing because they never appeared in debt actions. The best approach to this problem is to ask whether there are particular categories of creditor or debtor who are especially likely to remain hidden for this reason. Particularly important in this respect are the poorest individuals involved in credit. Although, as observed a moment ago, it has been stressed in previous studies that the relatively rich usually lent to the relatively poor, doubt has simultaneously been cast on the extent to which the participation of the poorest debtors is accurately reflected in manorial debt litigation. The argument made is that it was only worthwhile suing the comparatively wealthy for debts, since the poor could not pay.[2] If this were generally true, it could of course jeopardize attempts to make meaningful statements about the relative wealth and status of creditors and debtors.

However, as has been maintained at several points already, it is dangerous to overestimate the scale of any 'informal' village credit network in which defaulting debtors were never liable to be prosecuted in the manor court, and hence escape record. As argued in Chapter 2, the claim that the debt litigation evidence records even the poorest debtors is supported by the fact that many extremely small obligations were recovered in the manor court. To contemporaries, patently, even the smallest unpaid debts were worth collecting using the court.[3] Equally, however, it is unlikely that villagers were prepared to extend even small amounts of credit to people who did not have at least some movable property of low value, or a strong likelihood of obtaining such property in the future. That property was important because it could be taken in lieu of repayment if the debtor defaulted. However, the only local institution that enjoyed the authority to seize the debtor's goods and use them for the creditor's benefit—that is, to 'levy' a debt from movables—was of course the manor court itself; or at least, the manor court was the most important such institution.[4] Therefore, any creditor who gave credit to someone who possessed property of at least the same value as the debt had a strong incentive to use the manor court to recover the debt if necessary. This applied even if the debt and the goods were of low value. Hence one can expect even very poor borrowers—or at least those borrowers who had not become yet poorer since the time of the transaction—to appear in debt litigation.

That some seriously poor individuals were sued in debt in the manor courts is sometimes confirmed by reports made on their property as part of litigation procedure. For example, when Alice daughter of Alice le Clerk was sued in 1346 at Balsham in a plea of debt, it was reported that she possessed nothing but a piece of cloth, which was taken and kept until she appeared to answer the debt claim. Anyone who owned only a piece of cloth—referred to subsequently as a piece of blanket—can confidently be described as poor.[5]

[2] Dyer, *Standards*, 186; Dyer, 'Political life', 154.

[3] See also Briggs, 'Empowered or marginalized?', 36.

[4] Briggs, 'Manor court procedures', 548–9.

[5] LMA, ACC/1876/MR/02/010, mm.1, 2 (10 July 1346, 8 October 1346). In the first of these sessions it was reported that the object had been valued at the preceding session. Unfortunately, the relevant record is lost.

Presumably, however, that object was of a value at least equal to the debt she owed, or it would not have been worth prosecuting her. Evidence such as this suggests that if poor people really did borrow, then they ought to be present among the recorded debtors, even if they are perhaps not as well represented there as their wealthier counterparts. The only people who will certainly not appear as debtors in manorial litigation are those who borrowed without owning any property which could be seized in case of default, and logic suggests such borrowers were anyway virtually unheard of.

The second potential obstacle to the investigation of creditors and debtors using court rolls arises from the nature of litigation. Medieval litigation was not simply about recovering a debt or obtaining damages for a wrong. It could also function at times as a means of expressing conflict, perpetuating unconnected quarrels, or even of working out emotions of anger and hatred.[6] How can we be certain that a particular debt action brought to one of the courts represents a real credit relationship, rather than a vexatious suit based on a fictitious claim, brought to harass an enemy? The best way to deal with this is to ask what the court itself, or, more accurately, the villagers who made up the court juries, thought about the claims being made. Accordingly, the outcome of each debt case, where known, has been examined, and any action which concluded in the plaintiff being amerced for a 'false claim' or 'false plaint', or in the complete exoneration of the defendant, has been excluded from this chapter and the next. All the cases that remain are treated as representing bona fide credit relationships.[7]

The final point concerns the wider problem of the scope for using manorial records to reconstruct rural communities as a whole. Ideally, the characterization of the creditor and debtor groups attempted in the present chapter would proceed by asking what similarities and differences the two groups shared with the village population at large. This way of working would also be best because it would allow one to look at those who did *not* engage in credit networks, and to see how such people compared with those who definitely did. Unfortunately, such an approach is impractical and cannot be adopted here. For one thing, it is a matter of debate whether manorial court rolls can reliably be used to reconstruct entire village populations or manorial communities. What is certain is that such an enterprise requires a huge

[6] Schofield, 'Peasants and the manor court'; Smail, *Consumption of justice*, 1–28.

[7] For details see Appendix 2, which also describes how post-mortem cases and cases involving pledging are treated in order to isolate the persons who actually lent and borrowed, rather than those who simply brought or answered the case. The possibility remains, of course, that some defendants may have used their influence over the jurors to secure exoneration, but this is hard to test. Briggs, 'Creditors and debtors', gives figures on individuals which differ slightly from those here as they do not exclude litigants in cases terminated by 'false claim', 'false plaint', or the defendant's complete exoneration.

investment of time and labour.[8] Making such an investment would have forced this book to use a single set of court rolls only, and hence would have reduced its breadth. Rather than comparing creditors and debtors with the whole village population, therefore, the discussion that follows compares the creditor and debtor groups with each other. This approach is itself very revealing, and still allows one to answer the chapter's key questions about who the creditors and debtors were. Furthermore, as the next section shows, it is possible to gain a good sense of the share of the village population who did not engage in credit, without striving to reconstruct the entire community.

4.2 Village creditors and debtors within wider society

A simple yet crucial point about the identity of creditors and debtors is that, in this period, most credit received in English villages flowed from one villager to another. This was, overwhelmingly, peasant credit.

The credit received by members of village populations was rarely if ever provided by institutions. Parish clergy lent and borrowed, but as private individuals, not on behalf of the church. It is known that rural gilds, or fraternities, sometimes made loans to their members.[9] However, this was much more a phenomenon of the fifteenth and early sixteenth centuries than of the fourteenth. Gilds, and their lending activities, only begin to be mentioned frequently in local sources from that period. Although it is difficult to disentangle the actual pattern of gild activity from the survival patterns of the documents that record it, it seems likely that more gilds existed and were active after 1400 than before that date.[10] In the sources used for this book, only one debt case explicitly involving a gild appears. This was in 1311 at Balsham, when William Bertelote was sued by Robert Godroun and 'other brothers of the gild of St John the Baptist'.[11] However, even in this case it is not certain that a loan was involved, rather than a gild subscription, or indeed that a Balsham gild is referred to. Even if gilds were in existence in the fourteenth century in the places studied, which for the Cambridgeshire villages at least is uncertain, the court rolls offer hardly any evidence that they provided credit.[12]

[8] Briggs, 'What proportion?'.

[9] Dyer, *Age of transition?*, 185–6.

[10] Bainbridge, *Gilds*, 41; Dyer, 'Political life', 150; Dyer, *Age of transition?*, 76–8.

[11] LMA, ACC/1876/MR/02/001, m.5 (15 December 1311).

[12] Bainbridge, *Gilds*, 30–1, shows that just one of the six villages examined here—Littleport—is known to have had a gild before 1389. The earliest reference to a Littleport gild appears to date from 1377: *VCH Cambs.*, iv, 100. Documentary evidence shows the existence of gilds in the

Equally, landlords apparently played little part in providing credit to villagers. Of course, the line between lord and peasant is sometimes difficult to draw. Some parish clergy, especially the rectors whose glebe lands were run essentially as manors, should be regarded as lords. Yet as is shown below, it was precisely those wealthy incumbents who were least involved in village credit. Some of the plaintiffs in manorial debt litigation are shadowy figures about whom we know little beyond their names. This group possibly includes individuals who had a small number of tenants and thus, technically speaking, were lords. The village of Oakington is perhaps an especially likely source of such figures, as lordship there was fragmented, and there were several minor lords with just a few tenants. One of the most prominent lenders there in the 1330s and 1340s was John Rous, who normally litigated through his bailiff, Geoffrey. John held a freehold estate in Oakington of at least 58 acres, though it is not clear whether at this date this comprised a manor with tenants in the usual sense.[13] Yet even John, in spite of holding some land in other places, was to all intents and purposes an Oakington villager, albeit one who was unusually influential and well endowed with land.[14] He was fundamentally unlike those powerful, distant, and wealthy lords who held the manors of which the records are studied here.

There is little if any evidence in our court rolls that lords like the bishop of Ely lent directly to their peasant tenants. They may have extended credit to them indirectly, by allowing rent arrears or by making concessions on other seigniorial exactions. Yet this is hard to document using the court rolls, where it is rare to find references to tenants' rent arrears, other than demands that they be collected. The credit networks frequented by such high-status landlords were probably quite separate from those of the villagers. A glimpse of those lordly networks is sometimes provided by our court rolls, as in the exceptional entry of 1315 in which the prior of Newton Longville made use of the Horwood roll to record a recognizance for 34 marks owed to him by John Giffard of Whaddon, an individual not named elsewhere in these rolls.[15] More usually, however, the credit arrangements of landlords are to be found

---

remaining five Cambridgeshire villages for a date after 1389 (Bainbridge, *Gilds*, 30–1), which is almost certainly post-1400; the fourteenth-century court rolls confirm that by failing to mention gilds (with the Balsham exception). Gilds are recorded at Dry Drayton, Oakington, and Willingham for the early sixteenth century: *VCH Cambs.*, ix, 86, 206, 409.

[13] Briggs, 'Credit and the peasant household economy', 247.

[14] John's residence in Oakington is implied in a court roll entry that shows a new free tenant there swearing fealty to the abbot in the presence of John and 'other worthy neighbours': CUL, Q 3, m.35d (25 March 1340).

[15] NCA 3913, m.17 (12 August 1315). The Giffards of Whaddon were a prominent family. This borrower was probably the same man as the John Giffard recorded as keeper of Whaddon Chase in 1318: *VCH Bucks.*, iii, 439.

in non-manorial sources, which is unsurprising given the relatively exalted status of the people to and from whom they lent and borrowed.

The only exception to the observation that most villagers participated in credit ties only with other villagers lies in the role of urban lenders. A certain proportion of village credit was granted by outsiders. Section 4.3.3 below considers the frequency with which such external credit came from townspeople rather than villagers. That exception aside, however, one may safely say that most lending and borrowing involving residents of the villages studied brought together private individuals, who usually acted alone, but occasionally lent or borrowed jointly. Crucially, virtually all such individuals came from the peasant 'side' of the lord–peasant divide.

A second crucial point is that most of the villagers recorded as creditors and debtors were heads of households. The great majority of parties to debt actions are cited in the rolls without an indication of 'dependency status'. That is, they are not described by reference to another as 'son of', 'daughter of', and so on. Occasionally, people cited thus do appear as creditors or debtors. Alice daughter of Alice le Clerk, the poor debtor mentioned earlier, is an example. Such people were almost certainly resident in a household headed by another—typically a parent—but had become involved in credit in their own right. Slightly more common in debt litigation are servants, described as 'servant of' another in the records. Their presence as creditors and debtors makes sense in the light of the evidence, seen in Chapter 2, that some village debts consisted of arrears of wages. Overall, however, individuals cited in a form that indicates dependency status are rare. Of all the creditors and debtors from the seven villages, only fifty-two (2.9 per cent) are recorded using the 'son of', 'daughter of', or 'servant of' forms. This reflects the fact that most credit was given or received by the household head on behalf of the household as a whole, and also that he—or less commonly, she—had to answer for those obligations in court. When wives appear in debt litigation, they almost always appear jointly with their husbands. Such cases generally arose from instances in which the household's credit transactions had been personally handled by the wife, rather than by the head himself, as was normally the case. Irrespective of who did the actual lending and borrowing, however, the key point is that village credit was usually, if not invariably, extended between households, rather than individuals.[16]

How many of these households were involved in credit relationships? Our sources provide no easy way of discovering the proportion engaged in a credit arrangement at any one time. Nor do they allow us to observe the lending and borrowing 'histories' of all households.[17] What one can do, however, is to

[16] Briggs, 'Empowered or marginalized?'; Briggs, 'What proportion?'.

[17] For fuller discussion of these problems, and alternative solutions, see Briggs, 'What proportion?'.

focus on samples of households in existence at a particular date, and ask how many of them lent and borrowed during their lifetimes. This provides a minimum figure for the share of rural households affected by credit.

The samples of households are provided by two types of source. The first are the lists of taxpayers who contributed to the royal lay subsidies, or taxes on movable property. These are available for two different subsidies, those of 1315 and 1327. For all the villages apart from Horwood, the lists consist simply of the taxpaying household head's name, and the charge each had to pay.[18] The second source comprises lists of manorial tenants, or of those owing suit to (attendance at) the manor court. Since the vast majority of suitors were tenants, this amounts to much the same thing. In their specifics, the tenant/suitor lists are quite diverse. For Oakington and Drayton we have rentals; for Cottenham, a list of villein court suitors; for Horwood, a manorial extent; and for Balsham, a list of court suitors which can almost certainly be treated as equivalent to a list of manorial tenants.[19] However, each gives essentially the same information: the names of household heads who were resident in a village at a particular date.

Neither the subsidy rolls nor the tenant lists name all of a village's households. The subsidies were assessed only on those with saleable surplus goods at or above a minimum value, usually 10*s*., which means that some poorer households are omitted.[20] The tenant lists tell one only about those who held land from the relevant manors, which here means Crowland Abbey's manors in Oakington, Cottenham, and Drayton, Newton Longville Priory's manor in Great Horwood, and the bishop of Ely's manor in Balsham. Tenants of other manors in the village, and landless households, are omitted. However, these features do not prevent the lists offering useful snapshots of existing households, whose credit activities can then be traced.

[18] The tax charge represented a fraction—in the case of these two subsidies, a twentieth—of the total assessed value of each taxpayer's property. TNA, E 179/81/7 (Cambridgeshire and the Isle of Ely, twentieth of 1315); TNA, E 179/81/6 (Cambridgeshire and the Isle of Ely, twentieth of 1327, printed in Evelyn-White (ed.), *Cambridgeshire*); TNA, E 179/242/86 (Great Horwood, twentieth of 1327, which also gives the valuations of taxpayers' property).

[19] Rentals of 1344, Oakington and Dry Drayton: CUL, Q Box 8. Cottenham suitor list, *c.*1346: CUL, Q 4 (list between mm. 6 and 7). Extent of 1320, Great Horwood: NCA, 4503, and 9744 (the *Liber Niger*), fos. 37–40. Balsham suitor list, which was probably created to show individual contributions of each tenant to the recognition fine payable upon the accession of John de Hotham as bishop of Ely: LMA, ACC/1876/MR/02/001, m.12d (26 October 1316).

[20] Ten shillings was specified as the tax threshold in 1327. It is not clear that a minimum value of goods to be assessed was specified in instructions to chief taxers assessing the twentieth of 1315. Jenks, 'Lay subsidies', 30, notes a minimum for the fifteenth of that year only. Yet since the minimum 1315 tax charge in all places studied here was 6*d*., the minimum of 10*s*. nonetheless appears to have been observed in the assessment of the twentieth. The observations on the Drayton subsidy in Briggs, 'Creditors and debtors', 138, unfortunately incorporate errors concerning taxpayer numbers now eradicated in subsequent analysis of the data.

What this shows is that many households are never recorded as lending and borrowing (Tables 4.1 and 4.2). At one extreme, only four of Cottenham's seventy-three taxpaying households of 1315 with legible names can be traced in debt litigation. More generally, it is unusual to find more than half of all taxpayers or tenants displaying a record of credit participation. Furthermore, it must be remembered that the households that do leave such a record lent and borrowed at different points over several decades. They were not all involved in credit relationships simultaneously.

Does this prove that rural credit was unimportant, in that many people were unaffected by it, thus adding weight to the claim that the weaknesses of medieval English rural credit were greater than its strengths? There are several reasons why this is not necessarily the case. First, the credit relationships of some villages are less well represented in the court rolls than others. This is particularly true of Cottenham and Dry Drayton. The court that provides our records of the activities of Cottenham and Drayton residents was the abbot of Crowland's manor court at Oakington. When a tenant of the abbot's Oakington manor wished to sue an Oakington resident who was not a tenant of the same manor, he is likely to have used the Crowland abbey court rather than an alternative, owing to its convenience. However, when a tenant of the abbot's Cottenham manor wished to sue a Cottenham resident who was not a Crowland tenant, he is quite likely to have used an alternative manor court in Cottenham, rather than the Oakington court, which lay three miles away. The same goes for the abbot's tenants in Drayton. For this reason, the Oakington evidence concerning the number of households involved in credit probably gives a more faithful picture than that for Cottenham and Drayton.

One must also take into account the fact that we know only about defaulted debts that came to court. Some households, presumably, go unrecorded as creditor or debtor because the debts they were involved in were all repaid successfully. The number of such households can only be a matter of guesswork.[21] However, it is clear that the real number of households engaged in credit was greater than the recorded total. Hence the presence of tenant creditors and debtors at Oakington, Horwood, and Balsham—the villages for which there is the most reliable evidence—could have been substantially greater than is indicated by Table 4.2.[22]

Villages clearly varied in the quantity of households involved in credit. At Littleport, judging at least by the vast amount of debt litigation there, credit

[21] Briggs, 'What proportion?'

[22] Recall, also, that some Balsham debt disputes may have been recorded only in a series of market court rolls now lost. If this were the case, it might lead to underestimation of the number of Balsham households involved in credit.

Table 4.1 Taxpayers in 1315 and 1327 lay subsidies also recorded as creditors and debtors

	Total taxpayers	Taxpayers with names lost	Total identifiable taxpayers	Creditor only	Debtor only	Both creditor and debtor	Total creditors and debtors
1315							
Oakington	94	11	83	1	4	5	10
Cottenham	153	80	73	1	2	1	4
Drayton	63	17	46	9	7	2	18
Littleport	37	–	37	2	7	20	29
Balsham	84	25	59	4	9	10	23
1327							
Oakington	83	–	83	11	5	8	24
Cottenham[a]	132	–	132	4	7	5	16
Drayton	48	–	48	3	5	1	9
Littleport	31	–	31	5	3	17	25
Balsham	53	–	53	7	4	9	20
Great Horwood	42	–	42	8	5	10	23

Note: [a] Includes Westwick.
Sources: See Table 2.1 (court rolls); TNA, E 179/81/6, E 179/81/7, E 179/242/86.

Table 4.2 Manorial tenants and court suitors recorded as creditors and debtors

Village and tenant/suitor type	Individual tenants/suitors	Creditor only	Debtor only	Both creditor and debtor	Not in debt litigation
Oakington, 1344					
Free	12	3	0	0	9
Villein	38	5	7	15	11
Total	50	8	7	15	20
Cottenham, *c.* 1346					
Villein	50	6	11	5	28
Dry Drayton, 1344					
Free	6	0	3	0	3
Villein	35	3	5	3	24
Total	40[a]	3	8	3	26[a]
Great Horwood, 1320					
Free	10	1	4	1	4
Villein	45	6	8	11	20
Total	55	7	12	12	24
Balsham, 1316					
Free	19	2	2	4	11
Villein	92	11	19	11	51
Total	111	13	21	15	62

Notes: 'Villein' includes tenants of cottages and crofts. All recorded credit activity appears, irrespective of date. Male tenants who only ever appeared in debt litigation accompanied by females (usually wives) are included here as creditors or debtors; c.f. Briggs, 'Empowered or marginalized?', Table 7 and n. 46.

[a] Agatha, the widow of John Revesson, had a free holding and a cottage; she was not a creditor or debtor.

Sources: See Table 2.1 (court rolls), and n.19.

relationships were especially numerous. It is also notable that the majority of Littleport's taxpaying households are recorded in credit activity (Table 4.1). In a period of just over a decade, some 289 people appear in the rolls as creditors and debtors (see Figure 4.1 on p. 130). Most of these represent individual households. In contrast to its position today, fourteenth-century Littleport was not large relative to its neighbouring settlements within the Isle of Ely.[23] Therefore, even without allowing for the fact that some Littleport residents must have lent and borrowed without appearing in the record, one can only conclude that virtually all Littleport households must have participated in credit in the 1310s and early 1320s. In those villages where activity was most intense, therefore, English rural credit networks of this period were like those parts of contemporary southern Europe, or of early modern English towns, where almost everyone was involved.[24]

23 *VCH Cambs.*, iv, 96–7.

24 Drendel, 'Society and economy', 112–14; Gaulin and Menant, 'Crédit rural', 53–4, 60, citing Bocchi, 'I debiti'; Briggs, 'What proportion?'

4.3 Women, parish clergy, and non-residents as creditors and debtors

The typical credit relationship discussed in this book saw a male peasant household head from the lay population extending credit to someone with the same characteristics living in the same settlement. While typical, however, this type of relationship was not universal. Women, clergy, and non-residents were all involved, too. The purpose of this section is to establish the extent and significance of their involvement. The role of these groups reveals much about the strengths and weaknesses of rural credit.

4.3.1 Women

Women are often held to have had an important role in the credit networks of pre-industrial Europe, and in those current in its towns and cities especially. Where the medieval English countryside is concerned, however, there is a perplexing lack of correspondence between the levels of female involvement anticipated on the basis of knowledge of broadly similar times and places, and the limited evidence for such involvement in our main source, which is of course manorial debt litigation.

Historians have asked whether litigation evidence really tells the full story about the personal involvement of women in credit. Particular attention has focused on the position of married women, and the effects of coverture. Coverture was the common law principle which said that a married woman had no legal identity separate from that of her husband. Technically, she could not form contracts independently, nor could she sue or be sued in court in her own right. The principles of coverture observed in the common law courts were also observed in the manorial courts. The key question is, does the comparative rarity of wives in debt litigation accurately reflect the extent of their involvement in the credit networks of their communities? Or, alternatively, is the apparently restricted participation of married women in credit actually an illusion created by the distorting effects of coverture upon the surviving record? In theory, it could be that married women frequently contracted and formed debts independently in the rural economy. However, manor court disputes about the contracts and debts will not reveal this, because under coverture wives were represented in court by their husbands, and are therefore not mentioned in the recorded court proceedings.

An earlier article using the Oakington and Horwood rolls argued that, on balance, it seems that the debt litigation evidence does reveal the true extent of married women's participation in credit networks.[25] The court rolls give

[25] Briggs, 'Empowered or marginalized?'

little sign that married women lent and borrowed independently. In fact, in that study it was also claimed that knowledge of the rules of coverture may have worked to dissuade people from transacting with wives. The problem was that doing so risked legal complications. For instance, if one lent to a married woman and the debt was not repaid, one would not be able to bring legal proceedings against the woman herself, but would be forced to pursue her husband. That could lead to difficult and protracted negotiations. The husband could potentially deny knowledge of the debt, or prove difficult to bring to court to face the plaintiff's claims. In effect, a legal doctrine—coverture—had a potentially dramatic impact on economic practice.

Not everyone would accept this argument. Certainly, McIntosh has questioned the idea that manor court records really do reveal the true level of credit participation by married women.[26] McIntosh's grounds for saying this appear to be partly connected to the presence of what she calls the 'informal credit network'. According to McIntosh, many medieval credit relationships were established between people well known to one another on the basis of trust that debts would be repaid. In such relationships, the personal tie between the parties was such that it was rarely necessary to use courts of law to enforce the repayment of debts. Indeed, because the arrangements were so informal, and usually eschewed such safeguards as the use of pledges to witness debts, it would often have been impossible to use law courts to settle disputes, since the creditor was unable to supply adequate proof of outstanding obligations.[27] In this informal credit network, one could lend to or borrow from a wife without worrying about the implications of coverture, because the contracting parties were not expecting to need to resort to the law. However, as argued at several points already in this book, we should perhaps be sceptical about the existence of an informal village credit network undocumented by the court rolls. Furthermore, evidence presented by McIntosh from petitions brought to courts of equity, such as Chancery, from the later fifteenth century itself supports the notion that coverture made married women's legal standing doubtful, and made people wary of the legal complications of becoming involved in credit dealings with married women.[28]

It is undoubtedly true that more research is needed on the operation of coverture in medieval rural society, both in its impact on wives' ability to contract and in its influence on the participation of women in manor court litigation. The present discussion, however, stands by the earlier finding, arrived at through an analysis of the Oakington and Horwood material, that

[26] McIntosh, *Working women*, 96 n. 27.
[27] McIntosh, *Working women*, 86–90.
[28] McIntosh, 'Benefits and drawbacks', 427–9.

the court records accurately reflect the level of women's involvement in credit. It ventures to apply it to the Willingham, Littleport, and Balsham rolls also.

Most of the women who appear as creditors and debtors in the Oakington and Horwood records were not married, and were almost certainly widows.[29] This is to be expected, given the limited direct engagement of married women in credit. Even those not-married women, however, were not important players in credit networks. This judgement is based on the number of debt actions in which those women were recorded as creditor or debtor. Throughout this chapter and the next, the number of debt actions in which a person appears is treated as an indicator of the actual numbers of credit relationships—including unrecorded relationships—in which that individual participated, and it provides a useful way of comparing people. Only at Horwood, where widows were unusually numerous and prosperous within manorial society, is there any real sign of anyone resembling the important moneylending widow to whom attention has periodically been drawn by early modern historians.[30] Horwood's most important widow lender was probably Emma Isond, who remained unmarried between her husband's death in 1321 and her own in 1349, and is recorded in three credit relationships. The marked credit involvement of Horwood widows explains why the proportion of female creditors and debtors was largest there (Table 4.3), and was indeed

Table 4.3 Female creditors and debtors as a percentage of total

	Total creditors and debtors A	Female creditors and debtors B	Female creditors and debtors with 'dependency status'[a]	B as % A
Oakington, Cottenham, and Dry Drayton, 1291–1350	360	48	14	(13.3)
Oakington, Cottenham, and Dry Drayton, 1351–1400	402	40	10	(10.0)
Great Horwood, 1302–60	166	30	8	(18.1)
Willingham, 1377–1400	385	44	14	(11.4)
Littleport, 1316–27	289	38	17	(13.1)
Balsham, 1310–49	199	22	9	(11.1)

Notes: Joint parties, including husbands and wives appearing together, are counted as separate individuals.
[a] Individuals recorded in a debt case at least once by dependency status ('wife of', 'daughter of', 'servant of').
Sources: See Table 2.1.

[29] Briggs, 'Empowered or marginalized?', 29.
[30] Briggs, 'Empowered or marginalized?', 14, 34, and references therein; for a northern example of a widow creditor, see Jones, 'Some sources of loans', 289–90.

perhaps around the maximum one might expect from any contemporary village. In the remaining villages, the percentages of women among the creditors and debtors were remarkably similar. As at Horwood and the Crowland villages, the majority of the female creditors and debtors in the remaining locations are recorded without any indication of 'dependency status' (Table 4.3). Most, therefore, were almost certainly not-married household heads, a group which doubtless included many widows.[31]

It is also the case that the Willingham, Littleport, and Balsham rolls throw up few female creditors and debtors who can be described as significant or prolific, in terms of either the number of their recorded relationships or the size of their transactions. Only a handful of women are documented as creditor in more than two debt actions, and such women are not found at Balsham. At Willingham, the most significant lenders were Agnes Freman, who brought four debt actions between 1380 and 1390, including one in which she was found to be owed 3*s.* 1*d.* from numerous credit sales of ale, and Margaret Randolf, who brought five actions between 1377 and 1390, one of which saw her recover the large sum of 9*s.* 2*d.*[32] Littleport's most prominent female lenders were Isabella Belde, who successfully prosecuted four actions between 1317 and 1323, and Margaret Bolay, who in 1319–20 recovered four debts in as many cases, including one large sum of 8*s.* 7*d.*[33] To judge by the number of actions brought, these four women were probably even more intensely involved in extending credit than Emma Isond of Great Horwood. On the other hand, all four were much lower down than Emma in the hierarchy of creditors within their respective communities, as measured by number of actions brought. At Willingham, no woman appears among the top twenty-three lenders, each of whom acted in six or more debt cases, while at Littleport women are absent from the top twenty-seven lenders, each of whom initiated five or more cases.

As stated earlier, in English villages most credit was given and received by the household, rather than by individuals, and it was normally the head who carried out his or her household's credit transactions. It is therefore not surprising to find relatively few daughters, female servants, and wives among the

[31] Some of the Willingham, Littleport, and Balsham women described as 'wife of' in debt actions could actually have been relatively recently widowed women, who were often recorded in this way. Only an exhaustive study of the relevant court rolls could establish this.

[32] First appearances of Freman's actions: CRO, L1/177, mm.5 (9 June 1380), 28 (14 December 1386), and 36d (28 September 1390, two actions). First appearances of Randolf's actions: CRO, L1/177, mm.1–1d (30 November 1377), 26d (22 June 1386), 36d (28 September 1390, two actions), and 40 (7 June 1391).

[33] First appearances of Belde's actions: CRO, R 93/96, mm.3 (3 December 1317), 7 (18 July 1319), 16 (9 December 1322), and 17 (28 July 1323). First appearances of Bolay's actions: CRO, R 93/96, mm.7 (18 July 1319), 8 (11 December 1319), and 9 (21 July 1320, two actions).

creditors and debtors. The women enjoying the most significant degree of direct personal involvement in credit were naturally the not-married household heads. Even though we cannot know the proportion of all households headed by widows and singlewomen engaged in credit, we clearly should not play down the importance of the fact that such households were so engaged, even if the number of credit relationships in which they appeared was never especially large.

What do these findings on the place of women suggest about the strengths and weaknesses of medieval English rural credit? Married women did not normally have independent control over credit, but were affected by it only as members of a household. Was this a weakness of the credit system? Individualized, independent access to credit might in theory have given medieval wives their best chance of using that credit in the way that they, and not their husbands, thought best. However, to express surprise that such a level of independence did not really exist for married women is perhaps to have unrealistic or anachronistic expectations of the society under observation. In this sense, the central question previously posed—did women enjoy independent access to credit?—is perhaps an unfair one.[34] In any case, it is possible that wives privately shaped decisions about household credit. Therefore, the attenuated direct role of married women in credit should perhaps not be described as a significant weakness. If, as is sometimes suggested, relatively wealthy not-married women could in some contexts of early modern society accumulate reserves of cash significant enough to form an important source of capital for frequent lending, then the almost complete absence of not-married women with such characteristics in fourteenth-century rural society may be construed as something of a weakness. Certainly, no widow who could have been making a living out of moneylending has been encountered in the course of research for this book. Most widows were among the poorer members of medieval village society, and thus may have been just as likely to wish to borrow as to be in a position to lend. The presence of numerous widow debtors demonstrates that some of them, at least, did borrow on occasion.

4.3.2 Parish clergy

When asking 'who were the creditors and debtors?', there are good reasons for focusing on the parish clergy. That category, of course, covers a wide range, from wealthy rectors to unbeneficed chaplains employed on a short-term basis. As a consequence of their possession of surplus wealth from tithes, offerings, and the income from their glebe lands, the parish incumbents—the

[34] This is the question posed in Briggs, 'Empowered or marginalized?'.

rectors and vicars—were potentially well placed to extend credit to members of the village community. Lower in the clerical hierarchy were the unbeneficed chaplains or priests, who worked primarily for salaries, but could also expect revenues from other sources.[35] Yet even some of these unbeneficed clerics enjoyed resources that, in theory, allowed them to be more significant as creditors, and especially as moneylenders, than many of their lay neighbours.

The parish clergy also demand special attention because of what the literature of the time says about their involvement with credit. In the eyes of some contemporary writers, usurious lending was but one illustration of the avarice and lack of charity of priests, whose actions oppressed their parishioners. In *Handlyng Synne*, for example, Robert Mannyng of Brunne targeted usury as part of a general criticism of the covetousness and avarice of 'men of riche life, that have no charge of child nor wife / parsons, priests that have their rent / and others that have great extent'.[36] The author of the confessors' manual *Memoriale Presbiterorum* provides descriptions of 'cloaked usury' in which a priest is given the role of usurer. He writes, for example, of 'parish priests, given over to avarice', advancing the purchase price of grain to be delivered later at a time when the price will almost certainly have risen.[37]

This section asks whether parish clergy were as prominent as lenders as contemporaries believed, and indeed as they had the potential to be, given their wealth and influential position within the village. It also asks to what degree clerical lending fundamentally shaped the character of the rural credit market. Historians have often suspected that the English parish clergy were important sources of credit, and local clergy have been identified advancing large quantities of capital in parts of southern Europe.[38] However, a surer verdict on the impact of the parish clergy as lenders and borrowers can be reached only through examination of their activities alongside those of their lay counterparts.

Of the total number of creditors and debtors from the seven villages, forty-one individuals are described as either rector, parson, vicar, or chaplain. Collectively, these persons are recorded as creditor or debtor in 109 separate debt cases. Most of these men—twenty-eight—are recorded only as creditors, while nine are recorded only as debtors, and four as both creditor and

[35] Swanson, *Church and society*, 47–8; see also the payments owed to Thomas Tame chaplain in Chapter 6, p. 198 below.

[36] Mannyng, *Handlyng synne*, lines 5510–6080, quoted in Coulton, *Medieval village*, 285. Interestingly, given the geographical focus of this book, Mannyng's attack on covetousness and avarice includes the tale of a miser parson of Cambridgeshire: *Handlyng synne*, lines 6175–6234.

[37] Haren, *Sin and society*, 165–7. See also sections 2.1.4 and 3.3 above.

[38] Swanson, *Church and society*, 234–6; Swanson, 'Profits', 156; Drendel, 'Gens d'église'.

debtor. Thirty-one were chaplains, and only ten are described as vicar, rector, or parson, the latter name usually denoting a rector. Of these ten, three men are described by reference to a benefice outside the seven villages; an example is one Michael, vicar of Milton.[39] These three were presumably not residents of any of the seven villages.[40]

In fact, the most striking feature of the debt litigation evidence on clerics is the slight involvement of the incumbents of the seven villages. The rectors of Cottenham and Balsham are not recorded at all as creditors or debtors. A rector of Dry Drayton appears as defendant in just one debt action, while the involvement of the rector of Great Horwood extends to just two cases which show him as debtor.[41] Roger Weston, who had the living of Willingham in the later 1380s and early 1390s, is the only rector to appear in more than just a couple of debt cases. He prosecuted four actions between 1388 and 1392.[42] Oakington and Littleport were appropriated parishes in which the incumbent was a vicar, not a rector. These vicars were only slightly more fully engaged in village credit than the rectors just discussed. A vicar of Littleport is mentioned only once, when in 1321 William the vicar acknowledged a debt of 5*s*. to John de Mateshale of Colne.[43] No vicar of Oakington occurs in debt litigation there before the Black Death, but two vicars do so thereafter, the most important being John, who brought five debt plaints between 1366 and 1372.[44] Altogether, the incumbents of the villages studied here were involved in just fourteen debt cases.

To judge by the number of manorial debt cases in which they appeared, therefore, the rectors and vicars of these parishes were not significant figures in village credit. Why were the beneficed clergy so unimportant? A large part

[39] CRO, R 93/96, m.4 (27 July 1317). For this case, see p. 94 above (Chapter 3).

[40] There is some doubt about John Stowe, parson of the church of (Great) Ringstead (Norfolk?) (*Ryngestede Magna*), defendant in a Littleport debt case begun 7 January 1326 (CRO, R 93/96, m.23d). He may have lived in Littleport, or at least held taxable property there, as he appears in the 1315 lay subsidy assessment.

[41] For the case against Henry, the rector of Drayton, which ended in non-prosecution, see CUL, Q 6, mm.14–14d (30 April, 12 July 1367). In April 1305, Ralph son of Ralph began a debt case against Richard, rector of Great Horwood. Four court sessions later, in December 1305, Richard finally appeared to answer Ralph's charge that he owed him £8 10*s*. Richard successfully argued that he was not required to answer for a debt over 40*s*. without a royal writ: NCA, 3912, mm. 6d–8, 9 (8 April, 7 May, 29 May, 27 July, 1 December, and 22 December 1305). In the second case involving the rector of Horwood, Robert Ayswy successfully sued Robert Smith of Newton Longville, the former bailiff and executor of the rector, for a debt of 11*s*. 4*d*. arising from Ayswy's stipend during the four years he was in the rector's employ: NCA, 3913, m.4 (13 September 1309).

[42] CRO, L1/177, mm.31d (9 June 1388), and 43 (23 November 1392, three actions).

[43] A 'formal recognizance': CRO, R 93/96, m.11 (23 March 1321).

[44] First appearances of these cases: CUL, Q 6, m.13d (24 October 1366); Q 7, mm.1d (29 November 1368, two actions), 6d (29 July 1371), and 9 (25 October 1372).

of the answer must be that they were non-resident. The court rolls confirm that the rectors in particular played little direct part in village society. They were lords, and absentee lords at that, not peasants.[45] Non-residence gave the rectors few opportunities to encounter likely borrowers among members of the village population. In any case, giving credit to such persons was, on the whole, probably too lowly and perhaps too unprofitable an occupation for them.

The situation for the vicars is less clear cut. The vicars of Oakington and Littleport ought, in theory, to have resided in their parishes.[46] It is difficult to establish with certainty from the court rolls whether they in fact did so. The likelihood is that the vicars of Oakington, at least, were generally resident. For example, the vicar acted as pledge for individuals paying marriage licence fines, and in 1350 he was appointed as the plaintiff's attorney in a debt case.[47] Such functions would surely demand the vicar's residence in the parish. Yet no vicar of Oakington is recorded as creditor earlier than 1352, and no vicar of Littleport is recorded as creditor in the surviving rolls. It may well therefore have been some lack of incentive, rather than simply the lack of opportunity consequent upon non-residence, that prevented vicars from playing a greater role as creditors.

In the fourteenth century, the vicars of Oakington and Littleport and the frequently wealthy and powerful rectors of the remaining five villages all paid chaplains to assist them in their parochial duties, or to perform them in their place. It was the stipendiary chaplains of the villages studied who accounted for most of the recorded credit activity involving clerics in those places. The one particularly important exception to this—William Stevens, vicar of Little Horwood, active at Great Horwood—is discussed below. The most significant difference between the chaplains and the rectors, if not necessarily the vicars, was that the chaplains were resident. Daily contact with their parishioners gave the chaplains knowledge about potential borrowers and their circumstances that could be an important precondition for extending credit.

How significant were the activities of those parish clerics who did operate as creditors? The answer is, as ever, based upon the number of credit relationships in which an individual is recorded, and also upon the relative size of the debts involved. Many chaplains are recorded in just one or two relationships.

[45] For the high value of the livings of Balsham, Cottenham (where there was a clearly defined rectorial manor), Drayton, and Willingham, see *VCH Cambs.*, vi, 132; and ix, 65, 85, 409. See also Swanson, 'Profits', 154.

[46] Swanson, *Church and society*, 44.

[47] CUL, Q 2, m.22d (9 December 1320); Q 6, m.15 (11 December 1367); Q 5, m.2d (25 January 1350; attorney).

Some of these people were owed unusually large sums. For example, in 1302, after the death of Robert Porter, a Cottenham chaplain, his executors and, one presumes, kinsmen John and William Porter recovered a debt of 16*s.* owed to him by Robert Aleyn.[48]

On the whole, however, most of the priests do not stand out as particularly active or dominant figures in the credit networks of each village. There are three notable exceptions to this, clerics who were the most significant, or among the most significant, creditors in their communities. In order to understand why these clerics but not others built up a notable role as creditors, it is necessary to summarize their recorded debts, as well as other details known about them.

At Willingham, John Crouch the chaplain was joint sixth in the hierarchy of creditors, in terms of the number of actions brought as creditor. In his case, such actions totalled twelve between 1385 and 1400. He does not appear to have been much of a moneylender, although a debt of 36*s.* recovered by him in 1398 could conceivably have resulted from a loan.[49] Most of the debts owed to John for which details exist arose from deferred payments on sales of livestock. A total of 38*s.* 9*d.* was owed to him for steers purchased on credit in five separate transactions.[50] John was also recorded as a debtor in five cases between 1385 and 1397.[51] A notable feature of his career was the relatively long duration of his residence in the village. Many parochial chaplains must have come and gone quite swiftly from rural communities as they moved from post to post, an impression supported by the fact that chaplains often appear only sporadically in court rolls. John Crouch, however, appears in the clerical poll tax assessment of 1379, was still serving Willingham parish as chaplain in 1406, and is documented in manor court litigation as late as 1407.[52]

John Wyot, documented from 1297, was chaplain of Dry Drayton and, from 1316, vicar of nearby Comberton.[53] John appears to have held these two posts simultaneously from that date, probably living in Drayton throughout his life. This is suggested by the way he is named in manorial sources and land charters, and in an action of account he brought in the court of common pleas at Westminster in 1328. In this case, John sued another chaplain, Roger Hobekyn, to cause him to render his account as John's bailiff in

48 CUL, Q 1, m.19 (10 February 1302).

49 CRO, L1/177, m.64d (22 November 1398).

50 CRO, L1/177, mm.47 (15 July 1394), 58d–59 (19 September 1397, two actions), and 63 (4 September 1398); L1/178, m.2d (29 March 1400).

51 CRO, L1/177, mm.23 (13 March 1385), 51 (23 September 1395), 52 (28 October 1395), 55 (9 November 1396), and 58d (19 September 1397) (dates of first appearances of actions only).

52 *VCH Cambs.*, ix, 409; CRO, L1/178, mm.26–26d (28 June 1407).

53 Here several details are added which extend the preliminary account of Wyot in Briggs, 'Creditors and debtors', 138.

Comberton.[54] This suggests that John had appointed Roger to collect the Comberton parochial revenues, and perhaps to perform the cure of souls there also. In later life Wyot was one of village society's wealthier individuals. He was Drayton's largest contributor to the 1327 lay subsidy, with a tax charge of 5*s*. 4*d*., which equates to taxable temporal goods to the value of £5 6*s*. 8*d*.[55] He was also the most prolific pre-plague creditor in the Crowland villages, to judge by the Oakington debt litigation. He sued for debts in twelve cases between 1298 and 1320, including some substantial money debts which possibly represent loans. The largest of these was an obligation of 44*s*. 6*d*. recognized by Robert Kynnesone in 1311.[56]

The third key creditor from the parish clergy was William Stevens, vicar of Little Horwood. The village of Little Horwood, lying adjacent to Great Horwood, was not in this period a separate parish, but formed a chapelry within the parish of Winslow. Nonetheless, Little Horwood was served by its own vicar.[57] William is recorded as vicar there from 1311. By 1337 he is occasionally referred to as the 'former vicar' of Little Horwood, and he was dead by September 1343. Although strictly speaking resident outside Great Horwood, in reality his abode lay little over a mile from the larger settlement. William was doubtless well known in Great Horwood, not least because he owed suit at the manor court there.[58] Perhaps the crucial piece of information about him, however, is that he was the brother of Walter Stevens, the wealthiest villager in Great Horwood before the Black Death. Walter was the top contributor to the 1327 subsidy, with taxable goods assessed at £4 in value. Personally, Walter was of free status, but held among his various lands a messuage and virgate in villeinage.[59] In 1323 he paid a massive fine of 10 marks so that he would not have to act as either reeve or woodward, offices in which

[54] For the charters, see Briggs, 'Credit and the freehold land market'; for the common pleas appearances, (perhaps two separate actions), TNA, CP 40/274 m.128 (which also shows Wyot suing William Pyrt of Hinton in respect of his activities as John's bailiff in Dry Drayton), and CP 40/275 m.118d, as calendared in *Index of Placita de Banco*, 61.

[55] TNA, E 179/81/6, m.11. Lay subsidies only affected those goods of the parish clergy 'not annexed to their churches': Richardson, 'Parish clergy', 110.

[56] Wyot's debt actions (dates of first appearances): CUL, Q 1, mm.14 (2 November 1298), 17 (19 November 1302); Q 2, mm.2d (22 January 1306, three actions), 8d (7 December 1311, two), 10d (15 October 1313), 12d (13 December 1314), 15d (23 October 1316), 16d (10 February 1318), and 22d (9 December 1320).

[57] *VCH Bucks.*, iii, 376–9. Similarly, Little Horwood was part of the abbot of St Albans' manor of Winslow.

[58] The 1320 extent names William son of John Stevens among those owing suit at the two sessions of the view of frankpledge; as other evidence in this paragraph indicates, this man was almost certainly William the vicar. For default of suit of court by William, vicar of Little Horwood, see e.g. NCA, 3914, m.7 (8 October 1327).

[59] For his freehold land, see Chapter 5, p. 168 below.

the tenants of such holdings were liable to serve.[60] The nature of Walter's relationship to William is revealed by a 1313 debt case involving the two men, which describes them as brothers.[61] William was the most prolific creditor in the pre-plague village, with his brother not far behind him.[62] William is recorded as creditor in nine debt actions brought between 1306 and 1343, the last being a post-mortem action. Several large money debts were owed to him, including two of 16*s*. each, recovered in 1338 and 1339.[63]

These three, then, were the only parish clerics to become really prominent in their villages' credit markets. The credit networks in which John Wyot and William Stevens participated would have been very different without their involvement. It is unlikely that many villagers from the lay population were in a position to extend credit in the quantities and with the frequency that John and William did, some of it almost certainly in the form of loans rather than sales credit. It seems clear that John and William were able to lend in this way as a direct result of their advantageous economic position as parish clergy. The picture for John Crouch of Willingham is slightly different. There is less evidence that he was a moneylender, and little in the scale of his activities differentiates him greatly from other prolific creditors among the parish's layfolk. In other words, the fact that John Crouch was a priest did not serve to dictate the shape of his village's credit system.

Thus, while individual figures from the parish clergy could dominate village credit in the way one might expect given their access to cash and their above-average incomes, clerics did not do so in all villages at all times. The beneficed clergy, in particular, were not much involved. The credit networks of the beneficed clergy apparently engaged them with persons from more elevated social level, and are documented properly only in sources like the Statute Merchant certificates.[64] Like those affecting the greater landlords, the credit networks of the beneficed clergy appear to have been largely separate from those of the village.

Given the quantities of agricultural produce from tithes that must have come into the hands of incumbents and been sold locally, it does remain surprising that there are not more debt cases arising from credit sales made by rectors and vicars. The only example of this is provided by one of the debts

[60] NCA, 3913, m.33d (22 January 1323).
[61] NCA, 3913, m.13 (21 May 1313). In earlier court roll references to them, both are described as son of John Stevens.
[62] This excludes John Aschewy, whose twelve debt cases as plaintiff all appear in only a single court session of February 1349.
[63] NCA, 3914, mm.28, 30 (4 March 1338, 21 April 1339).
[64] Nightingale, 'English parochial clergy'. Around two-thirds of the credit by value analysed in this study was owed to rectors/parsons. As Swanson suggests, Nightingale's sources probably document only the higher end of lending by parochial clergy: Swanson, 'Profits', 156 n. 53.

recovered by Roger, rector of Willingham. In this case, Simon Palmer acknowledged 23*s*. 8*d*. to the rector 'for tithe lambs and a goose sold to him by John Houdeon his servant'.[65] Yet this is the only case where it is made explicit that a debt was connected with the collection of parochial revenues.

Most credit received by peasants from clerical sources came from the unbeneficed priests of their own villages. Yet many chaplains did not build up a significant role as creditor. As in the early modern period, members of the fourteenth-century parish clergy often participated in credit on much the same scale as people from the lay populace.[66] Chaplains varied in their incomes, which meant that some were simply better placed than others to lend. John Wyot's prominence as a creditor must have derived in large measure from his considerable accumulation of wealth. Crucial also, however, were the possession of local family connections and maintenance of close contact with a village's populace over a period of years. Existing studies show that a cleric who enjoyed such connections and contacts could also play a significant role in credit.[67] The case of the parish clergy reminds one, therefore, of the importance of personal knowledge in the formation of credit relationships. Were the credit relationships involving John Wyot and William Stevens with members of the local peasantry primarily exploitative arrangements in which clergy lent back to parishioners money extracted from them as tithe and other payments as part of a cycle leading ultimately to greater impoverishment? Or were they, by contrast, the means by which the village economy received a welcome injection of capital? That is the question to be addressed in the next chapter. What the investigation in this has established is that the wealth amassed by the clergy at parish level did not automatically become available to villagers as credit in any form.

4.3.3 Non-residents

Contact with outsiders involving credit could take one of several forms. A resident of a village could, most obviously, take a loan from an individual living elsewhere. Alternatively, he could buy on credit from the outsider. Matters could also work the other way round, with an outsider receiving the loan or purchasing on credit. Examples of all these arrangements occur in the court rolls. But just how significant were outsiders as providers or recipients of credit in relationships involving people from the seven villages? Addressing this question helps in the broader task of establishing the strengths and weaknesses of medieval rural credit. In particular, it helps one understand

[65] CRO, L1/177, m.31d (9 June 1388).
[66] Holderness, 'Clergy as money-lenders'.
[67] Swanson, 'Clergy and manorial society', 23–6 (Thomas Faleyn, chaplain of Alrewas, Staffs.).

how easy it was for villagers to obtain credit, either through loans or in the context of sales, from people not already known to them. Further, where loans in particular are concerned, it allows one to determine the extent to which villagers could access sources of capital, especially urban capital, that were potentially greater than those available in their immediate localities.[68]

The particular focus in this section is on the villagers as borrowers and outsiders as lenders. This is partly dictated by the evidence. Manorial lords did not have the power to 'distrain outside the fee'; that is, they could not compel a person to appear in their courts by seizing their goods, if that person did not have goods upon the territory under the lord's jurisdiction.[69] This is likely to have deterred villagers from suing an outsider for debt in the creditor's 'home' manor court. In all probability, therefore, the non-resident debtors of the inhabitants of the seven villages will be less well represented in the records than their creditors. This assumption is supported by information from the court rolls. Table 4.4 shows the creditors and debtors recorded as being *de* or 'of' another location, such as 'Laurence Suitor of Lolworth'. As the table indicates, non-resident creditors outnumber non-resident debtors.

The other reason for concentrating on outsiders as creditors is that it allows one to assess the penetration of urban capital into villages. The idea that most credit affecting the countryside flowed from the town is almost a commonplace of the literature on medieval European credit. The role in that story of Jewish lenders based in towns is also important.[70] Given the location of the Cambridgeshire villages studied (see Map 1.1), the towns scrutinized most closely here as possible sources of urban credit are Cambridge and Ely, 22nd and 30th respectively in terms of the ranking of English towns by numbers of taxpayers in the 1377 poll tax.[71] Additional evidence on creditors from these towns is gleaned from manorial court rolls pertaining to eleven further villages all lying within a 10-mile radius of Cambridge, from which the names of all non-resident creditors (forty-three in total) and non-resident debtors (thirty-six in total) have been extracted.[72] In the century before their expulsion from the town in 1275, the Jews of Cambridge had been an

68 For this latter issue, see especially Schofield, 'Access'.

69 On this point, and for general discussion of peasant litigation beyond the manor, see Briggs, 'Seigniorial control', and Briggs, 'Travelling'.

70 Drendel, 'Society and economy', 92–8; Gaulin and Menant, 'Crédit rural', 47–50; Toch, 'Geld und Kredit', 506–12; see also Wernham, *Salon-de-Provence*, 125–36, 146–50, who emphasizes, however, that credit was contracted only in villages in a narrow hinterland of Salon.

71 Palliser (ed.), *Cambridge urban history*, 758.

72 Barton (Lancaster manor), 1356–1400: Cambridge, Corpus Christi College Archives, XXXVII/1–2; Barton (Priory manor), 1326–47: Cambridge, King's College Archives, BAR/261 and BAR/296; Bottisham, 1320–72: TNA, SC 2/155/47–52; Foxton, 1276–1325: Cambridge, Trinity College Archives, Box 27, rolls 1–5; Fulbourn, 1361–1400: TNA, E 315/79; Grantchester, 1398–1400: Cambridge, King's College Archives, GRA/284–5; Great Abington, 1287–1400:

Table 4.4 Creditors and debtors explicitly identified as non-resident

	Oakington, Cottenham, and Dry Drayton, 1291–1400	Horwood, 1302–60	Willingham, 1377–1400	Littleport, 1316–27	Balsham, 1310–49	Total non-resident	All creditors and debtors
Creditors	9	8	19	10	12	58	1,080
Debtors	11	4	12	10	1	38	1,065
Total persons	20	12	30[a]	20	13	95[a]	1,780
All creditors and debtors	741	166	385	289	199		

Note: [a] Includes one non-resident who appeared as both creditor and debtor.
Sources: See Table 2.1.

important source of credit to inhabitants of the surrounding countryside, even if they appear to have catered primarily for those whom Dobson characterizes as the 'middle ranks of English rural society', rather than to the peasantry.[73] In the following century, did other townspeople take the Jews' place to perpetuate the importance of urban credit in the rural context?

The first point to note is that non-resident creditors were not numerically significant. Only 5.1 per cent of creditors in the six core Cambridgeshire villages are explicitly described as outsiders. This, however, must be treated very much as a minimum figure.[74] Court roll scribes often recorded the place of residence of an outsider inconsistently.[75] Consequently, some genuinely non-resident lenders are almost certainly not counted in Table 4.4. Outsiders whose place of residence is unrecorded are especially likely to be found among those who make only a single appearance in the court roll record.[76]

What were the places of origin of the non-residents with whom villagers established credit relations? Most of them lived close by, often in adjacent parishes, as can be seen from the map of Willingham's external credit contacts (Map 4.1). Of the seventy-nine non-residents involved in credit relations with villagers from the eleven settlements in Cambridge's hinterland, just five (6.3 per cent) came from 10 miles away or more. Where the non-resident was creditor, the average distance between the parties' residences was 3.6 miles; where the non-resident was debtor, the average was 3.1 miles.[77] In the villages in Table 4.4, the non-resident creditors and debtors originating 10 miles or more away from the village were somewhat more numerous, totalling twenty-three of ninety-five individuals (24.2 per cent). This largely reflects the presence of Littleport, whose external credit contacts extended over unusually large distances, a feature which will be discussed below.

That non-resident debtors often lived close to their creditors is perhaps unsurprising. Manorial lawsuits brought against persons living a substantial

---

CRO, 619/M1–2; Great Eversden, 1382–99: CUL, Q Box 11; Harston, 1313–1400: BL, Add. Ch. 18521, 18523–18525, 18530; Landbeach, 1327–98: Cambridge, Corpus Christi College Archives, XXXV/121–2; Meldreth, 1316–95: LMA, HO1/ST/E/079/1–18; Swaffham Prior, 1281–1377: CUL, EDC 7/13/2–5. Several court roll series have substantial gaps within the date range.

[73] Stokes, *Studies*, 252–79; Dobson, 'Jews', 13–14. See also Stacey, 'Jewish lending', 95–6, and Mundill, *England's Jewish solution*, 209.

[74] The possibility that Balsham market court rolls once existed and are now lost is again relevant. The village market is an obvious location for the contracting of debts involving non-residents. If such debts were incurred, and were recorded exclusively in a source now lost, then this has obvious implications for the estimation of Balsham's external credit ties.

[75] Briggs, 'Credit and the peasant household economy', 244, and references therein.

[76] Briggs, 'Rural credit', 198–203.

[77] All distances as the crow flies.

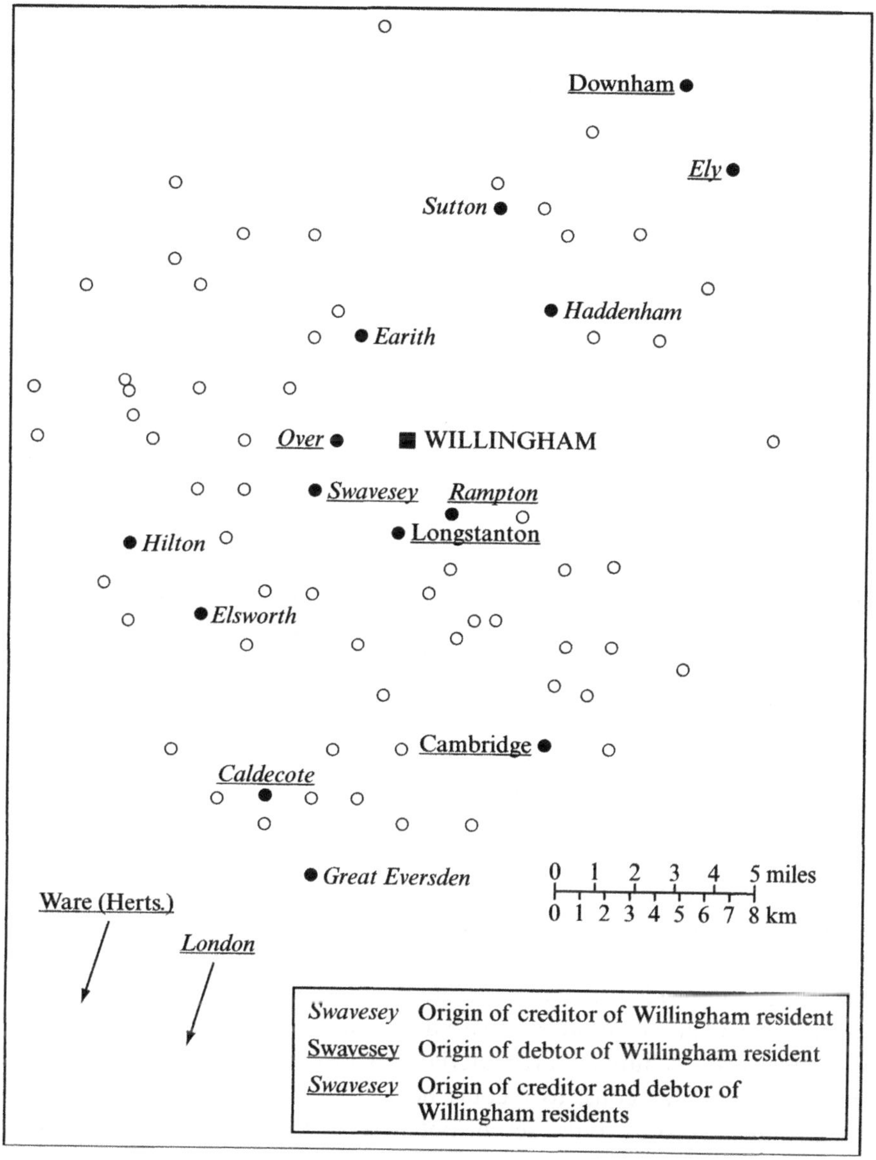

Map 4.1 Locations of non-resident creditors and debtors of Willingham residents, 1377–1400, plus sites of all towns and villages within a ten-mile radius of Willingham

Source: CRO, L1/177–8.

distance away were probably quite rare, since the limits to a lord's power to distrain outside his fee made it hard to secure the court appearance of such debtors. More weight can be placed on the generally close proximity of non-resident creditors to their village borrowers, as revealed by the manorial evidence. This suggests that credit relationships between people from different places developed best where the individuals concerned lived in close enough proximity to one another to make pre-existing contact likely. That said, we should not ignore those credit relationships involving villagers that were established over longer distances. The external creditors of Littleport residents came from places 9.6 miles away on average, while their external debtors lived an average of 11 miles away. This reflects not only the relatively large spaces between settlements in the fenland, but also the commercialized nature of a local economy based upon water transport.

How common in villages were urban creditors? It cannot be claimed that they are a numerically significant presence in the manorial sources. Just fourteen persons in the records of the six core Cambridgeshire villages and in those of the eleven additional settlements were urban creditors. With the exception of one John Brid, citizen of London, all these men came from Cambridge or Ely.[78] Of course, manorial court records alone cannot necessarily give a full picture of urban–rural credit. If villagers went to the town to contract loans or to buy on credit from townspeople, then we might expect many resulting unpaid debts to have been collected in the town's courts, rather than in the manor courts.[79] Cambridge borough court material with which to test this is, unfortunately, largely lacking, though a glimpse is provided by a draft court book of 1389–90. This confirms that villagers owed to town dwellers debts about which one would remain unaware if using manorial sources alone. However, the numbers involved are not overwhelming. Of a total of approximately 308 debt cases heard in the borough court over a period of around one year, only 34 (11.0 per cent) involved an urban plaintiff and a non-resident defendant from a rural location.[80] Nor does it seem likely that evidence of more extensive debts owed by villagers to townspeople was concealed in church court material now lost. To judge by the register of the bishop of Ely's consistory court held at Cambridge between 1374 and 1382, which records only seven potentially debt-related cases between

[78] Two creditors 'of Barnwell' are included in Cambridge here. Brid prosecuted William Grygge of Willingham: CRO, L1/177, m.42 (5 March 1392).

[79] See Kowaleski, *Exeter*, 279–93; Galloway, 'Urban hinterlands', 119–20; Dyer, 'Market towns', 19–24.

[80] CRO, Palmer/Barnard, Vol. I. There were a further sixteen debt cases in which a rural plaintiff sued a rural debtor. For use of this source, see also Lee, *Cambridge*, 98–100.

Cambridge residents and persons from the surrounding villages, such ties were not common.[81]

However, although people from the towns who gave credit to villagers were few in number, the quantities of credit they gave were comparatively large. Evidence is available for eight money debts owed to the Cambridge and Ely creditors known about from manorial sources, as detailed in the preceding paragraph. At least two of these were loans, as they are recorded in formal recognizances. Six of the eight debts were more than 20*s*. in value, and the average was just over 23*s*. The villager borrowers in these arrangements clearly had access to a quantity of credit significantly greater than was usually available from lenders within the village. The enhanced scope for further lending by the village borrower in such transactions meant that, in all probability, occasional large credits of this kind eventually affected more people within the village than just that initial borrower.[82]

The dominance of European rural credit by town lenders may to some extent be an illusion created by the overwhelmingly urban origins of the surviving sources.[83] Similarly, the considerable degree of isolation from outside involvement displayed by English village credit markets may be overstated by looking at matters primarily through manorial material. Also, non-residence has almost certainly been underestimated since only those people recorded in the '*de*' plus place name form, such as 'Laurence Suitor of Lolworth', have been counted as non-resident. Yet in spite of these factors, it is clear that although credit contacts with outsiders were certainly made, they were rare, compared with equivalent contacts with neighbours. One of the various conclusions to be drawn is that when peasants bought and sold in a range of local markets in order to raise cash and obtain essentials, credit sales were less common when trading with outsiders than when dealing with neighbours. Urban credit does not appear to have been particularly significant for villagers, in terms of the numbers of transactions made. With respect to credit, as in the medieval English economy more generally outside of London's hinterland, towns did not invariably dominate the countryside. Nonetheless, even lenders from towns like Cambridge and Ely could provide credit on a scale not readily available from intra-village sources. This suggests that the presence of urban lenders—or more typically, their absence—had the potential to shape substantially the character of rural credit.

[81] CUL, EDR D/2/1. Account is taken of all *fidei lesio* (i.e. debt) and testamentary cases with rural parties from outside the Isle of Ely.

[82] Schofield, 'Access'; Briggs, 'Credit and the peasant household economy'.

[83] For the urban origins of much Italian documentation, see Gaulin and Menant, 'Crédit rural', 59.

4.4 Creditors and debtors: mutually exclusive groups?

Having examined the key subgroups, it is time to return to consideration of the creditors and debtors of the seven villages as a whole. How many different people were involved? Were the groups of individual creditors and debtors of similar size, or quite different? And, in the villages studied, how significant were the creditor-debtors, a group regarded in existing studies of village credit as being of negligible importance?

Figure 4.1 shows the proportions of all individuals in each location recorded as creditor only, debtor only, or creditor-debtor. The figure makes the key point that the creditors and debtors were remarkably similar in terms of their overall numbers. Only at Littleport can the ratio of creditors to debtors be regarded as in any way low, at 0.8. In no village, however, did there exist a small clique of repeat lenders catering for a much larger set of borrowers. This was a basic finding of Clark's work on fifteenth-century Writtle, and it seems to represent an enduring characteristic of rural credit in medieval England.[84] It is in apparent contrast to the picture presented by the

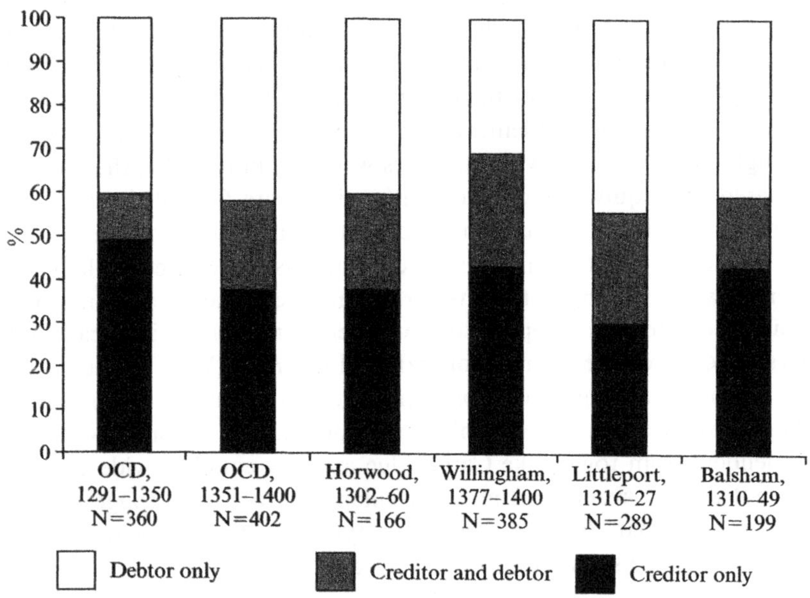

Figure 4.1 Percentages of persons acting as creditor only, debtor only, and as both

Notes: OCD: Oakington, Cottenham, and Dry Drayton. Joint parties, including husbands and wives appearing together, are counted as separate individuals.
Sources: See Table 2.1.

[84] Clark, 'Medieval debt litigation: Essex and Norfolk', 110–13.

available continental European studies, which often stress the existence of small groups of dominant creditor families.[85]

Another crucial area illustrated by Figure 4.1 is the numerical importance of the creditor-debtors, compared with those who appeared as either creditor only or debtor only. That some 10–25 per cent of known credit market participants borrowed as well as lent is undoubtedly significant. It is a reminder, for example, that involvement in credit could change over the life-cycle of a household, as a need to borrow gave way to an ability to lend. On the other hand, it is undeniable that most people known to have played a part in credit networks did so as either creditor or debtor, not both. This, of course, is something that previous commentators on pre-plague rural credit have remarked upon, though one cannot argue from Figure 4.1 that the creditor-debtors were less significant in the first half of the century than in the second across all villages. Nonetheless, a problem remains. Ought one to stress the substantial minority of creditor-debtors, whose presence suggests that credit did not necessarily polarize people into two mutually exclusive groups? Or alternatively, should most emphasis be given to the fact that so many people were limited to a single category of involvement in the credit market?

Unfortunately, a way out of this impasse cannot be provided through the use of comparable information from European studies. Instead, the way forward requires one to recognize that villagers were involved in credit to differing degrees, according to circumstances. Some people doubtless lent or borrowed just once or twice in their lives, at particularly significant junctures. Others, owing to the nature of their families and economic activities, lent and borrowed much more frequently, and for a wider variety of reasons. Consequently, it is not enough to look only at whether an individual acted as creditor only, debtor only, or both creditor and debtor. It is also essential to establish *how often* he acted in those roles. In doing so, it is possible to envisage two basic scenarios (Figure 4.2). In the first of these, the more intensively an individual was involved in credit, as measured by the number of credit relationships acted in, the more likely he was to have acted as creditor only or debtor only, but not as both (Figure 4.2 (a)). This scenario corresponds to the socially polarized credit network, composed of distinct classes of habitual lenders and habitual borrowers, as envisaged by existing studies of the later thirteenth and earlier fourteenth century. In the second scenario, by contrast, the more intensive an individual's involvement in credit, the more likely he was to have been a creditor-debtor (Figure 4.2 (b)). In this scenario, the credit network was composed of a core of very active participants who were not at all polarized into exclusive sets of creditors and debtors, plus a group of

[85] Drendel, 'Society and economy', 92–8; Drendel, 'Gens d'église', 84–5. This contrast was appreciated by Postan, 'Medieval agrarian society', 627.

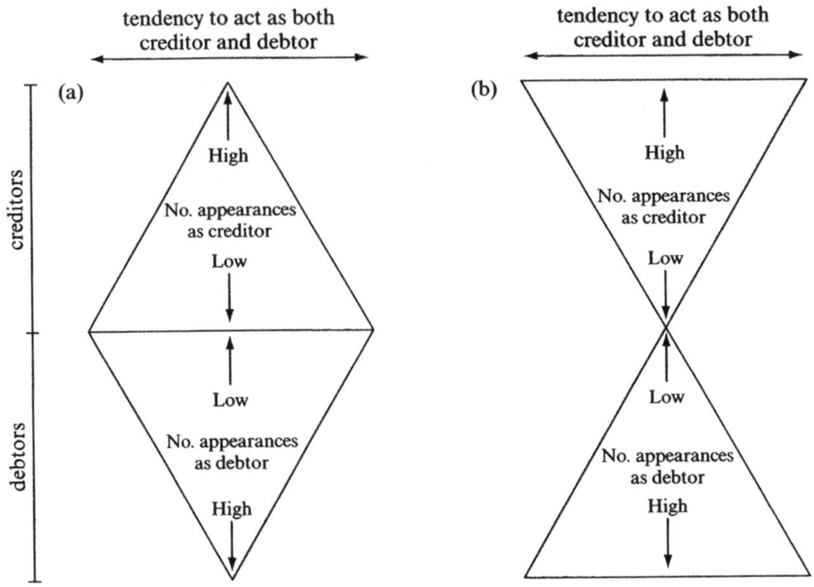

Figure 4.2 Two models of the relationship between intensity of involvement in credit and the tendency to act as both creditor and debtor

people who either lent or borrowed just once, or very occasionally. Although numerous, members of this second group were of marginal importance to the credit network as a whole.

Which of the two scenarios fits our evidence most closely? Table 4.5 compares individuals who are recorded as creditor or debtor in just one relationship with those who are recorded in multiple relationships, by reference to the percentages of creditor-debtors within each group. Without exception, the percentage of creditor-debtors was higher among those recorded in two or more relationships than it was among those recorded in just single relationships. Table 4.5 thus implies a situation in our villages closer to the scenario in Figure 4.2 (b) than to that in Figure 4.2 (a); that is, it was one in which the most intensively involved persons were not polarized into mutually exclusive groups.

To see how true a picture Table 4.5 gives, it is necessary to look more closely at individuals. The claim that credit networks were not necessarily polarized into serial creditors and serial debtors stands up least well to scrutiny in the cases of the Crowland villages before 1351 and Balsham. The example of John Wyot, chaplain of Dry Drayton (Section 4.3.2 above), shows that there were important repeat creditors in these villages who only ever lent. While not necessarily the most typical figure, Wyot was not alone in acting frequently as creditor only. At Balsham, for example, there were

Table 4.5 The percentages of individuals in several categories who acted as both creditor and debtor

	Oakington, Cottenham, and Dry Drayton, 1291–1350			Oakington, Cottenham, and Dry Drayton, 1351–1400			Horwood, 1302–60			Willingham, 1377–1400			Littleport, 1316–27			Balsham, 1310–49		
	A	B	C	A	B	C	A	B	C	A	B	C	A	B	C	A	B	C
(a)	153	19	(12.4)	140	37	(26.4)	68	22	(32.4)	146	26	(17.8)	95	27	(28.4)	86	21	(24.4)
(b)	119	16	(13.4)	162	33	(20.4)	67	16	(23.9)	119	31	(26.1)	111	25	(22.5)	78	17	(21.8)
(c)	61	19	(31.1)	93	44	(47.3)	31	14	(45.2)	120	73	(60.8)	66	47	(71.2)	32	11	(34.4)
(d)	65	22	(33.8)	88	48	(54.5)	36	20	(55.6)	99	68	(68.7)	91	49	(53.8)	35	15	(42.9)

Notes: Key: Rows: (a) creditor once only. (b) debtor once only. (c) creditor >once (d) debtor >once. Columns: A: Total individuals in category. B: Individuals in A who appeared as both creditor and debtor. C: B as % A. A Difference in Proportions test comparing row (a) with row (c), and row (b) with row (d), showed that the differences were statistically significant at the 95% level, with the exception of Balsham and Horwood, comparison of row (a) with row (c) (creditors).
Sources: See Table 2.1.

several repeat creditors who are never recorded as debtors. The most prominent was Chilman Lemmer, the most prolific lender in the Balsham rolls. Chilman recovered debts in nine actions between 1322 and 1340, including large sums of 7*s*. 9*d*. and 14*s*. 4*d*.[86] Furthermore, while these villages provide examples from among their most active creditors and debtors of individuals who both lent and borrowed, and thus may technically be called creditor-debtors, it often turns out on closer inspection that the individual concerned performed one role much more frequently than the other.

After closer inspection of the Crowland villages and Balsham, therefore, much evidence remains of a pre-plague situation where even those households most intensively involved in the credit network were substantially segregated into two groups, 'creditor only' and 'debtor only'. However, this situation is not found for all villages before 1349. In the figure of William Stevens, vicar of Little Horwood, Great Horwood clearly had at least one major lender who never borrowed. However, he was not typical. Of the fourteen Horwood persons recorded more than three times as creditor, eight also borrowed, while ten of the top fifteen borrowers—those borrowing twice or more—also lent. It is true that the prosperous and prolific creditor Walter Stevens appeared a notable eight times as lender, but just once as borrower.[87] However, many of the other most active creditors and debtors acted with more equal frequency in each capacity. A good example is Robert Saunders, who was creditor in five cases between 1321 and 1336 and debtor in six between 1306 and 1338.[88] At Littleport, furthermore, there was an even more striking lack of polarization among the most active credit market participants. Of the twenty-seven Littleport persons recorded in five or more cases as creditor, twenty-five also borrowed, while the thirty-three individuals appearing in the same number of cases as debtor included twenty-five people also recorded as creditors. There are numerous examples of Littleport residents who brought many cases as both creditor and debtor. John de Elm, for

[86] First appearances of Lemmer's actions: LMA, ACC/1876/MR/02/001, m.30 (29 January 1322); ACC/1876/MR/02/003, m.3d (9 February 1329); ACC/1876/MR/02/004, mm.1 (27 October 1330), and 2 (29 March 1331); ACC/1876/MR/02/006, mm.2d–3d (16 September 1333, 12 November 1334, 3 February 1335); ACC/1876/MR/02/007, m.6d (28 September 1339); ACC/1876/MR/02/008, m.1 (24 May 1340).

[87] First appearances of actions showing Stevens as creditor: NCA, 3913, mm.18d (13 September 1316), 20 (7 August 1317), 21 (17 February 1318, two actions), 23 (13 August 1319), 28–28d (13 July 1321, two actions), and 28d (11 September 1321); as debtor, NCA, 3913, m.13 (21 May 1313; in this case Walter's brother William, vicar of Little Horwood, was creditor).

[88] First appearances of actions showing Saunders as creditor: NCA, 3913, mm.28 (13 July 1321), and 30 (December 1321); NCA, 3914, mm.22d (April 1335), and 24 (2 July 1336, two). As debtor, NCA 3912, m.11 (6 December 1306); NCA, 3913, mm.18 (4 April 1316), 22 (28 October 1318), and 28 (13 July 1321); NCA, 3914, mm.23 (12 January 1336), and 28d (30 April 1338).

example, featured as creditor in eight actions between 1316 and 1320, and as debtor in ten actions between 1316 and 1322.[89]

For at least two pre-plague villages, therefore, one gains the strong impression that there was no great separation of the credit network's major players into two mutually exclusive groups, 'creditor only' and 'debtor only'. This impression is even stronger with the post-1350 evidence. This is what one would expect given the removal of the economic conditions which tended to polarize communities. In the Crowland villages between 1351 and 1400, twenty-seven individuals are known as creditors from five or more cases, of whom twenty also borrowed, while sixteen of the nineteen persons known as debtors from five or more cases also gave credit. Numerous individuals loomed large as both creditor and debtor simultaneously. Finally, at Willingham forty-one persons acted as creditor in five or more cases, of whom thirty-five also borrowed, while thirty-eight persons acted as debtor in five or more cases, including thirty-four who also lent. Admittedly one William Wykham, Willingham's most prolific lender with twenty-two cases, never appears as debtor. Yet three of the four next most important creditors after William also figure among Willingham's eleven most prolific debtors, that is, those recorded in ten or more cases. The record of an individual like William Torell of Willingham, who brought fifteen cases as creditor between 1378 and 1386, and nineteen as debtor between 1380 and 1387, does not conform at all to the notion of a fourteenth-century village in which those most heavily implicated in credit tended to feature exclusively as either inveterate lenders or inveterate borrowers.[90]

4.5 Creditors and debtors compared by wealth

The preceding section showed that in four of the six pre-plague villages studied—the three Crowland villages and Balsham—involvement in credit

[89] First appearances of actions showing Elm as creditor: CRO, R 93/96, mm.1 (13 August 1316), 2 (8 December 1316), 4 (27 July 1317, three actions), 3 (22 December 1317), 7 (18 July 1319), and 8d (23 May 1320); as debtor, CRO, R 93/96, mm.1 (13 August 1316), 2 (8 December 1316), 3 (22 December 1317), 6d (22 March 1319), 7 (18 July 1319), 9 (23 May 1320), 10 (24 October 1320), 15d (18 September 1321), 13 (8 December 1321), and 15 (28 September 1322).

[90] First appearances of actions showing Torell as creditor: CRO, L1/177, mm.1d–2 (18 February 1378), 4d (19 March 1380), 9 (16 February 1381), 12d (27 September 1381), 13d (22 September 1382), 15 (17 March 1383), 17d (4 December 1383), 18d (21 March 1384), 24 (6 September 1385, two actions), 26 (2 April 1386), and 28 (14 December 1386, four actions); as debtor: CRO, L1/177, mm.8 (18 December 1380, two actions), 9 (16 February 1381), 17 (4 December 1383), 18–18d (20 January 1384, two actions), 23d (13 July 1385), 24 (6 September 1385, five actions), 26 (2 April 1386), 27 (20 September 1386), and 30 (16 September 1387, five actions).

conformed relatively closely to the expectations generated by previous work on this period. In those villages, individuals who both lent and borrowed, although not absent, were never significant. More importantly, those who did the most lending tended to do very little borrowing, and vice versa. However, a different picture emerges from the two remaining pre-plague villages, Horwood and Littleport, and for the post-1350 villages. There, the households that dominated the credit market, in terms of the number of relationships formed, were highly likely to act as both lender and borrower. By contrast with the other four villages, at Horwood and Littleport it was the 'marginal players'—the individuals for whom just one or two credit relationships are recorded—who made up the bulk of the 'creditor only' and 'debtor only' groups.

However, no attempt has yet been made to address the other key proposition of extant work on the pre-plague period: that the creditors were generally wealthier than the debtors. The previous section looked at the roles households played in credit, but ignored the characteristics of those households. However, just because, in four pre-plague villages at least, creditors and debtors were quite polarized into two groups, it does not automatically follow that rich lenders lent to poor borrowers in those places. Equally, the evidence from Horwood and Littleport and from the post-plague villages of a large presence of creditor-debtors among the most frequent credit network participants does not necessarily mean that lending there took place between economic equals.

In this section, therefore, a comparison is made of the creditors, debtors, and creditor-debtors, to see how they differed in wealth. Wealth is measured by contributions to lay taxes assessed on movable goods, and by landholding. In the case of landholding, attention is restricted to Great Horwood, and to the Crowland villages before 1380, since the necessary detailed work could not be conducted for all places and periods. Comparing the relative wealth levels of creditors and debtors, and establishing absolute wealth levels within each group, is important not simply because it helps one to understand who the creditors and debtors were, but also because it sheds light on the purposes of credit and the nature of credit relationships, issues addressed directly elsewhere in this book.

4.5.1 Taxpaying

Lay subsidy returns do not necessarily provide straightforward information about the wealth of households, or about variations in wealth within the village. Historians continue to debate such issues as the proportion of rural households netted by the taxes, and the impact of undervaluation and conventional valuation of goods.[91] Nonetheless, these tax assessments do provide a useful means of assessing the relative standing of creditors and debtors, provided one adopts two assumptions traditionally made by historians who have used them. The first is that the tax lists omit poorer households. The second is that although the lists do not provide an exact measure of an individual's assets, they do nonetheless reflect relative wealth among the taxpayers. In other words, if Taxpayer A's tax charge was higher than that of Taxpayer B, then usually B can be regarded as poorer than A at the date of the assessment.[92]

Table 4.6 shows the number of creditors and debtors who appeared in debt litigation in two periods centred on the dates of the subsidies (1295–1335 and 1307–47). It indicates the percentage of people in each group

Table 4.6 The number of creditors and debtors in 1295–1335 and 1307–47 who were taxpayers in 1315 and 1327

	A	B	C	D	E	F
	All creditors	Taxpayer creditors	B as % of A	All debtors	Taxpayer debtors	E as % of D
1315 subsidy						
Oakington, Cottenham, and Dry Drayton, 1295–1335	102	19	(18.6)	93	20	(21.5)
Littleport, 1316–27	146	22	(15.1)	186	27	(14.5)
Balsham, 1310–35	72	13	(18.1)	86	17	(19.8)
1327 subsidy						
Oakington, Cottenham, and Dry Drayton, 1307–47	149	32	(21.5)	124	29	(23.4)
Littleport, 1316–27	146	22	(15.1)	186	20	(10.8)
Balsham, 1310–47	99	15	(15.2)	106	13	(12.3)
Great Horwood, 1307–47	63	17	(27.0)	68	14	(20.6)

Notes: Wives who appeared only with their husbands are excluded, as are non-residents of case study villages. No separate column is included for persons recorded as both creditor and debtor. Instead, such persons appear twice, once in columns A–C and once in columns D–F.

Sources: CUL, Q Boxes 3–4 rolls 1–4; NCA, 3912–3914; LMA, ACC/1876/MR/02/001–011; CRO, R 93/96; TNA, E 179/81/6, E 179/81/7, E 179/242/86.

[91] See Briggs, 'Taxation', 644, 656–7, and works cited therein. For recent reflections on the proportion of the population covered by the lay subsidies, see Campbell and Bartley, *England on the eve of the Black Death*, 321–9.

[92] For doubts about these suppositions, however, see Franklin (ed,), *Taxpayers*, 15–18. The Horwood 1327 lay subsidy return shows clear evidence of manipulation of the assessment; Briggs, 'Rural credit', 256–8. However, this does not invalidate its use as a rough ranking by wealth of a section of the population.

appearing as taxpayers on the subsidy lists. As can be seen from the table, only a minority of the recorded creditors and debtors also appear in the tax records. At the time of the taxes some creditors and debtors would have been either dead, able to evade payment, living elsewhere, or not in the position of taxpaying household head. Many absences, though, presumably demonstrate that a household was too poor to pay. If this is so, and the debtors really were generally poorer that the creditors, then one would expect to find taxpayers forming a smaller percentage of the debtor group than the creditor group.

However, a comparison of Table 4.6 columns C and F does not show this unequivocally. In three out of seven instances, in fact, the proportion of debtors paying the subsidy was greater than the proportion of creditors paying it. In another—Littleport in 1315—these proportions were very similar. In the remaining three instances, the taxpaying portion was larger among the creditors than the debtors, but in none was the margin dramatically different. Contribution to royal taxes, widely recognized as a hallmark of the better-off peasant households, was not a consistently greater tendency among creditors than it was among debtors.

As important as whether or not one paid tax, of course, was how much one paid. The figures on this issue show no general propensity for creditors to be better off than debtors in terms of movable wealth. Table 4.7 gives, for each subsidy, the median tax charges paid by creditors, debtors, and all tax-

Table. 4.7 Tax charges (in pence) of taxpaying creditors and debtors, 1315 and 1327

	Creditors	Debtors (median)	All taxpayers	Highest charge	Lowest charge (all taxpayers)	Total no. of taxpayers
1315 subsidy						
Oakington, Cottenham, and Dry Drayton[a]	25.00	23.50	18.50	120.00	6.00	310
Littleport	34.88	25.75	21.50	106.00	6.00	37[b]
Balsham	9.75	8.75	10.63	108.00	6.00	84
1327 subsidy						
Oakington, Cottenham, and Dry Drayton[a]	15.25	18.00	15.00	64.50	5.50	263
Littleport	12.38	12.38	12.00	104.00	6.00	31
Balsham	12.00	12.00	11.00	85.00	6.25	53
Horwood	16.00	16.00	15.50	48.00	10.00	42

Notes: The creditors and debtors in this table are those in columns B and E of Table 4.6.

[a]Cottenham list includes Westwick.

[b] Seven Littleport tax charges of 1315 are not fully legible and are excluded from consideration. The Littleport data is thus based on sixteen creditors' and twenty-three debtors' charges.

Sources: See Table 4.6.

payers. In 1327, the debtors paid, on average, tax charges that were the same as, or larger than, those of the creditors. In 1315, by contrast, it was the creditors who paid more.[93] Interestingly, in all but one instance the creditors and debtors contributed average charges that were higher than those of the taxpayers as a whole. Creditors and debtors—or at least, those creditors and debtors who paid the lay subsidies—did not belong to the poorest stratum of the village population, or even of the village's taxpaying population.

4.5.2 Landholding

The quantity of land owned by a peasant family was key to its overall wealth.[94] Our knowledge of the land held by the creditors and debtors of Oakington, Cottenham, Drayton, and Horwood is largely restricted to the property they held as part of the Crowland Abbey and Newton Longville Priory manors, as documented in the Oakington and Horwood court rolls, and in the tenant listings.[95] The tenant land in these manors consisted primarily of villein holdings, which owed both labour and money rent. In all four manors, there were several groups of holdings all of a standard area. At Horwood, the tenants comprised cottagers, half-virgaters (15 acres), and virgaters (30 acres); at Oakington, croftmen and cottars, 'five-acre men' (5-acre holdings), and 'fullondidmen' (10-acre holdings); at Cottenham, cottagers with 3 acres each, 5-acre tenants, and 10-acre tenants; and at Drayton, cottars and croftmen, half-virgaters (15 acres), and virgaters (30 acres).[96] There were also a number of free holdings of various sizes in each manor, none of which, it appears, exceeded 30 acres.[97] As was common on such 'midland' manors in this period, the standard villein units were not normally split up through permanent alienation of parts of the holding. Nor was it common to find more than one standard holding in the hands of a single tenant, though some tenants did begin to accumulate multiple holdings at Drayton and Cottenham in the years of land surplus after 1349. However, before the Black Death, at least, the landholding norm was for one tenant to possess a single unfragmented holding of standard size.[98]

[93] One should not place too much weight on the figures for Littleport in the 1315 subsidy (Table 4.7) because of the substantial proportion of illegible tax charges.

[94] For the detailed material summarized in this section, see Briggs, 'Rural credit', 204–86.

[95] For these sources, see above, n. 19.

[96] The Horwood virgate of 30 customary acres was equal to 35.7 modern statutory acres: Tompkins, 'Peasant society', 50. The areas of the Crowland holdings probably also represent customary rather than modern acres.

[97] The Crowland manor at Cottenham featured a 40-acre free holding in 1279–80, but it is not clear whether it survived unfragmented at this size into the early fourteenth century: *Rotuli hundredorum*, ii, 409.

[98] On the absence of accumulation at Horwood, see Tompkins, 'Peasant society', 53–4.

Ideally, we would have a comprehensive picture of land occupation for every creditor and debtor household. Unfortunately, our almost exclusive reliance on the surviving material pertaining to the Crowland and Newton Longville manors means that we cannot achieve this ideal. One potential problem is that creditors and debtors might hold land from several lords simultaneously. For example, a Cottenham creditor could have held land exclusively from a non-Crowland manor in that village, yet the survival of just the Crowland manorial records means that that person will appear to have been landless. The best one can do with respect to this problem is to make use of such additional information on landholding as survives. Thus the analysis incorporates information from a tenant list dated 1346/7 concerning one non-Crowland Oakington estate, the 'Picot Fee', and from twenty-one fourteenth-century Horwood charters.[99]

Another potential problem is subtenancy. The standard holdings described in manorial sources are well known to have been units of ownership, not of occupation. A tenant who held, say, a half-virgate was responsible for that holding's rent and dues, but we cannot be certain that that tenant actually cultivated the holding himself. He could have sublet it to others who worked the land. However, the subletting issue does not greatly jeopardize the analysis in this section. True, it has been shown that subtenancy was one of several factors which caused the reality of Great Horwood land occupation to differ from the landholding structure indicated by survey material. However, all the relevant factors that produced this situation, including subletting, only emerged significantly at the end of the fourteenth century at the earliest.[100] Furthermore, the pre-plague Oakington and Horwood court rolls give a fairly complete picture of the subletting of parts of standard holdings.[101] Although important, this subletting was probably not extensive enough to have caused the underlying pattern of land occupation to differ greatly from the pattern of ownership. In any case, this section uses landholding as an indicator of wealth, and tenancy of land was a prime determinant of wealth, irrespective of whether the head tenant sublet the land or farmed it himself.

The available evidence is therefore of a quality that justifies a comparison of creditors and debtors according to landholding. Tables 4.8 and 4.9 summarize information on the recorded landholdings of individual creditors and debtors.[102] With the exception of those wives who only ever appeared in debt litigation accompanied by their husbands, women as well as men are

[99] BL, Add. MS 5845, fos. 63–6; NCA, Horwood charters.

[100] Tompkins, 'Peasant society', 128–9.

[101] For leases, see especially Chapter 5 below.

[102] For further details on the attribution of landholdings in these tables, see Appendix 2.

Table 4.8 Landholding among creditors and debtors, 1291–1350

	Creditors			Debtors		
	A Acted as creditor only	B Also acted as debtor	C All creditors	D Acted as debtor only	E Also acted as creditor	F All debtors
Total individuals	205	72	277	184	74	258
Individuals at risk to display characteristics	145	70	215	171	72	243
No recorded landholding(s)	73 (50.3)	13 (18.6)	86 (40.0)	64 (37.4)	11 (15.3)	75 (30.9)
With recorded landholding(s)	72 (49.7)	57 (81.4)	129 (60.0)	107 (62.6)	61 (84.7)	168 (69.1)
With <10 ac. landholding(s)	35 (24.1)	16 (22.9)	51 (23.7)	33 (19.3)	16 (22.2)	49 (20.2)
With ≥10 ac. landholding(s)	37 (25.5)	41 (58.6)	78 (36.3)	74 (43.3)	45 (62.5)	119 (49.0)

Notes: Crowland villages and Great Horwood only. 'Individuals at risk to display characteristics' excludes creditors and debtors recorded in the court rolls only in personal litigation, and persons with stated external place of residence. In parentheses: persons with recorded landholdings and landholdings of benchmark size or greater as a percentage of individuals at risk to display characteristics. Differences in totals, columns B and E: column B shows the number of creditors between 1291 and 1350 who also appeared as debtor *at some point*. A small number of those creditors made their only appearance as debtor *after* 1350, in which case they will not also appear in column E, since column E contains debtors of the period 1291–1350 only.

Sources: CUL, Q Boxes 3–4 rolls 1–8, 12; NCA, 3912–3914; Q Box 8 (1344 rentals); NCA 4503, and 9744 fos. 37–40 (1320 extent, Horwood); NCA, Horwood charters; BL, Add. MS 5845, fos. 63–6.

Table 4.9 Landholding among creditors and debtors, 1351–80

	Creditors			Debtors		
	A Acted as creditor only	B Also acted as debtor	C All creditors	D Acted as debtor only	E Also acted as creditor	F All debtors
Total individuals	111	69	180	106	64	170
Individuals at risk to display characteristics	64	65	129	83	60	143
No recorded landholding(s)	34 (53.1)	19 (29.2)	53 (41.1)	43 (51.8)	15 (25.0)	58 (40.6)
With recorded landholding(s)	30 (46.9)	46 (70.8)	76 (58.9)	40 (48.2)	45 (75.0)	85 (59.4)
With <10 ac. landholding(s)	6 (9.4)	6 (9.2)	12 (9.3)	21 (25.3)	8 (13.3)	29 (20.3)
With ≥10 ac. landholding(s)	24 (37.5)	40 (61.5)	64 (49.6)	19 (22.9)	37 (61.7)	56 (39.2)

Notes: See Table 4.8. Differences in totals, columns B and E: column B shows the number of creditors between 1351 and 1380 who also appeared as debtor *at some point*. A small number of those creditors made their only appearance as debtor *before* 1351, in which case they will not also appear in column E, since column E contains debtors of the period 1351–80 only.
Sources: See Table 4.8.

included. The tables show the number of people who held land. They also indicate the number of landholders with a property or combination of properties of a benchmark size of 10 acres or more, and numbers with less than this amount of land.

Since the important question is whether or not an individual held land during the years in which he lent or borrowed, account is taken only of land held in the 'debt period', that is, the years preceding the person's appearance in litigation.[103] An individual who acted as both creditor and debtor has two separate periods under observation: one as creditor and one as debtor. This division is intended to take account of the possibility that individuals might typically lend but not borrow in particular phases of their lives, and borrow but not lend in others. We cannot assume that the landholding circumstances of such individuals were necessarily the same in each phase. A further feature requiring comment is that the total of individuals at risk to display landholding characteristics is smaller than the overall total of creditors and debtors. Excluded from the 'at risk' group are creditors and debtors recorded in the court rolls in connection with personal litigation, but in no other capacity. The fleeting court roll appearances made by these 'litigation only' individuals suggests they were probably not tenants of one of the four manors studied here. They are excluded because it is unfair to expect the records to contain information on their landholdings. Also excluded are the non-residents, those persons with place of residence explicitly given who were discussed in Section 4.3.3.

An examination of columns C and F of Table 4.8 shows that, before 1351, creditors and debtors held land to roughly the same extent. In fact, landholding was more common among the debtors than among the creditors, with 69.1 per cent of debtors holding land during their 'debt periods', as opposed to 60.0 per cent of creditors. Further, more debtors than creditors possessed landholdings totalling 10 acres or more. Smallholders with less than 10 acres were actually more common among the creditors than the debtors. These figures clearly suggest that, when these four pre-plague villages are considered together, a model of comparatively wealthy households extending credit to poorer households is not borne out by the evidence. Similar patterns are evident between 1351 and 1380 (Table 4.9, columns C and F). Here, too, landownership was just as common among debtors as it was among creditors. If anything, it was only after the Black Death that individuals well provided with land—that is, with holdings at or above 10 acres—became more numerous in the creditor group than the debtor group.

[103] For the 'debt period', see Appendix 2.

Before the Black Death, then, nearly 70 per cent of debtor households at risk to display landholding characteristics held land when they borrowed, and 49 per cent possessed at least a 10-acre holding. This latter group, clearly, were not poor or labouring households with little or no land in debt to a uniformly wealthy class of lenders. This point notwithstanding, however, Table 4.8 still leaves questions unanswered. Most importantly, what were the characteristics of those creditors and debtors in columns C and F of the table for whom we can pick up no landholding evidence in the sources? This group includes both those individuals not 'at risk' to display landholding characteristics, and those who were 'at risk', but for whom no landholding has been traced. It is highly improbable that all these people were genuinely landless. Unfortunately, however, we do not know how much land each owned. What is clear, though, is that if many of the apparently landless creditors in Table 4.8 were actually well endowed with land, and many of the apparently landless debtors were actually poorly provided with land or indeed landless, then the assumption of existing work—that richer villagers generally lent to poorer—would receive a significant boost.

To investigate this, one must abandon aggregation and return again to the court roll information on individuals. Such evidence concerning the apparently landless is naturally scarce, as the individuals of interest here are among the least well documented. On the whole, however, this evidence offers little threat to the argument that most creditors and debtors were broadly equivalent in wealth, as made on the basis of the taxpaying and landholding data reviewed already.

A few creditors without recorded land really were landless, notably those employees who became 'creditors' through wages arrears.[104] At the other end of the spectrum, one cannot eliminate the possibility that some of the patchily documented, ostensibly landless creditors were actually exceptionally wealthy villagers. After all, as the case of the substantial freeholder creditor John Rous of Oakington demonstrates, where the right evidence happens to survive, we can sometimes show that such people existed.[105] Oakington, however, is probably exceptional among the four villages in having a social and landholding structure within which it was at all likely that villagers would be found possessing much more than around 30 acres of land. Most preplague creditors for whom no sign of landholding is traceable, therefore, were probably not noticeably wealthier than the 60 per cent for whom we do have such evidence. This supposition is supported by the presence of several apparently landless creditors who were closely tied to the activities of the manor and its court and were presumably manorial tenants. An example of

[104] See Section 2.1.2.

[105] For Rous, see p. 106 above.

such a creditor is William Danewell of Oakington, who is mentioned several times between 1339 and 1348 as the lord's bailiff, and acted five times as a personal pledge.[106] William leased land several times from others but, for reasons that are unclear, no record of a tenancy held in his own right can be found.

The court roll histories of apparently landless debtors were searched for signs that they were genuinely landless, or made their livings primarily by means other than through their own holdings. In trying to identify such debtors, several types of court roll information were given close attention. The most important were offences at harvest time, such as illegal gleaning or taking sheaves; offences on the commons, such as digging peat turves without right; and being taken into the household of another, which was potentially typical of the casual worker. A total of 124 apparently landless debtors—28 from Horwood and 96 from the Crowland villages from the period 1291–1380—were investigated to see whether they displayed these or similar characteristics.[107] It should be stressed that ninety-seven of these debtors are recorded in one debt case only, so collectively they did not constitute major players in their respective credit networks.

None of the twenty-eight Horwood debtors investigated could be connected with activities characteristic of the landless poor, and there is no firm evidence to suggest that any of them were genuinely landless. In the case of the Crowland villages, evidence indicates that ten of the ninety-six individuals engaged in activities characteristic of landless families of low economic status. As for the remainder, it is unlikely that many of them were genuinely unsupported by land. There are numerous reasons why the landholdings of these people might escape record. For example, at least four men clearly present the appearance of landlessness simply because they lived elsewhere, as is shown by the chevage payments they made to the abbot.[108]

There is no intention here to suggest that individuals or households without land adequate by itself to support a family never borrowed. Specific cases prove that they did. A telling example is that of William Cole, whose court roll biography extends to just four entries in the records of two court sessions of 1342 and 1345. These reveal that William dwelt in the house of Agatha Tankret of Cottenham; that he had sold turves illegally; that he ought to have

[106] For Danewell as bailiff, see, for example, CUL, Q 3, m.57d (3 July 1344). 'Bailiff' at Oakington was a generic term used to denote any manorial officer except the aletaster: Page, *Estates*, 73.

[107] Some of these debtors appeared both before and after 1350.

[108] Chevage was a payment made by villeins to the lord for permission to live off the manor. Chevage payments of apparently landless debtors: CUL, Q 1, m.3d (3 September 1293, Nicholas Valet); Q 1, m.6 (26 May 1295, Henry Kylle); Q 2, m.28d (1 October 1324, Nicholas Schayl); and Q 6, m.3d (15 April 1361, William Gilbert, who was a debtor before 1349).

been in a tithing, or unit of local peacekeeping, but was not; and that he owed John Pepiz a debt of ½*d*.[109] Reading between the lines, it appears William was a landless and presumably unmarried young man who had perhaps recently arrived in Cottenham, was trying to establish himself in the village, and in doing so had contracted a petty debt to a wealthier villager. However, in his circumstances as the presumably landless subordinate member of another's household, and in the context of his indebtedness, he is not typical of the majority of borrowers studied in this book.

4.6 Conclusion: 'horizontal' credit

Throughout the fourteenth century, most rural credit relationships involved peasant households from the lay community. The individuals who directly handled credit transactions were usually male, but that minority of households headed by not-married women did also lend and borrow on a modest scale. Townspeople and rural clergy were numerically unimportant, but where they were present, the quantities of credit they gave were among the largest extended to rural households. No one, whether resident in town or country, appears to have made a living purely from lending to peasants, though there were several figures whose wealth from other sources was sufficient to allow them to develop a fairly specialized sideline as credit providers. The English countryside therefore differed markedly from parts of southern Europe. In that zone, peasants requiring credit were much more likely than their English counterparts to turn not to their neighbours, but to a narrow set of local moneylending families, many of whom resided in nearby towns. For the southern European peasants, Jews no doubt formed an important group within this body of urban lenders, but no such source of credit was available to the English in this period. This chapter has thus largely confirmed Postan's forty-year-old speculation that lending to English villagers was not the preserve of 'professional usurers', but was 'disseminated all through the upper ranks of village society'.[110]

In some villages, lending, and indeed borrowing, was so widely disseminated that almost everyone must have been involved in it. This was plainly the case at Littleport around 1320. Yet it is also very important to recognize that people engaged in credit to differing degrees. In all places it is possible to identify a core of repeat creditors and repeat debtors, and a periphery of individuals who probably only ever made one or two credit contracts in their lifetimes. The core participants between them usually accounted for the majority

[109] CUL, Q 3, m.48d (16 September 1342); Q 4, m.3d (16 April 1345).
[110] Postan, 'Medieval agrarian society', 627.

of a village's credit relationships. In the Crowland villages and at Balsham before the Black Death, participants in credit networks from both the core and the periphery were largely, though not completely, polarized into two groups: those who only lent and those who only borrowed. In pre-Black Death Horwood and Littleport, by contrast, and in all places thereafter, it is evident that those who engaged most intensively in credit tended both to lend and to borrow, often during a single period.

Although creditors and debtors formed relatively distinct groups in some places, this does not necessarily mean that the former were invariably better off than the latter. There were undoubtedly several prolific creditors whose landholding and taxpaying characteristics mark them out as substantially wealthier than almost all their fellow villagers. John Rous of Oakington, John Wyot of Drayton, and Walter Stevens of Horwood all fall into this category. On the whole, however, creditors and debtors were roughly equal in their landed and movable wealth. Most credit relationships were 'horizontal'. The presence of a large body of lenders and borrowers for whom we have no landholding information might appear to throw some doubt on this claim. However, a closer examination of those individuals suggests there were few debtors who genuinely possessed very little or no land. Borrowers of low wealth and status ought to crop up in the litigation evidence if they actually received credit on any scale, yet what one finds is that their presence there is limited.

What does all this mean for the strengths and weaknesses of rural credit in medieval England? A situation in which peasants relied most heavily on neighbours for credit might imply that there were weaknesses which prevented them from tapping more substantial and resilient sources from which to borrow, especially those lying outside the village. Such weaknesses might particularly have restricted the supply of cash loans. On the other hand, it may be that villagers borrowed primarily from a variety of neighbours because that was the arrangement that was least costly and most efficient. To test whether the English system of disseminated lending represents a strength or weakness, a good approach is to see whether the supply of credit could meet demand at crisis periods. Thus, this matter is addressed through the discussion in Chapter 6.

Another potential weakness attributed to rural credit is that its primary function was to depress and expropriate a class of recurrent borrowers, while advantaging only an entirely separate class of recurrent lenders. To discover whether this really was the outcome of credit relationships is the objective of the next chapter. However, the present chapter provides important evidence upon which that subsequent discussion is based. It does not appear likely that a significant consequence of credit was that the landless became overburdened with debt as they sought to improve their livelihood through acquisition of land. This cannot have been the case, simply because most credit was extended between those who already held land. Hence a major weakness of the rural credit system was not that it induced the poor to take on ultimately catastrophic obligations in a bid to enter the privileged ranks of the landed. Rather, a key weakness was the opposite: in these 'midland' villages, most credit circulated only among the landed peasant households—most notably, the 10-acre holders, the half-virgaters, and the virgaters—while any landless and labouring families scraping a living below them were largely excluded from its benefits.

Any claim that village credit served only to create a class of struggling debtors and a class of ever-richer creditors receives a further blow from other evidence presented in this chapter. When the most heavily indebted persons also figured frequently among the community's most active creditors, as was the case at Littleport and at Horwood before the Black Death, and in all villages thereafter, then it is hard to argue that households were rigidly segregated into successful lenders and failing borrowers. That said, not all places were like these. In four pre-plague villages, there was quite a sharp divide between the serial creditors and serial debtors. Furthermore, even though in those villages the creditors were not generally better off than the debtors, in the objective sense of their landholding and taxpaying status, the possibility nonetheless remains that credit was a route by which the lenders advanced their position at the expense of the borrowers. Within any group of, say, half-virgater households, fortunes could vary widely, and debt relations could become the means by which a superficially homogeneous group became separated into the successful and the unsuccessful. In short, even horizontal credit had the potential to be exploitative and unproductive. It is the purpose of the chapter which follows to see how far this was the case.

5

Credit and social relations

The starting point of Chapter 4 was the consensus view of the nature of participants in later thirteenth- and early fourteenth-century rural credit. That view developed almost as a by-product of some of the most influential previous work on the agrarian society and economy of those decades of crisis. It suggested that village creditors were usually richer than village debtors, and that there was typically little commingling of the two groups. Yet the preceding analysis has suggested that that picture conceals a more complex reality. In fact, in the villages studied here, creditors and debtors displayed fairly similar wealth indicators. To be sure, creditor-debtors were often not numerous overall. However, both before the Black Death—in some places, at least—and after it, the households who were most active in credit often operated as both creditor and debtor.

The preceding chapter thus provided some important answers to the question: who were the creditors and debtors? However, the significance of its findings will not be fully clear until a series of related problems have been addressed. Most of these form part of the larger question at the heart of the present chapter, which is, what were the nature and consequences of the relationships between creditors and debtors, both for the individuals involved, and for village society at large?

The dominant view of pre-plague creditors and debtors explored in the previous chapter also provides us with a concomitant picture of the most typical creditor–debtor relationships. In this view the wealthier peasants, a group increasingly perceived by historians as key to the fate of the entire pre-plague economy, used their ability to give credit to poorer peasants primarily as a means of consolidating their position of power within the village in an era of rising land values and economic insecurity. Members of the wealthier strata might advance credit to poorer families with which the latter could buy land, or lease it at a rack-rent from the fortunate head tenants.[1] Alternatively, the elite peasants would be in an ideal position to service demands for credit arising from the exigencies faced by more vulnerable villagers, most obviously a

[1] Campbell, 'Agrarian problem', 53–4, 61–4.

shortage of food. In both scenarios, the poor peasant might, at worst, be obliged to alienate some or all of any land he held to meet the debts he had been forced to contract. Members of the wealthy creditor class would be among the most likely candidates to buy up such property.[2] At the very least, credit relationships of this kind could create a dependence of poor borrower upon rich lender, which the lender might capitalize upon in various ways. Conceivably, for example, the lender may have imposed conditions on the giving of credit, whereby the lender required the borrower to provide him with labour, or to come to him first for any future credit needs.

In this view, therefore, the majority of credit relationships were in some sense exploitative, in that they saw lasting benefits accrue only to the creditor at the expense of the debtor. While creditors profited, debtors simply became yet poorer, or might even suffer the outright catastrophe of wholesale loss of land, as a consequence of their borrowing. Any village in which such relationships were the norm, and in which there was little attempt to halt their consequences, was presumably a harsh environment in which signs of 'moral economy' were attenuated. Any such village would, to borrow Schofield's telling description of Hinderclay in the difficult 1290s, have become a place of 'winners and losers'.[3]

It should be stressed that all the commentators whose work is referred to above would doubtless insist that some pre-plague credit relationships did not conform in either their character or their effects to the model outlined. Acquisitive behaviour, including that driven by credit, had its limits, and was in any case not incompatible with social co-operation and the bonds of community.[4] Furthermore, credit may often simply have been of marginal importance compared with other contemporary economic or demographic processes which produced similar effects of social stratification or recurrent poverty. Thus, in presenting the view that pre-plague credit relationships were generally exploitative, and brought lasting benefits only to creditors, there is naturally a danger that it may be endowed with a coherence and force it does not merit given its expression in existing historical writing. Nonetheless, it must equally be admitted that this view also has a clear logic, and fits well with many generally agreed characteristics of English agrarian society before the Black Death. Furthermore, the idea that credit relationships

[2] Razi, *Life, marriage and death*, 82, 87–8, and Razi, 'Family, land and the village community', 5–6, 9 (indebted peasants sold land to wealthier peasants); Schofield, 'L'endettement', 87–8 (pre-plague debts perhaps contracted mainly out of need); Schofield, 'Credit and the peasant land market', 792–5, and Schofield, 'Manorial court rolls', 261–3 (poorer borrowers alienated land to wealthier lenders); Campbell, 'Agrarian problem', 52–5 (borrowing to acquire land, and foreclosure).

[3] Schofield, 'Dearth', 14.

[4] Razi, 'Family, land and the village community', 11.

usually had negative consequences for peasant debtors is also present in the literature on continental European rural credit, especially that which belongs to the 'old view' of pre-industrial credit as primarily a route to poverty and expropriation.[5]

How convincing is such a picture of rural credit relations in the early fourteenth century and their consequences? Earlier chapters have reviewed various pieces of evidence which already suggest that a large number of credit relationships could not have conformed to a model in which poorer households borrowed from markedly richer in transactions which further impoverished the former and increased the power of the latter. For instance, Chapter 2 showed that much credit was not extended for reasons of exigency. Furthermore, Chapter 4 showed that much credit was extended horizontally between households which, in terms of their landholding and taxpaying characteristics, appear roughly equal in wealth. Such evidence invites scepticism concerning the idea that village credit functioned essentially as a mechanism through which the rich could take advantage of the comparatively poor as the latter sought help to meet basic needs. However, in spite of some of the trends to the contrary discussed earlier in the book, it remains possible that credit relationships in the villages studied could be described as exploitative, in that they advanced the lenders' interests only, and led to greater dependency and increasing difficulties among debtors. In this chapter, therefore, the question of credit relations and their consequences is subjected to closer investigation. As in the preceding chapter, the focus is on the period before 1349, which is of course the era with which the model of credit relations under scrutiny is most closely identified. The evidence concerning the latter part of the century provides a control and a comparison.

5.1 The impoverishment and exploitation of debtors: case studies

To show from litigation evidence that an early fourteenth-century peasant was in debt, even repeatedly so, is not enough in itself to demonstrate that he or his household was experiencing difficulties through being party to an exploitative relationship, let alone that that household was facing ruin and unable to reproduce itself. When discussing economic contexts more 'positive' than that of the early fourteenth century, historians tend to regard the

[5] For example, Duby, *Rural economy*, 285, and Berthe, 'Marché', which assumes that major individual buyers of land acquired the properties of the indebted. Drendel observes that although it has long been a commonplace to argue that indebtedness was a significant mechanism in the transfer of large amounts of peasant property into urban ownership, this thesis has rarely been tested empirically: 'Le crédit', 297 n. 77.

indebtedness of individuals or households in a correspondingly optimistic light. Thus, being in debt during the years of economic expansion witnessed in certain later fourteenth-century towns, for example, has been regarded as evidence of a full participation in profitable commercial activity.[6] Similarly, it is difficult to argue that those Willingham residents shown by litigation to have been indebted in the 1380s following livestock purchases were involved in exploitative credit relationships that served to accelerate a descent into poverty. Being taken to court for debt can thus be seen as compatible with individual economic prosperity in some periods, and there is no real reason why this possibility should not exist for the early fourteenth century also. It must be remembered that in most manor courts, a large number of debt plaints were terminated via a 'licence to agree' or by the plaintiff's non-prosecution.[7] Most of those cases were followed by an out-of-court settlement, with the lawsuit itself serving merely as a prompt to the debtor to initiate repayment. Many debtors were probably sued not because they were in dire economic straits and were unable to honour their debts without further jeopardizing their financial prospects, but because it made financial sense to them to wait until the last possible moment before meeting their obligations.[8]

Instead, to identify the potentially debt-driven economic failure of households, it is necessary to generate individual case histories using the full range of biographical details provided by the sources.[9] One historian has defined the problem, and the best approach to it, particularly well. Drendel concludes a lengthy discussion of the prevalence and forms of lending in Trets with what he regards as the most important question concerning rural credit, namely, whether or not the 'predominant kinds of credit . . . aided or destroyed the economic fortunes of the agriculturalist'. As he continues, 'some borrowers were clearly successful, others were poor, but what role credit played in their fortune and success cannot be answered with statistics'.[10] Whether one is using continental notarial registers or English manorial court rolls, what is needed is thus the detailed, qualitative approach entailed by the reconstruction of individual debtors' biographies.

In the English context, it is undoubtedly possible to identify personal or household histories which offer evidence both of indebtedness and of potentially credit-driven impoverishment and the related exploitation of a debtor by other villagers. The possible signs of impoverishment and exploitation are various. They include the permanent alienation or temporary leasing of land;

[6] Kowaleski, *Exeter*, 349.
[7] Briggs, 'Manor court procedures', 543.
[8] Briggs, 'Credit and the peasant household economy', 247.
[9] For use of this method in a similar context, see Schofield, 'Manorial court rolls', 261–5.
[10] Drendel, 'Society and economy', 133.

the surrendering of land through 'impotence'; evidence of involvement in crime or of flight from the community, which may sometimes reveal an individual's inability to provide for his family; the failure to maintain a tenement; and even, in certain circumstances, a report of a death.

In virtually any pre-plague village, whether in eastern or western England, one can find examples of indebted peasants who show such signs of distress or difficulty. Thus Thomas Collin of Hawne, a township within Halesowen manor (Worcestershire), became indebted in the 1290s, was forced to sell off most of his land prior to his death in 1312, and thus could not provide for his daughters, while at the end of the 1290s Henry Crane of Hinderclay was in a similar 'spiral of debt and land sale'.[11]

Substantially similar case histories may be found in the records used in this study. For instance, Robert Salden of Great Horwood, a half-virgater who acted as affeeror (a setter of manor court amercements) and juror, experienced a decline in fortunes in the 1310s. In that decade he is recorded as a lessor of land, and debtor in six different cases. Robert owed some heavy debts. For instance, in 1312 he acknowledged a debt of 19*s.* to Sabina Baynard. In 1317, the forfeiture of the land belonging to Robert, who had by then disappeared, was announced on the grounds that he was a fugitive and 'of ill fame'. The initial belief appears to have been that Robert should lose his tenurial rights as a consequence of a criminal indictment or conviction. Yet after Robert's death, extended enquiries into this holding were conducted, and in 1331 a jury found that there was no evidence that Robert had been indicted or convicted.[12] Even if the manorial jurors later could not swear that Robert ought to have forfeited on grounds of his criminality, it does at least appear that in 1317 Robert had fled the village under suspicion of a crime. On the other hand, even if Robert's mounting debts did prompt him to some unrecorded desperate act at the height of the Great Famine, one cannot show that his situation was exploited directly by his creditors. For example, none of Robert's leases of land was made in favour of one of his known creditors.

A more overt example of excessive debt leading to disaster for a borrower is that of William Fraunce of Dry Drayton.[13] William's history of indebtedness appears to have begun with an attempt to expand his resources through acquisition, in 1303, of a virgate of land.[14] Thereafter he was repeatedly sued

[11] Razi, 'Family, land and the village community', 5–6; Schofield, 'Dearth', 14.

[12] . . .*fugitivus et male fame*. . .: NCA, 3913, m.21 (29 October 1317). For the enquiry into Salden's lands, see Poos and Bonfield (eds.), *Select cases*, xcvii–xcix. Start dates of plaints revealing Salden as debtor: 3913, mm.6d (29 July 1310), 12d (8 December 1312), 16 (15 March 1316), 18 (4 May 1316), 19 (7 October 1316), and 22 (16 December 1318). As creditor: NCA, 3913, m.17d (9 February 1316, two actions).

[13] For additional detail on William's case, see Briggs, 'Creditors and debtors', 138–9.

[14] See p. 52 above.

for debt, and sometime in mid-1316 he disappeared from the village, leaving a vacant holding to the lord.[15] In a later reference to this holding, the court roll states that William lost it because he was hanged for a felony.[16] The severity of William's decline appears to have been exacerbated by his involvement with one particular lender, and there is little doubt that that lender also profited directly from William's misfortunes. The lender was John Wyot, the chaplain of Drayton and prolific creditor, discussed earlier.[17] John was the creditor in three of the twelve debt actions brought against William. In 1316, it was John who took the departed William's land from the lord for a term of four years.[18]

The court roll entries that record the debts of Fraunce to Wyot show that the latter was quite relentless in using the court to pursue what was due to him. For instance, while in October 1313 John allowed that William should have until the following February to repay some of his outstanding debts, he simultaneously made the unusually severe demand that 11*s.* should be levied 'from day to day' from the debtor's goods.[19] In the end, John secured what was due to him by obtaining William's land. If any credit relationship in the rolls studied in this book merits the term 'exploitative', this is it. It is worth emphasizing, however, that by 1314, the community at large was showing unease with the tenor of relations between the two men. In December of that year, an exceptional agreement between John and William was recorded in the court roll. In it, the parties made a concord 'concerning all contracts, plaints and demands from the beginning of the world, unto this day'. The agreement specified that William should pay John 8*s.* 8*d.*, which presumably represented a consolidation of his various debts to John.[20] The wider body of court suitors had presumably urged such a concord in an effort to stem the effects of John's demands upon his impoverished debtor.

Both Robert Salden and William Fraunce were reasonably well-off or aspiring men who fell into debt, became involved in crime or fell under suspicion of crime, lost their land, and died outside their communities.[21] But how typical were they? The mounting indebtedness of both men coincided with some of the worst periods of the century in terms of overall agrarian

[15] William is referred to in a session of 28 April 1316 as the pledge of a man who brewed against the assize. The next mention of him is the note of his vacant holding in the record of the session of 23 October of that year: see CUL, Q 2, mm.14d, 15d.

[16] CUL, Q 3, m. 16 (16 May 1332).

[17] Section 4.3.2.

[18] CUL, Q 2, m.15d (23 October 1316).

[19] CUL, Q 2, m.10d (15 October 1313).

[20] CUL, Q 2, m.12d (13 December 1314).

[21] On the links between economic distress and high rates of crime in this period, see Hanawalt, *Crime*.

conditions. At Drayton, the hardships of the Great Famine and subsequent agrarian crisis, and indeed of the remaining pre-plague years, appear to have been unusually severe, perhaps owing to peculiar environmental disadvantages of the village.[22] In the second decade of the fourteenth century, and in especially vulnerable places like Drayton in particular, debts that at other times might have been sustainable were instead likely to trigger disaster. Thus while for Robert and William, and for numerous other contemporary villagers, credit relations were closely associated with impoverishment and exploitation, theirs was not necessarily the modal experience for the pre-plague era as a whole, or for all villages.

To achieve a fuller picture of the nature and consequences of credit relations, therefore, three further aspects of land transfer and debt relations are examined. The first involves a return to the issue of the subletting of land and debt. The second is the issue of whether debtors lost their land through permanent alienations that may conceivably have been precipitated by debt, with a special focus on any alienations of land made to an individual's creditor. The final, connected area concerns the propensity of creditors to accumulate land. These topics are addressed using the Oakington and Horwood rolls via a combination of aggregative analysis and the biographical approach advocated by Drendel as the best route to understanding the effects of credit use on medieval cultivators. After endorsing this methodology, Drendel gives us the example of Petrus Savardi, a Trets peasant of modest wealth documented from 1324 to 1341. Petrus accumulated a series of heavy debts in the 1330s as his financial situation deteriorated. However, although Petrus sold land at the end of his life, this does not appear to have been a 'crisis' sale, and Petrus's surviving will shows he was able to make modest bequests to his family.[23] What strikes one most about his case, perhaps, is his willingness to take advantage of his continued creditworthiness by repeatedly borrowing, while simultaneously avoiding disaster. As the following sections show, the biographies of several contemporary English villagers, like that of this Provençal peasant, show that it is quite possible for evidence of extensive indebtedness to co-exist with clear signs of the avoidance of economic failure, or even with signs of considerable prosperity.

[22] For example, in view of the impact of the 'hard years' on the tenants, the lord gave permission in 1322 that for the twelve years following the Drayton homage would be required to have just half their sheep in the lord's fold: Q 2, m.23 (16 January 1322). See also *VCH Cambs.*, ix, 79; Ravensdale, 'Population changes', 207.

[23] Drendel, 'Society and economy', 133–6.

5.2 Temporary subletting and credit relations

As we have seen, the standard-sized customary holdings of Oakington, Cottenham, Drayton, and Horwood were kept largely unfragmented. Rather than selling portions of their holdings outright, tenants made adjustments to them by means of short-term inter-peasant leases of parcels covering half an acre on average. The court rolls give a relatively comprehensive picture of this leasing, or subletting, activity. Even leases of one year or 'cropping' required a seigniorial licence. Leases made without such a licence were liable to be reported to the court and noted in the record. This book uses all 426 recorded peasant leases, both licensed and initially unlicensed. Chapter 3 pointed to the significant link between subletting and credit relationships. It explored the possibility that short-term leases were used as means to secure new extensions of credit. The conclusion reached was that while one cannot exclude the possibility that leases were employed in this way, it was probably exceptional. Perhaps a more important dimension of the link between leasing and debt was the creation of a lease to repay a debt, or to raise money to ease more general financial difficulties towards which debt was a contributing factor. This is the relationship between leasing and indebtedness explored in this section.[24]

The leasing of peasant land has tended to be viewed together with the outright sale of land as part of a response to debt which shows that rural credit relations were frequently deleterious in their character and consequences.[25] The most common assumption appears to be that only really severe problems would have prompted individuals to shed land on either a temporary or a permanent basis. It is also arguable that those peasants who leased land, like those who sold it, were normally worse off afterwards because they had lost a vital part of their means of growing foodstuffs at a time when average landholdings were small and grain prices generally were rising.

Part of what follows is intended to modify this basic assumption that evidence of leasing by debtors is indicative of rural credit's essentially damaging repercussions. The main aim of this section, however, is simply to look at the extent of involvement in leasing among the creditors and, especially, the debtors. Table 5.1 provides support for the idea that leases of land were often carried out by debtors, and that many of the leases were intended to liquidate debts. More than 50 per cent of lessors were also recorded as debtors. It is also significant that the lessees of land included a substantial

[24] For a preliminary examination of leasing by individual debtors, see Briggs, 'Creditors and debtors'.

[25] See e.g. Razi, *Life, marriage and death*, 37; Schofield, 'Dearth', 15.

Table 5.1 Identifiable lessors and lessees recorded as creditor and/or debtor, Oakington (with Cottenham and Dry Drayton) and Great Horwood

	Total individuals	Recorded as creditor only		Recorded as debtor only		Recorded as both creditor & debtor		Recorded as neither	
		No.	(%)	No.	(%)	No.	(%)	No.	(%)
Oakington, Cottenham, and Dry Drayton, 1291–1350									
Lessors	64	2	(3.1)	26	(40.6)	7	(10.9)	29	(45.3)
Lessees	111	32	(28.8)	12	(10.8)	10	(9.0)	57	(51.4)
Great Horwood, 1302–50									
Lessors	35	2	(5.7)	9	(25.7)	9	(25.7)	15	(42.9)
Lessees	83	12	(14.5)	11	(13.3)	9	(10.8)	51	(61.4)

Sources: CUL, Q Boxes 3–4 rolls 1–5 and 12; NCA, 3912–3914.

number of known creditors, especially in the Crowland villages. This suggests the possibility that some leases were made in favour of creditors as a form of debt repayment.

It must of course be stressed that for the majority of debtors there is no record that they sublet land. Table 5.1 reveals that known debtor-lessors comprise just thirty-three individuals from Oakington, Cottenham, and Drayton, and eighteen individuals from Horwood. Those figures should be compared with the pre-1351 overall totals of debtors, namely 184 individuals in the Crowland villages and 96 at Horwood. Thus even if one recognizes that some lessors may have borrowed but were never recorded as defendants in debt litigation, it remains clear that leasing was a practice pursued by a minority of borrowers only. Yet given that, how far did leasing play a part in case histories in which debt was associated with impoverishment and exploitation?

5.2.1 Oakington

For a small core of people mostly active in one village and in one period—Oakington in the 1330s and 1340s—the connection between severe indebtedness and frequent subletting was profound.[26] In Oakington, Cottenham, and Drayton, just seven lessors made 145 leases between them, or 55 per cent of the total from those places. These seven included five Oakington men who appeared among the Crowland villages' top eleven debtors of the period 1291–1350, that is, those who acted as debtor in six or more credit relationships. It makes sense to focus on those individuals.

[26] For these debtors, see also Briggs, 'Credit and the peasant household economy'.

William Atte Touneshend was the tenant of an Oakington 10-acre 'full land' who is recorded as debtor in seven cases between 1340 and 1348, and made a remarkable thirty-four leases between 1338 and 1347 at a median area of 3 rods (0.75 acres). Notable evidence to suggest that William was facing difficulties comes from a report in October 1346 which stated that he was no longer capable of cultivating and maintaining his land.[27] Around one year later, William surrendered his holding, but retained to himself six selions of land and a dwelling as part of a retirement arrangement.[28] William Atte Touneshend appears to have survived the Black Death and apparently did well thereafter, in 1350 recovering from an executor a legacy of one quarter of barley left to him by a man who had presumably died in the plague, and in 1351 acquiring a cottage.[29] These activities in the immediate post-plague period demonstrate that although the indebted William had been declared 'impotent' in 1346, he was nonetheless able to provide himself with ample economic security thereafter.[30]

Richard Massely was a smallholder who possessed a messuage with a croft and 4 acres. He was involved as debtor in six cases between 1341 and 1343, and in the years 1337–42 made ten leases of median area 3 rods. At the end of the 1330s Richard began a decline that left its mark in the court rolls. Between 1339 and 1341 he was presented several times for 'wasting his goods at the tavern and elsewhere', and for making waste in his tenement.[31] In 1342 it was reported that he was unable to put right the neglect of his holding, and the record of the same court session contains the grant of Richard's property to Robert son of Thomas Sperner. If the entry fine of 30*s*. is anything to go by, the condition of the holding cannot have been too bad. The court rolls show that in 1335 Richard Massely had a wife, Christiana, but by 1342 he was alone, apparently a widower. A retirement agreement was made when Richard gave up his holding which saw the former smallholder, now apparently without any family of his own, given two butts of land in the croft plus the right to live in 'a certain chamber within the messuage, namely a room

[27] CUL, Q 4, m.9d (11 October 1346).

[28] CUL, Q 4, m.16 (7 November 1347). The holding was taken by one William son of Walter. The relevant court roll entry is badly faded, but it almost certainly states that William Atte Touneshend paid a fine of 30*s*. in order to secure this retirement arrangement. The ability to make a payment of this size would suggest William remained basically prosperous at this time in spite of his indebtedness.

[29] CUL, Q 5, mm.5d (28 October 1350), and 7d (18 October 1351).

[30] It is just possible that the 'William Atte Touneshend' mentioned in the court rolls after 1347 is actually the debtor William's younger brother, who was also named William. In the one reference to him in the court rolls, this younger William was cited as 'William Atte Touneshend junior', presumably in an attempt to distinguish him from his landholding elder brother. After 1347, however, the court rolls use only the form 'William Atte Touneshend'. The scribes did not add 'junior', which they presumably would have done if they had wanted to denote the younger man.

[31] CUL, Q 3, mm.31d (1 July 1339), 40d (29 January 1341), and 44d (19 October 1341).

which Richard's father inhabited, which he shall hold for as long as he remains alone and without a wife'.[32]

William Kylle senior was the tenant of an Oakington 10-acre 'full land' who is recorded as debtor in twenty-two debt cases between 1307 and 1347. Some large debts were claimed from him, including, in 1327, one massive debt of 41*s*. arising from a grain purchase.[33] Between 1337 and 1348 William made twenty-two leases with a median area of one acre. He was reported dead in the court of 25 July 1349. Apart from the leases, the only possible sign that William's debt burden was having negative consequences upon his livelihood is an isolated report in 1342 of ruinous buildings in his possession, and by itself this is hardly conclusive.[34]

John Kylle was tenant of a 5-acre holding. He appeared as debtor in sixteen cases between 1323 and 1348, in the most notable of which he acknowledged an obligation of 16*s*. 2*d*. arising from a loan.[35] In the period 1325–49 he made sixteen leases with a median area of 2.5 acres. Like William Kylle senior, John almost certainly died in the Black Death. His last recorded act while alive was to make two short leases to William de Danewell in May 1349, but by the following January he was dead. In 1348 he was given a day by which to repair a barn (*grangia*), but beyond this there is no evidence other than the leases to suggest that this individual was struggling to maintain himself or his family as a consequence of his frequent and heavy borrowing.[36]

No debtor recorded in the Oakington rolls is known to have engaged in more credit relationships than Geoffrey King, a holder of a 10-acre 'full land' who appears in twenty-seven debt cases between 1337 and 1359. Geoffrey also made twenty-four leases between 1337 and 1348, with a median area of one acre. Geoffrey was presented twice for making waste in his tenement, in 1335 and again in 1339. On the latter occasion he was also presented along with Richard Massely for 'wasting his goods at the tavern and elsewhere', though in Geoffrey's case this report was a one-off.[37] Like that of William Atte Touneshend, Geoffrey's career underwent something of an upturn after the Black Death, which he survived. In November 1349 Geoffrey appears in the records for the first time as manorial juror, and he served regularly in that role thereafter.[38] In 1358 he took a toft from the lord as a leasehold, and he died sometime between April 1361 and July 1364.[39]

[32] CUL, Q 3, m.50 (16 November 1342).
[33] CUL, Q 3, m.6d (26 October 1327).
[34] CUL, Q 3, m.46d (17 April 1342).
[35] CUL, Q 4, m.16 (8 October 1347).
[36] CUL, Q 4, m.14 (2 May 1348).
[37] CUL, Q 3, mm.20d (10 May 1335), and 31d (1 July 1339).
[38] CUL, Q 5, m.1 (20 November 1349).
[39] CUL, Q 5, m.21 (7 February 1358).

Does the evidence concerning these five men show that leasing was part of a downward spiral to which indebtedness was a major contributing factor? In three cases—William Kylle senior, John Kylle, and Geoffrey King—there really are no significant signs apart from the leases themselves that debt had a negative long-term effect on the men and families concerned. Significantly, all three left completely intact holdings on their deaths, though none of the holdings was taken over by an heir.[40] For the two other Oakington men—William Atte Touneshend and Richard Massely—there is more convincing evidence that the individuals concerned were struggling to maintain their farms, that heavy debts were both cause and symptom of that struggle, and that the leases may thus represent an attempt to stave off the surrender of the holding. However, other factors may have exacerbated the effects of debt upon William and Richard. It is notable that the retirement arrangements of both William and Richard made provision only for the retiring man. It is explicitly stated that Richard had no wife at his retirement, and one may argue from silence that William was in the same position.[41] No children of Richard or of William are noted in the rolls. Quite possibly, therefore, the unusually small size of the family living on the holding in each case meant that the struggle to maintain it when heavily indebted was less likely to succeed than it was in families where the tenant was accompanied by a wife and several children.

5.2.2 Great Horwood

At Great Horwood, the link between leasing and debt was weaker than it was for a hardcore of Oakington peasants in the two decades before 1349. Horwood presents the same pattern of a small number of individuals accounting for a large number of leases. Between them, for instance, John Godwin and John Payn made eighty leases, some 49 per cent of the total. However, the most frequent Horwood lessors did not include many recurrent debtors, as they did at Oakington. John Godwin, for example, is not recorded at all as creditor or debtor. Much short-term leasing was apparently unrelated to indebtedness.

Only two of the twelve Horwood lessors who made three or more leases feature among the ten most frequent debtors. One of these, John Payn, held

[40] William Kylle had at least two sons and a daughter, Geoffrey King had at least one son and one daughter, John Kylle no recorded children.

[41] Interestingly, William, like Richard, was said to have received as his retirement dwelling a small chamber (*receptaculum*) which his father had inhabited. In William's case, this is a reference to the retirement of his own father in 1335, who apparently (like his son some twelve years later) had no wife when he retired. It was in 1335 that the debtor William took over the holding; see CUL, Q 3, m.28d (28 October 1335).

a messuage and half-virgate. In many ways John Payn provides an example of a frequently indebted villager who suffered economic failure, and whose numerous leases can be seen as part of an effort to avert that failure. He is recorded as debtor in five cases of the period 1317–47. He also made thirty-nine leases between 1315 and 1347, the median size being 0.5 acres. Like others already discussed, in the period of Great Famine and agrarian crisis John's name became associated in his community with crime. In 1321, a report of his indictment was made to the court, and his holding was forfeited to the lord.[42] One can only speculate whether the alleged offence was of a type likely to constitute a response to economic difficulties. Yet if the offence were of this kind, it would naturally combine with the evidence of John's debts to support an interpretation of increasing distress, which the resort to leasing was an attempt to ameliorate.

In the following year, John appears to have been exonerated, and his land was restored to him.[43] Yet his troubles continued. In 1327 and again in 1335 he was presented for having ruinous buildings.[44] After 1330, John's short-term leases became more numerous, and in 1348 a further report of neglect on his holding led to its seizure by the lord.[45] Later that year, John was stated to be incapable of holding and maintaining his property, and in 1349, on the eve of the plague, the messuage and half-virgate were surrendered to the use of Nicholas le Yremongere.[46] A provision was made for the maintenance of John, now some 60 years old, on the holding.[47]

For John Payn, indebtedness was part of a wider pattern of economic insecurity and association with crime. In his case, short-term leases were clearly employed as a way of putting off the forced surrender of the holding. In the end this loss came, though only after many years of struggle. John had just one recorded son, also called John. However, this son apparently left the village around 1328 as a young man, perhaps unconvinced of his father's capacity to pass on to him a holding in good condition.[48]

The other frequent Horwood debtor who also made numerous leases was Hugh Neel. Hugh was well endowed with land after entering his father's virgate in 1305. Prior to 1317, Hugh was quite successful. In 1310 he gave the lord one quarter of oats so that his son Richard could have licence to enter

[42] NCA, 3913, mm.26d, 31d (28 February 1321, referred to again 27 August 1322).

[43] NCA, 3913, m.32d (6 November 1322).

[44] NCA, 3914, mm.6d, 22d (15 July 1327, April 1335).

[45] NCA, 3914, m.47 (15 July 1348).

[46] NCA, 3914, mm.47d, 51d (1 October 1348, 25 February 1349).

[47] He was placed in tithing in 1302, at which date he was probably twelve years old: NCA, 3912, m.3d (27 November 1302).

[48] NCA, 3914, m.8d (2 November 1328), the first of many reports of default of suit of court and of chevage payments.

holy orders, and in August 1316 he gave the same Richard a freehold messuage and house in Horwood.[49] Earlier in the same year Hugh had also paid 2*s*. to hold a cottage 'of small value' in addition to his virgate.[50] Then began a period of quite rapidly mounting difficulties. Hugh was debtor in four actions between 1316 and 1322, and in 1321 he was presented for letting a building collapse.[51] In the year 1322 Hugh made nine leases at a median 0.5 acres, and in 1323 he surrendered his holding 'through incapacity'. Richard Brut took the holding, and undertook to maintain Hugh and his wife, Sibyl, in their retirement.[52]

As in the case of John Payn, Hugh Neel's career suggests a pattern of debt associated with the inability to run a holding. In both cases, too, leasing was part of an attempt to put off the moment at which the holding could no longer be maintained. It should be remembered, however, that Hugh's indebtedness and rapid journey towards the loss of his land coincided with the exceptional years of the Great Famine and its aftermath. Furthermore, Hugh's case cannot simply be described as a debt-driven 'failure'. Prior to the Famine, Hugh had already set up his only known offspring with a house and a secure career. With his son gone, the labour at Hugh's disposal was probably depleted, as is suggested by a reference in 1317 to his amercement for 'receiving against the assize', which should probably be taken as evidence that Hugh was hiring live-in labour at this date.[53] Given the choice between retirement and continuing the struggle to work his holding, Hugh chose the former. Richard Brut appears to have received Hugh's holding in good order in 1323—he paid 5 marks as an entry fine—and the maintenance agreement was generous, allowing annually to Hugh and Sibyl five and a half quarters of grain, and a linen shirt and breeches for Hugh.[54] Hugh Neel and his family did not 'lose everything' as a result of his borrowing. Instead, debt combined with a shrinking household prompted him to choose an early retirement which, by the standards of his time, must have been relatively comfortable.

To summarize: the relationship between leasing and debt was not straightforward. Many leases were unrelated to credit. Many debtors did not lease land as a way of coping with their debts and their effects, apparently because there was no need to. Yet others, like Richard Massely, did so, and it is likely that for some such people the creation of a lease was an unwelcome

[49] NCA, 3913, m.6 (25 May 1310); NCA, Horwood charter 44 (29 August 1316).

[50] NCA, 3913, m.17d (9 February 1316).

[51] NCA, 3913, m.27d (22 May 1321).

[52] NCA, 3913, m.33d (22 January 1323); Poos and Bonfield (eds.), *Select cases*, 51–2.

[53] NCA, 3913, m.20 (13 May 1317).

[54] Hugh also received one mark in cash from Richard at the transfer. Compare the provisions made in other maintenance agreements documented in Dyer, *Standards*, 151–4.

step that the lessor was forced into because of debt. It is also quite possible that in some cases the granting of leases did little to ameliorate the debtor's situation. The investigation of the relationship between debt and temporary subletting thus suggests that for people such as Massely, credit relations were largely negative in their nature and consequences. After all, Massely, Atte Touneshend, Payn, and Neel all ending up losing their land, even if that loss essentially meant the forced retirement of the tenant, rather than an entire family of parents and children all losing their livelihoods.

However, other debtors who leased were not in difficulties because of debt, nor was their leasing part of a general slide towards catastrophe. Several of the Oakington debtors borrowed heavily—in some cases extremely heavily—and also made many leases. However, in the longer term they remained prosperous. For them, leasing appears to have been a routine method of raising cash to pay for debts arising from investment credit transactions. It did not signal disaster. If Campbell's assumption is correct, short-term leases in pre-plague England must have fetched high rents.[55] It was the possession of land, and the ability to sublet it, which made and kept borrowers such as William Kylle and Geoffrey King creditworthy. People without holdings to sublet are thus likely to have had a harder time attracting credit, and hence probably appear much more rarely in the manor court records as borrowers.

A final, important question about temporary leasing and debt concerns the degree to which borrowers leased land directly to people who were their creditors. If this was happening on any significant scale, then one could reasonably claim to have identified an exploitative dimension to credit relations. Any village in which many of the lands of borrowers were placed under the effective control of their lenders in the form of leases would arguably have been a place in which credit permitted members of one class to exercise a personal hold over the members of another. Since about half of all lessors in both the Crowland villages and Horwood were also debtors, it is potentially possible that a significant number of leases were made directly between a debtor and his creditor, perhaps as a form of debt repayment.

The issue is investigated by examining 'pairings' of lessors and lessees, and of creditors and debtors. Lessor A's leases to lessee B represent one 'pairing', just as creditor A's debt cases with debtor B represent one 'pairing'.[56] As Table 5.2 shows, before 1351 the four villages under scrutiny generated 324 different pairings or combinations of lessors and lessees, and 528 different creditor–debtor pairings. However, there was very little overlap between the

[55] Campbell, 'Agrarian problem', 55. We are rarely if ever told the inter-peasant rental arrangement.

[56] See Section 5.5 for fuller detail on the creditor–debtor pairing.

Table 5.2 Lessor–lessee 'pairings' of individuals also found in creditor–debtor relationships, Oakington (with Cottenham and Drayton) and Great Horwood

	Discrete lessor–lessee pairings[a] A	Discrete creditor–debtor pairings B	Pairings in A also found among pairings in B[b] C	C as % A
Oakington, Cottenham, and Dry Drayton, 1291–1350	172	363	21	12.2
Great Horwood, 1302–50	152	165	3	2.0
Total	324	528	24	7.4

Notes: [a]That is, lessor A and lessee B, lessor C and lessee D, etc.
[b] Lessor–lessee pairings with debtor as lessor and creditor as lessee.
Sources: See Table 5.1.

two categories of pairing. In only 24 instances out of a possible 324 did an individual create a lease to the benefit of someone from whom he is also known to have borrowed. Hence one must conclude that when borrowers made short-term leases as part of an effort to liquidate debts, they did not usually lease directly to their lenders. This restricted the degree to which credit relations led to a direct personal control by lenders over borrowers and their property.

5.3 Did debtors lose their land?

The previous section gave some examples of heavily indebted individuals who were forced to lease portions of their lands, and then eventually surrendered their entire holdings. The aim of this section is to go beyond these examples, and to discover just how common the giving up of land was among debtors more generally. For most of the people discussed in the previous section, 'losing land' effectively meant being forced into a retirement in which the person concerned would be supported on the holding by the new tenant. Debtors such as Richard Massely of Oakington seem often to have been relatively old individuals struggling to keep up a holding with the aid of just a couple of other family members, or even by themselves. The surrender of land by such people did not normally mean the loss of the primary resource of a growing family, or involve the denial of future landed security to the debtor's children. To be sure, such a precipitate shift into retirement for a villager lacking the labour power to maintain his property must have been traumatic enough. However, much more serious than this would have been the loss of land outside the family by a peasant in his prime. A particular effort is therefore made to trace situations of this type.

Attention is focused on *inter vivos* sales or involuntary surrenders of land made by known debtors before 1351. For each debtor, the individual's 'debt period' and the ten years following the end of the 'debt period' have been examined to look for such transfers or surrenders.[57] It is fairly obvious that any pre-mortem alienation of land was potentially something which the tenant was forced into through circumstances, rather than something he deliberately chose to do. Most alienations in these villages involved complete standard holdings, which a peasant would not have relinquished lightly. An obvious circumstance which might stimulate such a transfer was an intolerable level of debt.

Twenty-seven debtors from the Crowland villages and ten Horwood debtors made *inter vivos* transfers or surrenders in this category. Included among these are the retirements of Massely, Atte Touneshend, Payn, and Neel discussed in the previous section. The thirty-seven transferors comprised, respectively, 14.7 per cent and 10.4 per cent of all debtors of the period.[58] By contrast, just 2.3 per cent of creditors from the Crowland villages and 9.1 per cent of Horwood creditors transferred their land in this way. Hence in Cambridgeshire at least, the *inter vivos* alienation of land was much more a characteristic of debtors than it was of creditors. Only four of the thirty-seven 'sellers' made transfers in favour of kin. It is almost certain that some of the remaining 'sellers' involved in such alienations made them out of desperation. John Hogg is a likely candidate. In 1321, after demand was made of him in court that he should render the arrears of customs and services due from a messuage and virgate in Drayton, John responded that he was no longer able to hold the tenement owing to his impotence. The property was taken into the lord's possession.[59] Another example is that of John Roger, whose Drayton messuage and virgate were taken by the lord sometime between 1321 and 1325, again as a consequence of the tenant's impotence.[60] A final likely example of severe distress leading to loss of land concerns John Gerard, who in February 1318 transferred a 30-acre holding (a virgate) in Drayton to John Ruter, after apparently being in possession of it for only five years.[61] All these men gave up the basis of their livelihoods, the court rolls

[57] This includes any transfers of freehold land for which evidence exists. For the 'debt period', see Appendix 2.

[58] Totals of debtors before 1351: 184 in the Crowland villages; 96 at Horwood.

[59] CUL, Q 2, m.23d (10 November 1321).

[60] CUL, Q 3, m.1 (27 April 1325).

[61] CUL, Q 2, m.16 (10 February 1318). This John Gerard is not the same as the Oakington man discussed on p. 195 below.

record no retirement arrangement or other provision for their subsequent support, and we do not know what happened to them afterwards.

However, one is still left with the problem of determining how many of these transfers were primarily stimulated by the seller's debt burden, rather than by other, albeit connected, forces. In reconstructing individual case histories from the court rolls one must always make inferences on the basis of disparate information. The source never explicitly suggests the role of debt or of any other factor or event in precipitating transfers. Combinations of differing considerations must have led to the loss of land in each peasant's case. One very pertinent question, however, is to ask whether the debtors who lost their land really were carrying too much debt. On this issue, it is notable that twenty-seven of the thirty-seven persons who made *inter vivos* transfers or surrenders are recorded as debtor in just one or two debt cases. For instance, the three Drayton men mentioned in the preceding paragraph all appeared as debtor in 1316 in one action only. One gains the strong impression that debt was not really the main problem for such individuals. Other factors like poor yields and livestock disease, all of which can be only dimly perceived in the court rolls, were doubtless often enough in themselves to precipitate disaster, even in the absence of serious debt. Of the twenty-seven debtors from Oakington, Cottenham, and Drayton who shed land permanently in *inter vivos* transfers, seventeen lived in Drayton. Agrarian problems in that particular village in the four decades preceding 1349 were bad enough to generate numerous vacant holdings even without the incidence of heavy peasant debt. It is highly significant that the lord had great difficulties in acquiring replacement tenants to take the Drayton virgates surrendered by John Hogg and John Roger.[62] One is even tempted to suggest that some of the apparently indigent transferors of Drayton land might have weathered their crises somewhat better had they been able to borrow more extensively, rather than less.

5.4 Did creditors accumulate debtors' land?

A minority of debtors, therefore, were forced through distress to give up entire holdings during their lifetimes. It cannot be demonstrated that intolerable debts were the primary cause of such surrenders, though they can hardly

[62] In 1323, John Gilberd paid the lord 4*s*. so that he would not have to take Hogg's Drayton holding, but would be allowed instead to wait until a holding became vacant in Cottenham: CUL, Q 2, m.25d (12 January 1323). In 1325, John Reynal the reeve and Thomas Attepond presented that four men had been found who were capable of taking on John Roger's vacant tenement: Q 3, m.1 (27 April 1325).

have helped. Yet what about the land transactions of creditors? As debtors shed land, albeit in relatively small numbers, did creditors accumulate that land? Chapter 3's findings on the limited use of customary land as security suggest that foreclosures on mortgages are unlikely to have been common. Nonetheless, it would have been possible in theory for a creditor to take a debtor's land as a form of repayment. If village credit promoted the acquisition of property by lenders as borrowers lost it, then it must surely be described as a force leading to social polarization, impoverishment, and, potentially, exploitation. An even stronger case for this could be made if it were found that particular creditors were taking the land of those to whom they had extended credit.

The rarity with which the *inter vivos* transfers of debtors were made to the benefit of creditors is, however, striking. The land sold or surrendered by the thirty-seven debtors discussed in the previous section fell into the hands of a known creditor in just five instances. Even that figure exaggerates the extent to which creditors bought up the vacated holdings of impoverished debtors, since two of the five transactions represented an exchange between a pair of Oakington men of some unusually small parcels of land.[63] Even more notable is the fact that no *inter vivos* transfer can be traced involving a debtor passing land to someone known to be his creditor.

Earlier in this chapter we encountered the story of William Fraunce's involvement with his creditor John Wyot the chaplain, which arguably forms our court rolls' prime example of an exploitative credit relationship. John acquired the land of his debtor after many years' pursuit of him, but he did not do so by forcing William to give up his property during the latter's lifetime. Instead, John only obtained William's virgate as a result of the latter's sudden death and the resulting vacancy of the property. The analysis in the present section shows that the acquisition of a debtor's land by his creditor during the debtor's lifetime was an eventuality for which no evidence can be discovered in the Oakington and Horwood sources. This substantially reduces any justification for calling credit relations in these villages 'exploitative'.

It is perhaps not surprising that no creditor can be found buying up his debtor's land. Accumulation of multiple villein holdings by any individual peasant was rare in the Crowland villages and at Horwood before the Black Death, apparently as a combined result of seigniorial policy and local custom. Where it did occur, the accumulation of multiple villein holdings was really a later fourteenth-century phenomenon. Occasionally before 1349, a

[63] William Wright sold to Andrew Noteman a vacant place in Oakington next to the cemetery, in exchange for which Andrew gave William two customary selions, both, apparently, being permanent transfers: CUL, Q 3, m.32 (18 October 1339).

virgater would be permitted to hold, say, a cottage in addition to his main holding, yet this was exceptional, as was implied by the language of the court roll on those occasions when fines to do so were paid. For instance, in 1316 John Isond of Horwood was permitted to hold one croft and cottage 'beyond his half-virgate' (*preter dimidiam virgatam suam*). Evidently, special note was required of the fact that small properties were being added to John's basic 'allowance'.[64] Furthermore, since the standard villein holdings could not normally be broken up, there was little tendency for creditors to acquire fragments of a debtor's holding via permanent alienation.

Of course, with the sources available it is only possible to spot creditors' acquisitions of debtors' land in these villages if the property transferred belonged to the documented manors. For this reason, any debtor-to-creditor transfers of land not pertaining to the Crowland and Newton Longville manors will be hidden from view. The scope for the omission of freehold land sales from our analysis is also quite significant. The court rolls cannot be assumed to provide a comprehensive record of the freehold land market.[65] Some telling pieces of evidence on this point relate to Walter Stevens, the wealthiest peasant in pre-plague Horwood, and one of the village's major creditors. Walter held a messuage and virgate in villeinage which at his death in November 1344 passed to Ralph, his principal heir.[66] Yet Walter was also reported on three occasions during his lifetime to have acquired additional freehold land, on one instance to the extent of 22.5 acres.[67] It was almost certainly this land which Walter used to make several pre-mortem endowments totalling more than 33 acres to his four sons early in 1344, shortly before his death.[68] The information on Walter's freehold acquisitions is unusually full, but even so, and in spite of the survival of a number of contemporary Horwood charters, we cannot ascertain from whom he acquired his freehold acres. It is possible, of course, that these purchases represent land Walter had accumulated from his debtors.

These caveats aside, it is clear that if there was any systematic movement of property from recurrent borrowers to recurrent lenders, it was a very muted phenomenon in the villages under scrutiny. The 'midland' pattern of landholding, once again, appears to have reduced the scope for exploitative social relations consequent upon the use of credit. By contrast, in East

[64] NCA, 3913, m.17d (9 February 1316).
[65] Briggs, 'Credit and the freehold land market', and references therein.
[66] NCA, 3914, m.44 (November 1344).
[67] NCA, 3913, m.36 (8 May 1324); NCA, 3914, m.13d (14 June 1331); NCA, 3912, m.11d (6 January 1338).
[68] NCA, 3912, m.1d (1 March, 9 April 1344). The tenurial status of this land is not specified but it was stated to be part either 'of the fee of the earl of Gloucester' or 'of the fee of the lord prior', and is highly likely to have been freehold.

Anglia proper, where the permanent alienation of fragments of land co-existed with the relatively unrestricted accumulation of multiple parcels, debt apparently generated much greater potential for the widespread transfer of property from subordinate to dominant social groups in the village.

5.5 'Debt accumulation' and 'reciprocal indebtedness'

This section moves on from the temporary or permanent transfer of land to consider a further way of looking at the nature and consequences of village credit relationships. The focus is on the useful concepts of 'debt accumulation' and 'reciprocal indebtedness', as developed by Clark in her pioneering work. Debt accumulation was the repeated extension of credit in one direction only between a particular pair of individuals. The key characteristic of debt accumulation was the tie of dependency it created between a particular debtor and his creditor. Where one individual repeatedly sought and received credit from another, it is likely that the borrower would be increasingly beholden to the lender and obliged to do his bidding. Sometimes, that repeat lending was clearly not intended simply to squeeze the borrower for every penny possible. Instead, in such contexts the aim was to give the borrower repeat credit in an effort to cultivate ties with him, for instance with a view to conducting future trade with the borrower. This is the way in which Clark interpreted some of the debt accumulation relationships she identified in fifteenth-century Writtle, for example. In the early fourteenth-century context, however, it is probably safest to assume that debt accumulation represented a highly unequal relationship, in terms of the balance of power between the parties and of the lasting benefits gained through the association. The individual who came back to the same lender for help had clearly found in that lender a valuable source of credit that could be tapped more than once, perhaps even when other sources had failed. Yet in the decades before the Black Death, the borrower in such situations must rarely have operated from a strong bargaining position, and the negative aspects of such relationships were probably as strong as the positive. Extensive evidence of debt accumulation in that period should thus be interpreted as characteristic of credit relations in which the resources and livelihoods of particular debtors came increasingly under the personal control of members of a village creditor class.

Reciprocal indebtedness was very different. It was the presence of reciprocal indebtedness, rather than debt accumulation, which received greatest emphasis in Clark's study of Writtle. Reciprocal indebtedness describes the situation in which person A's extension of credit to person B was matched by a separate debt case showing person B's extension of credit to person A.

Sometimes, reciprocal indebtedness could involve multiple extensions of credit in either direction. One may assume that any pair of parties involved in reciprocal indebtedness engaged in a much more equal relationship than any pair involved in debt accumulation. Reciprocal indebtedness relationships represent associations that worked to the advantage of both parties. To be sure, extensions of credit made as part of a pattern of reciprocal indebtedness could, like any credit transaction, end in dispute. Had they not done so, we would of course be unaware of their existence. However, this point does not invalidate the claim that a village credit market dominated by reciprocal indebtedness was unlikely to have featured a great deal of exploitation of debtors by creditors.

In order to assess the extent of debt accumulation and reciprocal indebtedness, an analysis based on the characteristics of 'pairings' of creditors and debtors is employed.[69] One unique pairing of a particular creditor with a particular debtor is contained, for example, in the Littleport debt case brought by creditor Adam Hakeney against debtor William Albyn in 1316.[70] The bottom row of Table 5.3 indicates the total number of unique pairings of creditors and debtors recorded in each court roll series. Crucially, it was possible for any one of those unique pairings to crop up in more than one debt action. Thus, for instance, at Balsham John Edmond sued Henry Grigge once in March 1337, and then again in a separate action in February 1347.[71] This is an instance of debt accumulation, that is, of the same pairing occurring in more than one debt case. Alternatively, it was possible for a particular pairing to reappear elsewhere in reversed form, as a separate pairing. So, for example, at Willingham in March 1380 Adam Cherl prosecuted Thomas Lawe for debt, and then later, in July 1385, Thomas sued Adam.[72] That is an instance of reciprocal indebtedness, that is, of two different pairings which appear at least once in the form 'A v B' and at least once in the form 'B v A'. As we have seen, virtually every debt case in the rolls studied involved the recovery of just one debt arising from a single, discrete credit relationship.[73] Therefore, if a particular pairing of creditor and debtors is recorded in more than one debt case, we may assume that the people involved interacted with

[69] For Writtle debt accumulation and reciprocal indebtedness, see Clark, 'English vill', 265–70, and Clark, 'Medieval debt litigation: Essex and Norfolk', 149. Clark's quantitative findings here are not in a form which permits direct comparison with my own; see Briggs, 'Rural credit', 156–60.

[70] CRO, R 93/96, m.1 (13 August 1316).

[71] LMA, ACC/1876/MR/02/007, m.1d (26 March 1337); ACC/1876/MR/02/010, m.3 (19 February 1347).

[72] CRO, L1/177, mm.4d (19 March 1380), and 23d (13 July 1385).

[73] See Chapter 2.

Table 5.3 The extent of 'debt accumulation' and 'reciprocal indebtedness'

	Number of discrete creditor–debtor pairings											
	Oakington, Cottenham, and Dry Drayton 1291–1350		Oakington, Cottenham, and Dry Drayton 1351–1400		Horwood 1302–60		Willingham 1377–1400		Littleport 1316–27		Balsham 1310–49	
	No.	% total	No.	% total	No.	% total	No.	% total	No.	% total	No.	% total
'Debt accumulation'	29	(8.0)	42	(9.2)	9	(4.7)	49	(7.6)	53	(11.1)	5	(2.7)
'Reciprocal indebtedness'	4	(1.1)	16	(3.5)	4	(2.1)	61	(9.5)	44	(9.2)	2	(1.1)
Neither	330	(90.9)	397	(87.3)	178	(93.2)	535	(82.9)	380	(79.7)	179	(96.2)
Total pairings	363	(100.0)	455	(100.0)	191	(100.0)	645	(100.0)	477	(100.0)	186	(100.0)

Notes: The 'debt accumulation' row totals discrete pairings that occur in more than 1 case. The 'reciprocal indebtedness' row includes both a pairing and its reversal, i.e. A v B and B v A = two pairings. Joint parties including husbands and wives appearing together are counted as separate individuals.
Sources: See Table 2.1.

one another on more occasions than did the participants in any creditor–debtor pairing that was recorded in just one debt case.

Table 5.3 indicates those creditor–debtor pairings which recur, or crop up in reversed form, and consequently represent instances of either debt accumulation or reciprocal indebtedness. The most striking feature of Table 5.3 is that the vast majority of pairings are recorded in just one debt case only, and were never reversed. Those pairings therefore involved neither debt accumulation nor reciprocal indebtedness. The proportion of pairings in this category ranged from 79.7 per cent (Littleport) to 96.2 per cent (Balsham). This means that, as far as we know, most credit ties between particular individuals were one-off associations. Thus if an individual borrowed repeatedly, as many undoubtedly did, he usually went to a number of different individuals to obtain credit, rather than going back again to the same creditor. Similarly, if a borrower subsequently found himself in a position to extend credit, which again was a common occurrence, he did not necessarily feel obliged to lend to an erstwhile creditor.

Overall, debt accumulation was slightly more significant than reciprocal indebtedness. As intimated earlier, if one makes the assumption that a significant outcome of pre-plague credit relations was the increasing impoverishment and exploitation of debtors, then one would expect to be able to identify considerable evidence of debt accumulation in this period. However, even at Littleport, where it was most common, debt accumulation cannot be described as extensive, as it affected only 11 per cent of creditor–debtor pairings. Nor was debt accumulation much more common at Littleport than reciprocal indebtedness. It should also be added that most debt accumulation relationships consisted of just two debt actions. Only 28 of the total of 187 debt accumulation pairings in Table 5.3 consisted of three or more debt actions, and the maximum was six actions. Thus one cannot argue that it was common for a debtor to return again and again to a particular lender to establish multiple credit transactions, with all the potential for increasing personal dependence that such a scenario might have entailed.

As suggested earlier, lending and borrowing in most English villages was highly 'disseminated', in the sense that many different people participated in these activities from time to time, and neither was the preserve of a few families. The evidence on debt accumulation and reciprocal indebtedness should not be surprising in the light of that earlier argument, showing as it does the large number of one-off relationships between particular pairings of individuals. In the context of the present chapter, the evidence reviewed in this section has given support for the idea that exploitation and control of one individual by another was a fairly uncommon outcome of credit relations, even in the context of the economic extremes and social pressures of the pre-plague decades.

5.6 Conclusion: limits to impoverishment and exploitation through credit

The idea of debt as a malign force within the village has a long tradition in writing on European agrarian societies. Marx wrote of the 'parasite of usury' that seized hold of the petty cultivator, destroying his productive capacities and his freedom.[74] A more directly traceable influence on historians of fourteenth-century English rural society was perhaps R.H. Tawney, who in several historical writings bemoaned what he saw as the exploitative effects of moneylending on the small producer.[75] In the polemics of the Soviet era, of course, the destructive provision of credit to the poorer portions of a village population was among the activities attributed to wealthy peasant proprietors, and thus became but one component of the rich peasant's putative status as an enemy of the people.[76] It would be a gross distortion indeed to suggest that any recent work by a historian of the English middle ages has maintained any conscious connection with an ideology so tragic in its consequences. It is nonetheless the case that the term *kulak*, which some historians have used to denote the prosperous medieval villager, inevitably carries disparaging overtones of exploitation and rapacity.[77]

There is a long-established discourse, therefore, which maintains that the rural credit that existed in the pre-modern period was just as likely to make things worse for people and for relations within their communities as it was to improve matters. More recently, and more specifically, those historians of the earlier fourteenth century who have considered the issue have tended to conclude that credit largely reflected and reinforced the growing polarization of peasant society, and the dominance of a wealthy village elite within it.

In putting these assumptions to the test, this chapter has certainly identified peasants in the pre-plague period for whom credit relations were disastrous in their nature and outcome. Indebted peasants like Robert Salden of Great Horwood forfeited their livelihoods, and in some cases were forced to leave their villages. Furthermore, it must be stressed that impoverished borrowers like Robert were not often drawn from among the smallholders.

[74] Above, p. 9.

[75] Tawney, *Agrarian problem*, 108–10, considers the predicament of the small cultivator in 'the clutches of the usurer'; for discussion of Tawney's attitude, as revealed in the introduction to his edition of Thomas Wilson's *Discourse upon usury*, see also Holderness, 'Clergy as moneylenders', 195–6, and Schofield, 'Social economy', 38.

[76] Lewin, *Russian peasants*, 71–8.

[77] For reservations about the use of *kulak* in the medieval English context, see Smith, 'English peasantry', 349, and Raftis, *Peasant economic development*, 129. For a recent brief defence of such a use of the term, see Dyer and Schofield, 'Recent works', 36. More generally, see Shanin, *Russia*, 156–8.

Rather, there were half- and full-virgaters among those debtors compelled to give up their lands. Thus although, as Chapter 4 showed, creditors and debtors were roughly equal in their formal wealth characteristics, fortunes could vary within any one class of tenants. As a result, it remained possible for ostensibly 'horizontal' credit relations to become effectively 'vertical' in character, as successful half-virgaters, for example, lent to less successful half-virgaters. It was evidently upon that sort of situation that Razi laid particular stress in his brief discussion of these matters in relation to another 'midland' manor, that of Halesowen.[78]

However, such evidence falls short of demonstrating that the nature and effects of credit upon individual fortunes and the tenor of village life were generally pernicious. It is true that some 13 per cent of debtors from Oakington, Cottenham, Drayton, and Horwood are known to have surrendered land whilst still alive. That is not an entirely negligible proportion. However, many of those losses of land by peasant debtors occurred in the second decade of the century, when conditions were exceptionally bad. Outside that decade, pre-plague surrenders of land by debtors are thinner on the ground. It is also the case that holdings were especially likely to have been given up through poverty in Dry Drayton, a village whose sufferings from the 1310s onwards were unusually severe. Furthermore, although the role of the tenant's excessive debt burden in precipitating several of the losses of land can hardly be doubted, in many other instances the number of outstanding debts owed by the surrendering party appears to have been rather small. Often it was not solely or even mainly the debt factor that tipped a peasant over the edge. The debts borne by numerous Oakington borrowers of the 1330s and 1340s were generally more numerous and heavier than those borne by their Drayton counterparts of the 1310s. However, the outcomes were different, with numerous losses of debtors' lands in Drayton, but relatively few such surrenders in Oakington. It seems clear that other factors made the Drayton borrowers especially vulnerable to catastrophe, even though their debts were comparatively limited. It is also possible that Oakington borrowers like Geoffrey King avoided catastrophe precisely because they, unlike the earlier Drayton tenants, could rely on such a good supply of credit. Lending to Oakington residents was probably encouraged in the later 1330s and 1340s by the enhanced debt recovery mechanisms of the manor court that had been put in place since *c.*1325.[79] Although Razi never claimed that the outright loss of property was common in pre-plague Halesowen, he discussed debt almost exclusively in the context of such losses. This chapter has attempted

[78] Razi, *Life, marriage and death*, 75–98.
[79] Briggs, 'Manor court procedures', 551–6.

to correct the balance by stressing that most credit relationships did not result in negative consequences for the borrower.

It is also difficult to maintain that credit led to relations of exploitation or dependency involving particular creditors with particular debtors. Repeat extensions of credit from one particular individual to another can be traced, but they were outnumbered by credit transactions between parties who are not known to have come together on more than one occasion. Thus the highly personalized ties of obligation and control implied by debt accumulation were not extensive. Landholding customs meant few creditors were in a position to capitalize upon the misfortunes of their borrowers by taking their landed property via permanent transfers, and in fact few did so. Certainly, creditors often became the beneficiaries of short-term leases of land. Generally speaking, however, they did not come by this route to control directly the property of people to whom they are known to have extended credit.

In the villages studied here, with their 'midland' tenurial systems, most people therefore borrowed without encountering serious long-term economic problems, and without suffering obvious exploitation at the hands of creditors. This is in large part a reflection of the fact that many of the borrowers were relatively wealthy, often displaying the same basic economic characteristics as those from whom they sought loans or made credit purchases. As Chapter 2 showed, much credit was contracted for investment purposes and not for reasons of exigency. It is therefore not surprising that many heavy borrowers do not show signs of long-term economic difficulties, as their borrowing may ultimately have made them better off, not worse. There is little support, for example, for the supposition that poorer families took land as subtenants and became debtors in the process. Instead, as Table 5.1 shows, debtors are generally easiest to find among the lessors, not among the lessees. Landed borrowers could lease parts of their properties in order to pay off their debts, and these lands could form the effective security for further borrowing, even if they were not formally pledged as collateral. There would no doubt have been more widespread evidence of a connection between impoverishment and indebtedness had more landless persons or persons with very little land been admitted to the village credit network as borrowers than was the case in reality. Indeed, it is quite possible that such a pattern of borrowing was more widely encountered in East Anglia proper, and that this is why the historians working on those counties have tended to find stronger connections between credit, poverty, and exploitation than have been uncovered in this chapter.

6

The credit supply

As we have seen, credit was obtained in medieval English villages via a number of different transaction types. For example, in the most common type, the 'deferred payment', an individual would buy an item with provision for later payment. A borrower could also arrange to remunerate a lender in future for services received, such as ploughing or custody of animals. In the most straightforward type of transaction, an individual would take a loan of money or goods. A loan was also contracted, in effect, when a producer sold a commodity for an immediate payment, with delivery of the goods to follow. This, the 'purchase price advance', appears to have been the sort of transaction that often underlay the Littleport sedge debts and Oakington malt debts, as was argued in Chapter 2.

All these different transactions furnished a borrower with credit which could be used either for 'exigency' purposes, that is, in an effort to maintain production and consumption at its previous level, or for 'investment' purposes, that is, with the proactive aim of increasing future production or consumption. However, irrespective of the purposes for which credit was sought, it is clear that the vast majority of credit transactions discussed in this book sprang from the same basic scenario. Virtually all transactions arose because an individual wished or needed to obtain goods or services or to discharge an obligation at a time when immediate full cash payment from that individual's own resources was either impossible or inadvisable owing to the need to preserve an emergency fund. A major reason for cash payment in full being impossible or inadvisable was that in the society under investigation, income was generally irregular, being concentrated at various key points in the agricultural year. Thus in this monetized society credit structures naturally grew up which allowed people to cope with the lack of temporal coincidence between their needs and their access to adequate quantities of the normal means of payment, which was coined money.[1]

By its very existence, the debt evidence used in this book shows that people were not necessarily required to make immediate cash payment in full

[1] On the monetized rural economy, see Dyer, 'Peasants and coins'; Mayhew, 'Money in the late medieval countryside'.

from their own resources whenever they obtained goods or services, or to discharge an obligation. Thus an individual who did not have enough money to buy a cow but wished to obtain one immediately was not necessarily obliged to forgo the advantages of immediate possession of this resource. Rather, as numerous debt cases show, a cow could be bought on credit. The question at the heart of this chapter, however, concerns the extent to which individuals could invariably be found who were willing to sell a cow on credit, or indeed to lend via any other of the village credit mechanisms. It is quite possible that changes in conditions meant that many potential creditors were very willing to lend in some years, but that hardly any wished to do so at other times. In other words, the credit supply was not constant. It is also quite possible that the credit supply did not increase and decrease in line with demand. The resilience of the credit supply is certainly a central consideration in assessing the strengths and weaknesses of any rural credit system.

The weaknesses of the English rural credit supply in the fourteenth century have attracted more attention than the strengths.[2] This period had more than its fair share of contingent circumstances which may have made it temporarily impractical or unwise to extend credit.[3] First, food shortages and high prices caused by harvest failure, and, second, a lack of coin, could undermine the creditor's confidence in the ability of debtors to repay. In addition, as has commonly been argued, and this book has confirmed, most credit obtained by English peasants came not from specialists or outsiders to some extent cushioned from the vicissitudes of the agrarian economy, but from fellow peasants and neighbours. Thus any difficult conditions, like harvest failure, that swelled the pool of would-be recipients of exigency credit also affected the most important category of potential lenders. In the language of development economics, the two groups—creditors and debtors—were subject to 'covariate risk'. Other conditions characteristic of the fourteenth century could also interrupt the credit supply, most obviously the excess mortality caused by epidemic disease. This could suddenly remove influential creditors or curtail lending as creditors gave priority instead to recovering debts from the estates of deceased borrowers. This chapter's aim is to discover whether the actual effects of these factors on the credit supply were as devastating as has been assumed.

It is important to note that the factors of dearth and price volatility, coin shortage, and crisis mortality do not exhaust the list of influences upon readiness to offer credit. My earlier study of court procedures at Oakington and Horwood was primarily concerned with patterns of debt litigation, not the

[2] Schofield, 'Dearth', 16–17; Bailey, 'Peasant welfare', 243–4.
[3] For a useful summary, see Nightingale, 'Money and credit', 67.

underlying volume of lending.[4] Nonetheless, it suggested ways in which the credit supply could be influenced by the legal environment in which creditors operated. Put simply, where they were available—and they did not develop everywhere—fast and efficient debt recovery mechanisms provided by the manor court appear to have encouraged lending even when conditions were otherwise unpropitious. The influence of the local curial environment upon the credit supply is a feature returned to in the chapter's conclusion.

6.1 Changes in credit supply: problems of the sources

As in several of its predecessors, it is necessary to preface this chapter with some remarks on the limitations of the debt litigation evidence for the matter in hand. Manorial debt litigation perhaps falls furthest short of one's ideal as a source when one tries to use it as a guide to changes in amount of credit extended. Students of rural credit in European regions of notarial culture have access to dated credit acts recorded at each transaction's inception. Although the users of such sources must contend with other problems arising from the patchy and urban-biased survival of registers, their chances of obtaining an accurate picture of the amount of new credit created at any one point in time are better than those of the historian of English debt litigation. The only court roll debt entries known for certain to record the inception of a credit transaction are the rare 'formal recognizances'. By contrast, the manorial debt plaints proper represent only that share of defaulted debts that were brought to court. Even if the rate of default were constant,[5] which seems a dangerous assumption to make at the village level, we still could not read off the total of transactions from the number of plaints, as the number of plaints primarily reflects the propensity to litigate, and this almost certainly changed over time. Such problems are compounded by the fact that a plaint came to court at an interval following the creation of the disputed debt that is usually—if not always—unknown.

Thus relatively high annual numbers of plaints have been interpreted as showing diametrically different underlying trends in the creation of new credit. In the latter half of the fourteenth century and in the sixteenth century, a large amount of debt litigation is usually taken to mean a large amount of credit, consonant with periods of intense commercial activity.[6] At

[4] Briggs, 'Manor court procedures'.

[5] For work adopting this assumption, see Nightingale, 'Money and credit', 63; Nightingale, 'Norwich, London, and the regional integration of Norfolk's economy', 84.

[6] Britnell, *Growth and decline*, 101; Kowaleski, *Exeter*, 349; Muldrew, *Economy of obligation*, 216–26.

other times, a large amount of debt litigation is taken to denote a simultaneous cessation in new credit. This argument has been made, for example, about upturns in debt litigation at times and in places in the sixteenth century when mortality rose because of food shortages and high prices.[7] It has also been made about the earlier fourteenth century. Where that period is concerned, such observations about the relationship between quantities of litigation and quantities of new credit have so far involved little more than speculation. However, this chapter develops a method whereby one may infer changes in credit supply from changes in debt litigation. The key to this method, as the next section shows, is first to establish the average delay between a credit transaction's inception and its first appearance in the record as a debt plaint. Once this is done, it becomes possible in certain circumstances to reconstruct a pattern of new credit extension from the pattern of debt litigation evident at a later point in time.

6.2 Dearth and high prices

The years 1290 to 1331, which are the focus of this section, represent the climax of a long period of rising average grain prices. They are also well known as years of marked grain price volatility.[8] The general price rise of which these decades represent the final phase has complex causes, reflecting, variously, long-term trends in population growth, grain yields, and the money supply. Here we are concerned solely with short-term price fluctuations and their impact. The many sharp price increases that characterize these years are usually regarded, as they are here, as the outcome of poor harvests in a period when population was pressing hard on resources.[9] Of all sub-periods of the later middle ages, this is the most obvious one to examine to find out whether the credit supply could continue to flow even at a time when large numbers of rural families were struggling to feed themselves.

Figures 6.1 to 6.4 show the totals of new debt plaints brought to the courts of Oakington, Horwood, Balsham, and Littleport in each accounting year running from Michaelmas (29 September).[10] D.L. Farmer's 'national' grain price index, included in these graphs, is the basis for identification of

[7] Muldrew, *Economy of obligation*, 226–7.

[8] On the implications for the peasantry, see Bailey, 'Peasant welfare', 234–5.

[9] For the strong correlation between demesne grain yields and prices, especially in the first half of the fourteenth century, see Campbell, *Three centuries*.

[10] In Figures 6.1 to 6.6, 1300 denotes the accounting year 1299–1300, and so on. As in Figures 3.1 and 3.2, half the 'unknown' actions are entered here as 0.5 actions. All actions (debt and 'unknown') terminated as 'false claim' or 'false plaint', or with the defendant's complete exoneration, are excluded from Figures 6.1 to 6.5.

dearth years.[11] For the Cambridgeshire locations, supplementary local price data from the account rolls of the Crowland manors exists (Figure 6.6). Like the national data, this material is presented here as a composite index of the sale price of several grains.[12] The Cambridgeshire series largely confirms the pattern of high price years indicated by the national index, demonstrating that locally, as well as nationally, 1297–8, 1304–5, 1309–10, and 1321–2 were years of exceptionally high prices, or part of a run of such years. The only really surprising feature of this Cambridgeshire data is the relatively low price year 1295–6, which is unexpected given the wider pattern. In the absence of Crowland accounts for 1293–5, one is forced to assume that in those years higher than average prices prevailed in Cambridgeshire as well as in the country more generally, even though doubt exists as to whether high prices persisted locally into 1295–6.[13] In addition to 1293–6, the other years not covered by the Crowland accounts but given close attention here are the famine years 1315–17 and the years 1330–2. Although we have no local price data from these dates, their status as high price years of subsistence crisis is not in doubt.[14]

In order to investigate the impact of dearth on credit supply, we need not only to identify the key years of inadequate harvest. We also need to estimate the average time that elapsed between the creation of a debt and its first appearance in the record. Fortunately, information on the age of debts at the point when they were first sued in court is not entirely lacking. One option is to use the small number of debt cases, seventeen in all, that tell us the date of the disputed transaction. If these few informative examples are typical, then debts should be regarded as approximately 36 months old on average by the time they got to court.[15] However, this figure probably gives an unrealistically large estimate of the average interval.[16] It is distinctly possible that the date of transaction was specified in these seventeen cases precisely because the debt was exceptionally old. One can easily imagine that the date of

[11] Farmer, 'Prices and wages', 790–1.

[12] The Crowland price index is an average of the indexes for wheat, rye, drage, and peas. The series to 1322 is based on accounts covering all three Crowland manors, that from 1360–99 on Oakington accounts only, since that is all that survives. CUL, Q Boxes 1, 2, 6, and 8 (Crowland manorial accounts).

[13] Note that 1295–6 was not a year of outstandingly high prices everywhere, as, for example, at Hinderclay (Suffolk): Schofield, 'Social economy', 44.

[14] Jordan, *Great Famine*; Campbell, 'Population pressure', 112.

[15] The median of all values. A Balsham case begun in July 1346 tells us that the disputed loan was made some 38 months earlier in April 1343, while a June 1318 case from Horwood states that the loan in question was made 'three years ago'. Seven Oakington cases from 1291–1400 provide the transaction date. The Willingham records provide similar information, albeit from the last quarter of the century, in eight suits.

[16] For use of this measure see, however, Briggs, 'Manor court procedures', 553.

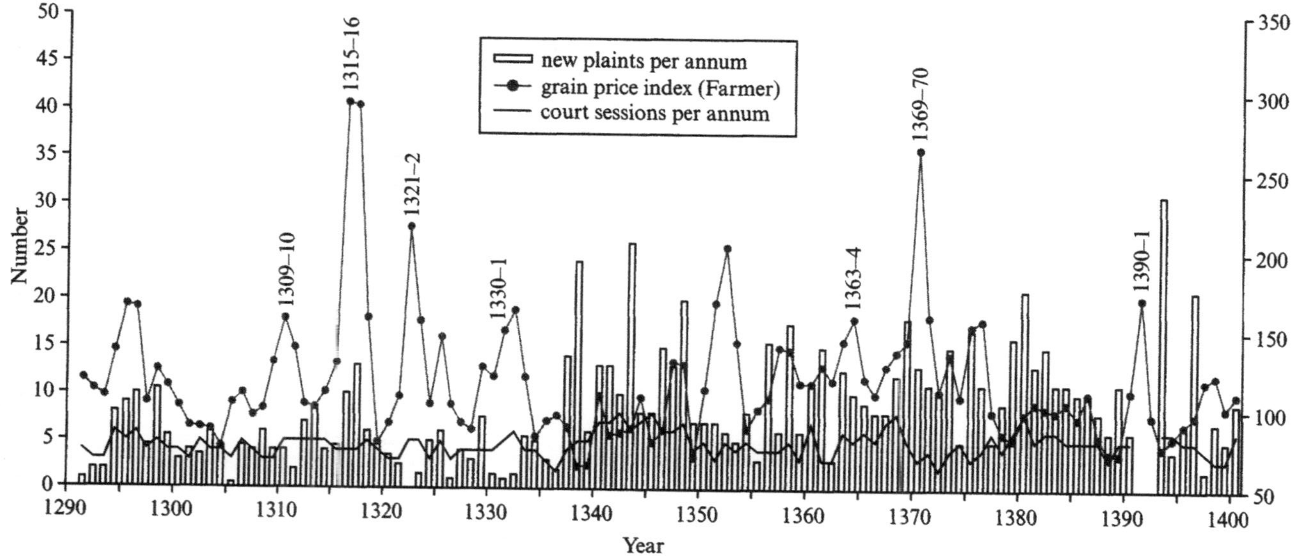

Figure 6.1 Oakington: new debt plaints plus half 'unknowns' per annum, 1291–1400

Note: 1300 is harvest year 1299–1300.
Sources: See Table 2.1 (court rolls); Farmer, 'Prices and wages', 790–1; Farmer, 'Prices and wages, 1350–1500', 502–3.

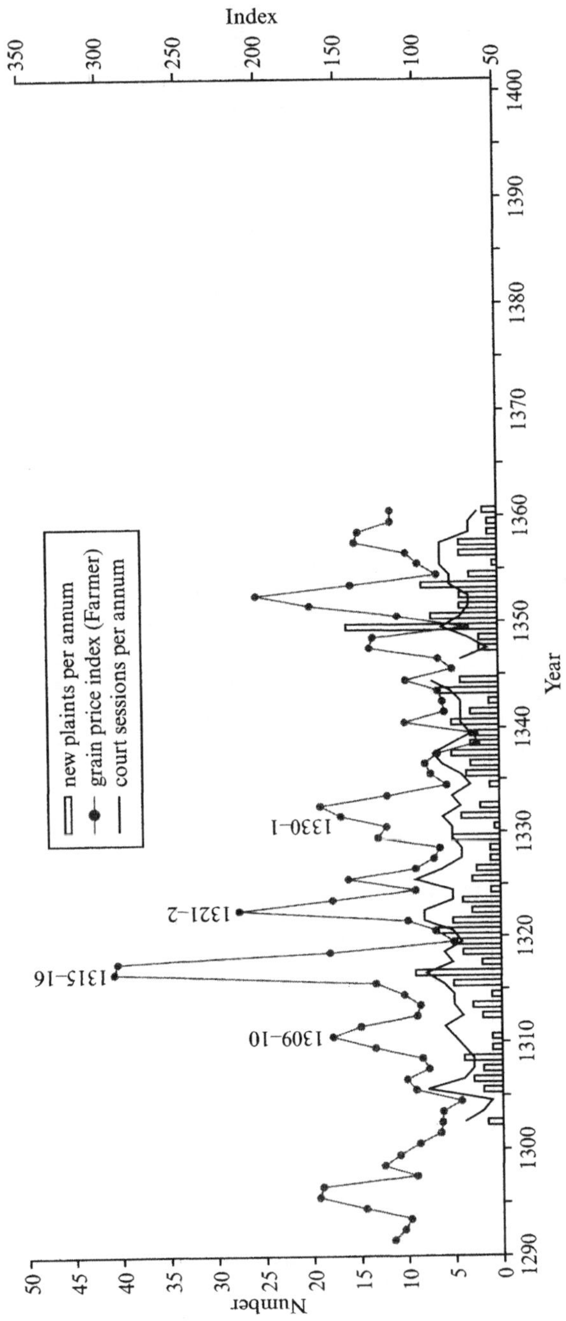

Figure 6.2 Great Horwood: new debt plaints plus half 'unknowns' per annum, 1302–60

Note: 1300 is harvest year 1299–1300.
Sources: See Figure 6.1.

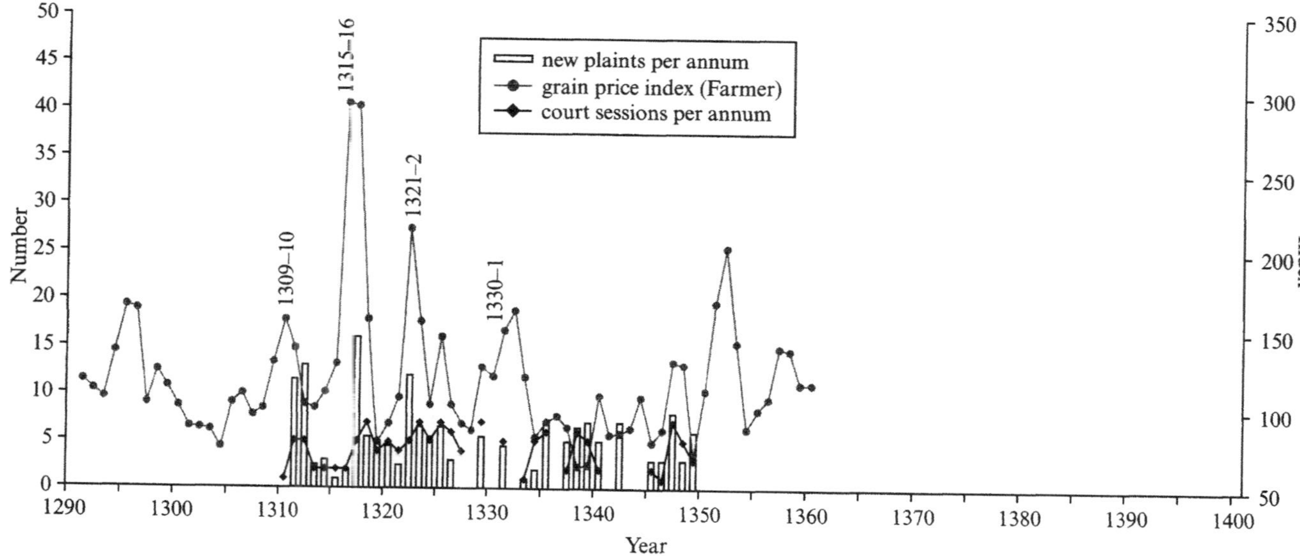

Figure 6.3 Balsham: new debt plaints plus half 'unknowns' per annum, 1310–49

Note: 1300 is harvest year 1299–1300.
Sources: See Figure 6.1.

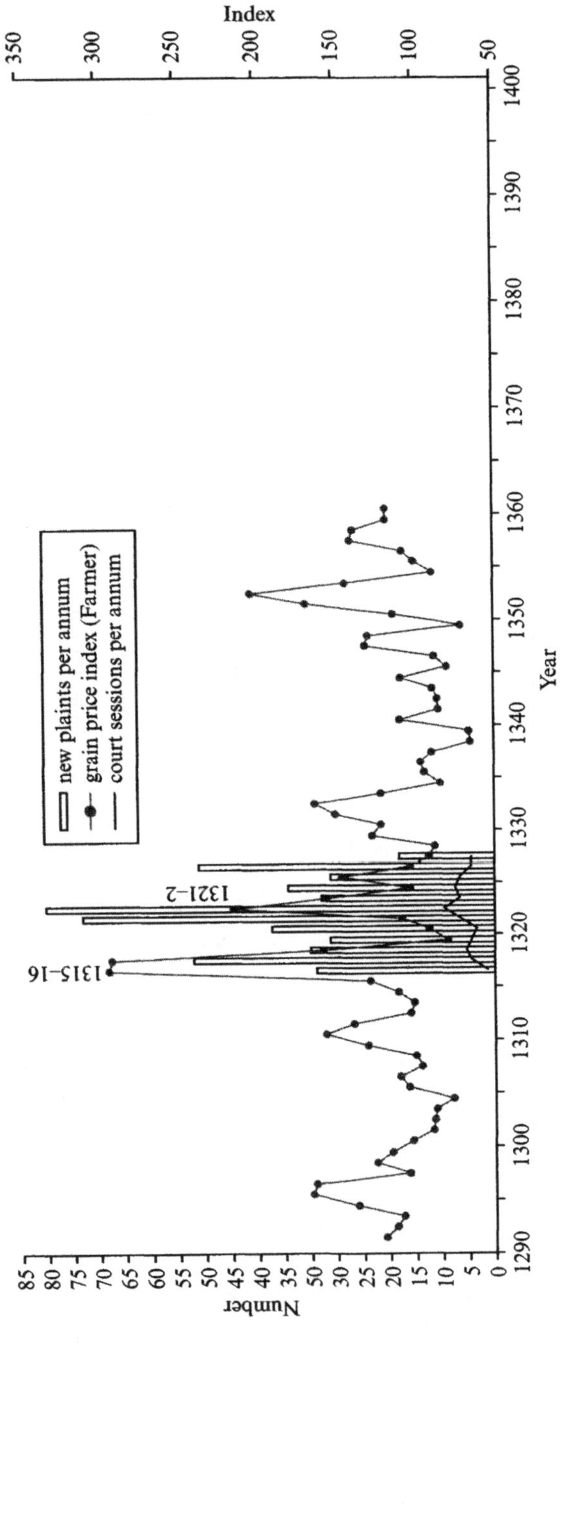

Figure 6.4 Littleport: new debt plaints plus half 'unknowns' per annum, 1316–27

Note: 1300 is harvest year 1299–1300.
Sources: See Figure 6.1.

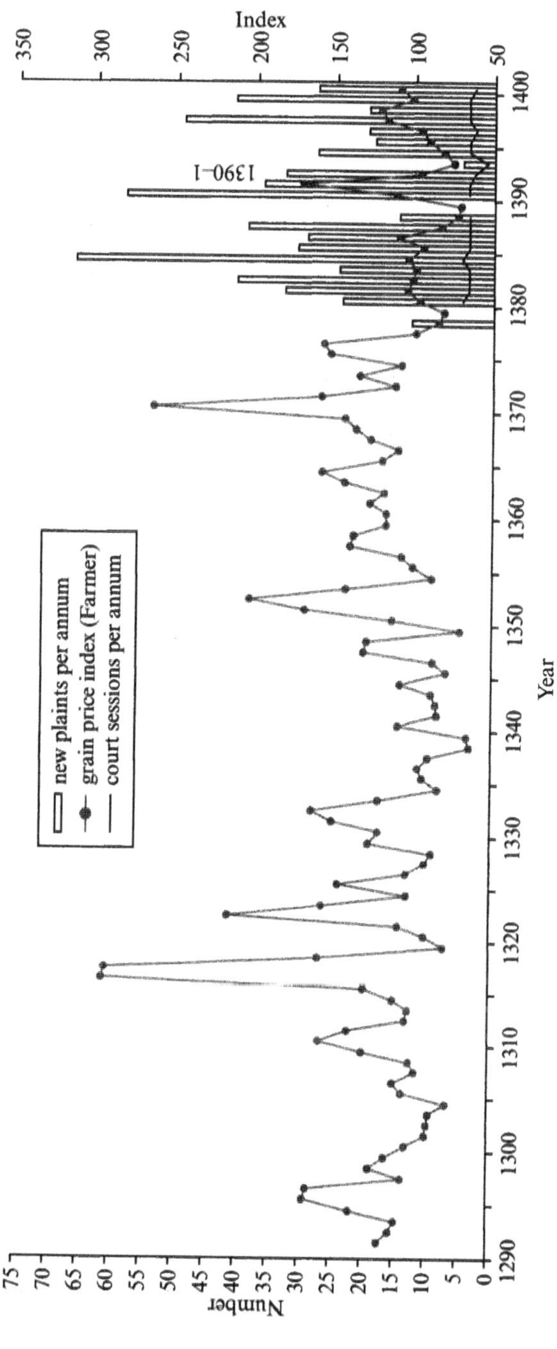

Figure 6.5 Willingham: new debt plaints plus half 'unknowns' per annum, 1377–1400

Note: 1300 is harvest year 1299–1300.
Sources: See Figure 6.1.

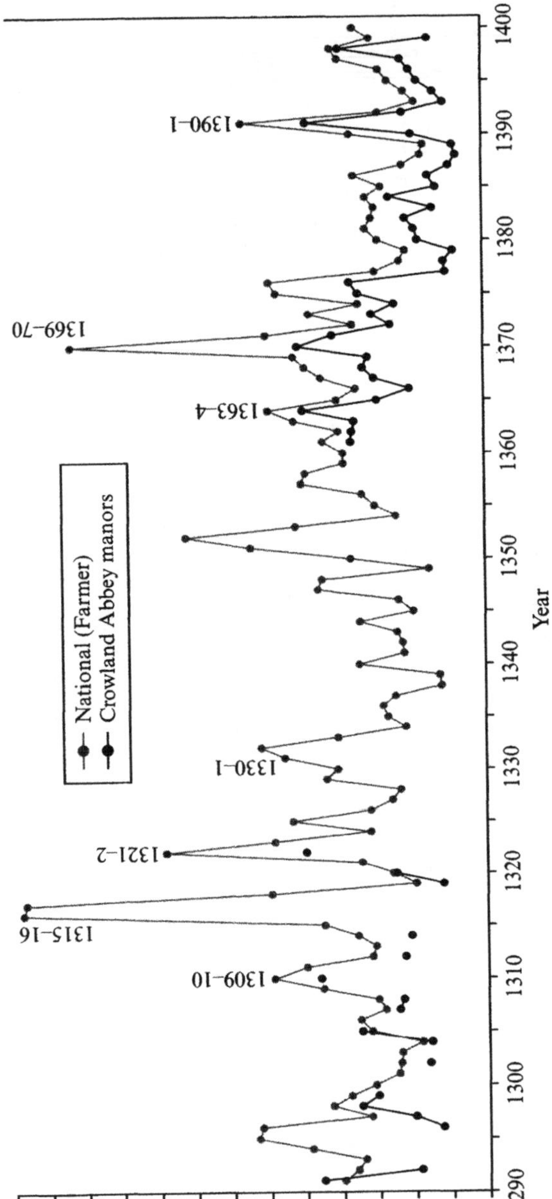

Figure 6.6 Grain price indexes: Crowland Abbey manors and 'national' series

Note: 1300 is harvest year 1299–1300. In Crowland index, 1298–9 = 100, in 'national' index 1330–1 to 1346–7 = 100.
Sources: Crowland account rolls (see text); Farmer, 'Prices and wages', 790–1; Farmer, 'Prices and wages, 1350–1500', 502–3.

transaction might be an issue of particular contention in actions about matters that happened too long ago for witnesses to be available, and hence that that date would be especially likely to appear in the court record's summary of such a case.[17] Also, some of the seventeen debt cases on which the figure is based clearly came to court an unusually long time after the due date for repayment. In one case this was because the original creditor had died, and the dispute was being prosecuted by his executor.[18] In another, it happened because the creditor had lent to a married woman and attempted to recover the debt from her husband. The husband had been refusing to pay, perhaps for some time, before he was taken to court. Once there, he continued to deny the obligation.[19]

A more realistic estimate of the average interval between transaction and plaint initiation is 330 days, or just less than eleven months. This is arrived at by combining the small amount of direct information we have on the loan term (the interval between transaction date and due date) with the information from an additional sixty-six cases for which we know both the due date and the plaint initiation date.[20] Although it is clear that lending did take place over terms in excess of one year, there is little doubt the typical loan term was quite short. The available data suggest a median loan term of 61 days.[21] The sixty-six cases giving the due date–plaint initiation interval suggest an average of 269 days.[22] Even the combined average of 330 days is perhaps an overestimate, as sixteen of the sixty-six cases saw exceptional delays in coming to court following default, either because they involved executors or because the creditor, after fruitlessly pursuing the principal defaulting debtor, had chosen instead to try to recover the obligation from the debtor's personal sureties. Such cases involving executors or pledges form a much larger proportion of those sixty-six cases that mention the due date than they do of the total corpus of debt actions. In spite of that caveat, the 330 day figure constitutes the best available estimate of the average age of a debt by the time of its first appearance in court, and it is the estimate used in what follows.

The coincidence between dearth and increased debt recovery is well attested.[23] Causal explanations for it come readily to hand. First, defaulted debt is likely to have been relatively common at such times, as debtors had to

[17] For pledges as witnesses, see Section 3.4.3.

[18] Willingham, CRO, L1/177, m.10d (29 November 1381). Thomas Marchall recovered 14*s*. 10*d*. from William Grygge, owed for a horse purchased from Elias Outy four years earlier when Elias was alive.

[19] For this Horwood case, see Briggs, 'Empowered or marginalized?', 29 n. 33.

[20] Eighteen Willingham, six Balsham, thirty-five Oakington, and seven Horwood cases.

[21] Section 3.2.2.

[22] The median of all sixty-six values.

[23] Schofield, 'Dearth'; Schofield, 'Social economy'; Dyer, *Standards*, 266.

spend more than usual on food and seed corn, and consequently had less for debt repayment. Default took the form either of failure to make repayment on a prearranged due date or, in 'on demand' transactions, of failure to repay when the creditor requested.[24] Crisis years would also have affected creditors. As we have seen, creditors often belonged to the same wealth and landholding bracket as their debtors. Both groups featured numerous 10-acre tenants, half-virgaters, and virgaters, yet possession even of holdings of this size did not necessarily make a peasant impervious to the effects of harvest failure.[25] In crisis years creditors would have been quicker both to request 'on demand' repayments and to sue upon default than in years of adequate harvest, especially if they themselves were running short of food. Given these conditions and their effects, it is extremely likely that, where there were roughly equal numbers of extant credit relationships in a high price year and in an average or low price year, the high price year would have produced a higher rate of both default and litigation following default than the year of average or low prices.

Thus the remainder of this chapter adopts the following assumption. Where a year of above-average prices did not also generate an above-average total of new debt plaints, then this must reflect a relatively low or declining total of extant credit relationships in that year. That, in turn, is taken as evidence of contraction in the quantity of new credit created some eleven months earlier. We are now in a position to return to the annual totals of debt plaints in an effort to understand the effects of dearth on the credit supply (Figures 6.1 to 6.4).

As already intimated, the most notable phases of high prices, as indicated by the 'national' price index in conjunction with the Crowland index, were 1293–6, 1297–8, 1304–6, 1308–11, 1315–17, 1321–2, and 1330–2. In many of these years, annual totals of new debt plaints exceeded the average for the period to 1331.[26] Most obviously, plaint totals at Oakington, Horwood, and Balsham peaked in the famine years 1315–17. Furthermore, above-average quantities of debt litigation arose at Balsham in 1310–11, suggesting an association with the high price years 1309–11, and did so again in 1321–2. At Oakington, the high price years 1294–6 and 1297–8 coincided with litigation levels at roughly double the average there for the period 1290–1331. Lastly,

[24] For this difference, see Section 3.2.1.

[25] See Kitsikopoulos, 'Standards of living', for the argument that some 18 acres was the minimum necessary to guarantee a family's subsistence and investment in the holding, even in normal years.

[26] Mean average of new plaints per annum to 1330–1: Oakington, 4.7; Horwood, 2.7; Balsham, 5.5; Littleport, 42.5. 'National' grain price index average, 1290–1 to 1330–1=126.7.

the peak in annual totals of Littleport debt plaints was reached in the crisis year 1321–2.[27]

Perhaps surprisingly, however, in other years of exceptionally high grain prices this pattern of intensified debt recovery is not evident. In fact, in several such years, annual totals of new suits at Oakington and Horwood either fall below the average for the period to 1331, or drop to zero. At Oakington, the years in this category are 1304–5, 1310–11, 1321–2, and 1330–1. At Horwood, there was only one new suit in 1309–10.[28] Also, at Balsham in 1330–1, the count of new debt actions dropped slightly below average, at 4.5 plaints. In short, some dearth years brought a flurry of debt litigation, while others saw a marked fall in such litigation. What does this contrast reveal about changes in the credit supply?

For all these crisis years, the direction taken by totals of new plaints—whether up or down—reflects the supply of credit some eleven months previously. Because the Great Famine years 1315–17 are in many ways exceptional, fuller discussion of them is reserved for the end of this section. What seems to have been happening in the other years, however, is illustrated by the following: in early summer 1321, say, potential local creditors would already have known by the state of the weather and of the standing crop that the harvest of 1321 was likely to be poor. They would also have known that 1321–2 was likely to be a hard year for both themselves and others. Creditors knew that if they lent now, some debtors might have trouble repaying some few months hence. In such circumstances, it might make sense to withhold credit. To do so would result in fewer debt ties, fewer defaults, and low litigation levels eleven months later in 1322. It is this situation that we see reflected in the low litigation levels evident in several notable high price years. Essentially, potential creditors had withdrawn credit in anticipation of difficult circumstances in the coming year. Yet this did not always happen. In numerous high price years, as we have seen, the flow of new actions in the case study courts rose above the average. These represent occasions on which, for one reason or another, the credit supply had not faltered in the previous year, even though creditors probably knew that there were hard times ahead. The most notable instance of this is the overall peak in Littleport debt actions of 1321–2. Although some of those debts would undoubtedly have been quite old, they cannot all have been so, if the average delay between transaction and lawsuit was only eleven months on average. Much of the lending that became the subject of litigation at Littleport in 1322 must therefore have

[27] For conditions in 1321–2, see Kershaw, 'Great Famine', 97.

[28] At Horwood, plaint totals in 1321–2 and 1330–1 were above average but only marginally so, at three and four plaints respectively.

taken place on the eve of the poor harvest of 1321.[29] Such access to credit may have made a big difference to many in coping with one of the most difficult periods of grain shortage of the early fourteenth century.

What we perhaps most want to know, however, is not the amount of new credit extended in the run up to a crisis year, but the amount extended in the crisis year itself. In other words, to what extent was credit simply unobtainable during dearth conditions? To investigate this, the focus is placed on lending in three high price years: 1309–10, 1321–2, and 1330–1. These years are selected partly because they give the most scope for comparison of the various courts. Furthermore, for two of the three years we have Crowland price data which confirm that in the vicinity of Cambridge, as elsewhere, these were years of substantial upturn in grain prices. Any new debts that were formed in these years and were subsequently subject to default and litigation would have ended up in court eleven months later on average, that is, mostly within the years 1310–11, 1322–3, and 1331–2 respectively.

Prices remained above average in each year in this latter group. This means that if the quantity of new credit extended in 1309–10, 1321–2, and 1330–1 had remained static or grown, then we should see an above-average total of debt plaints in 1310–11, 1322–3, and 1331–2. On the whole, however, we do not see this, which suggests that the credit supply generally contracted in the three selected dearth years. Only Balsham in 1310–11 exhibited the well above-average total of new debt plaints that one would expect had there been any significant creation of new debts in the crisis year 1309–10. At Horwood and Balsham in 1322–3, the total of new plaints was somewhat above average, suggesting that some new credit was made available in 1321–2. Aside from this, the available data show counts of new plaints dropping below average in the case study courts in all relevant years, even falling to zero in 1310–11 at Horwood, in spite of the fact that six court sessions were held there in that 12-month period. Taken together, this evidence does not rule out the possibility that some new credit was offered and taken up in some locations in the three selected crisis years. At Littleport, most notably, thirty debt actions were begun in 1322–3, which is a large number for a manor court in any period of the later middle ages, and is suggestive of substantial credit activity in the preceding year. However, the overall message from Figures 6.1 to 6.4 is that if peasants were looking to local credit networks to offer a lifeline in crisis years, they are likely to have found creditors much less willing to lend than in periods without food scarcity.

What happened to credit supplies during the worst subsistence crisis of the period, the Great Famine of 1315–17? One cannot obtain reliable debt

[29] Forty-seven of the 80.5 Littleport actions of 1321–2 were begun in four court sessions held June–September 1322.

plaint totals for Littleport and Balsham in 1315–16, since there are only a handful of surviving records for court sessions in that year. At better documented Oakington and Horwood, however, debt plaint totals were clearly markedly above average in 1315–16. Furthermore, totals of new actions were well above average at Oakington, Balsham, and Littleport in 1316–17 also. According to the logic of the earlier discussion, this evidence suggests, first, that, at least in the three Crowland villages and at Horwood, the credit supply did not contract in anticipation of the dearth of 1315–16, and second, that in all places except Horwood, substantial lending occurred even in 1315–16. Should we really accept such an optimistic picture of the fate of the credit supply?

Although there is evidence to support such a picture, several caveats apply. Particularly significant is the role of debt cases pursued against personal sureties or pledges. It seems a fair assumption that creditors would only seek to sue a pledge once they had exhausted all possibility of securing repayment from the principal debtor. By the time that a case against pledges was initiated, therefore, the disputed debt was probably exceptionally old. Of the 151 debt actions begun in the four courts in 1315–17, at least 15, or just less than 10 per cent, were brought against pledges. This proportion represents a minimum, since the defendant's status as a pledge would not be recorded in cases terminated at an early stage through a 'licence to agree' or plaintiff's non-prosecution. It is also notable that actions against pledges were disproportionately concentrated in the Great Famine years: the fifteen actions represent 26.3 per cent of all pre-1351 debt actions against pledges, of which there were fifty-seven in total.[30] In sum, there is reason to think that the debt litigation upturn in 1315–16 is partly a sign of creditors making increasingly desperate efforts to recover long-standing debts, and not simply an indication of an expansion in the formation of credit ties during the previous year.

Furthermore, the idea that credit continued to be extended in 1315–16 should not be pushed too far, at least for the Crowland villages. The vast majority of the Oakington debt cases of 1316–17 were initiated in October to December 1316. Only two debt actions were begun at Oakington in 1317 itself.[31] In other words, using the eleven-month figure for the average interval between transaction and recovery suggests that new credit had largely disappeared by the start of 1316. Even the two 1317 actions perhaps involved debts of unusually long standing. In the first of them, William Kylle and Walter

[30] These figures on cases against pledges include debt cases terminated by 'false claim' or 'false plaint', or the defendant's complete exoneration, and exclude 'unknown' actions. For the increased propensity to sue against pledges in the Great Famine period, see also Schofield, 'Social economy', 57.

[31] There were two 'unknown' cases also.

Harger admitted owing John Alberd 18*d.* as pledges of principal debtor Eustace Norman. In the second, Henry Wyot and Robert Sped, as executors of Robert Aleyn, sued John Osbern, and the case was settled by licence to agree.[32] These are both cases where the interval between transaction and plaint probably exceeded the average of eleven months.

The same point cannot so easily be made, however, about Balsham or Littleport. At Balsham there were a respectable nine debt cases begun in the calendar year 1317, which speaks of a continued extension of credit eleven or so months earlier. In one particularly detailed case that first appears in May 1317, the debtor, Hugh Ryvel, acknowledged owing one bushel of beans to John Sutor 'which he ought to have paid on the feast of the Exaltation of the Holy Cross last past', that is, on 14 September 1316.[33] Applying the average loan term in this case suggests that credit had been extended in early July 1316, a period in which the loan of even a bushel of beans might have been particularly welcome.[34] At Littleport, a striking fifty debt actions were initiated in the calendar year 1317, many of which must concern loans made in 1316. Of particular interest is a case of June 1317, in which Robert le Charet' sued John Albyn for 19*s.* 'from an old debt' (*ex veteri debito*).[35] This is the only time such a phrase appears in the Littleport rolls. One possible interpretation is that the debt was given its special description because it was exceptional in being unlike all other debts, which were not 'old'. In 1315–16, therefore, credit supplies at Balsham and Littleport appear to have held up well, just as they did in the years of less severe dearth discussed earlier.

A picture thus emerges of a lack of uniformity in the extent to which high prices were associated with interruption in credit availability. One probable explanation for this is that years known to historians as times of general dearth varied greatly in their local effects. It was partly because of this that credit was better able to cope in some places than others. For example, the villagers of Littleport were relatively well placed to obtain cash with which to buy food when their own grain reserves ran short. They had access to fen products such as fish, sedge, and turves, which could conceivably continue to find a market and provide income even at times of harvest failure. Such a comparatively high degree of resilience to dearth conditions may partly explain why credit continued to flow there between 1316 and 1327. Elsewhere, things were different. Dry Drayton suffered particularly badly in 1315–22,

32 CUL, Q 2, mm.15, 16d (12 March and 27 October 1317, 10 February 1318).

33 LMA, ACC/1876/MR/02/001, m.15d (10 May 1317).

34 It is of course theoretically possible that the transaction here was actually a 'purchase price advance', not a loan in kind. If so, the borrower would have received an effective cash loan around July 1316.

35 CRO, R 93/96, m.1d (21 June 1317).

and thereafter, as we have seen. This feature is doubtless reflected in the evidence just reviewed concerning the withdrawal of credit in problem years in the Crowland villages. The economy and social structure of each village examined here differed slightly from that of the others, and this is one reason why the credit networks of each overcame early fourteenth-century harvest failure and its related problems with varying success.

6.3 Mortality

When investigating changes in the rural credit supply, a second obvious influence to consider is that of sudden increases in death rates above 'normal' levels. Some of historians' chief questions about the period covered by this book concern the impact of the Black Death, and of the further plague outbreaks that followed. The present section is primarily concerned with identifying the extent and nature of any disruption to the credit supply caused by plague deaths. However, excess mortality in the fourteenth century was not solely the consequence of epidemic disease. The early fourteenth-century episodes of dearth in an era of population pressure, discussed in the previous section, frequently had an effect beyond a simple reduction in the resources available for debt repayment. They also brought about crisis mortality through starvation, most obviously in 1315–17, when local studies suggest some 10–15 per cent of the population died.[36] Accordingly, this section also tries to keep in view the effects of dearth-related mortality upon credit supply.

Few years, of course, would have been without randomly timed deaths of individual rural creditors and debtors, yet such isolated deaths would usually affect just one small part of the larger village credit network at a time. Moreover, the disruptive effects of such deaths may have been less than those occurring in periods of plague or famine. This is because in 'normal' conditions, people were probably able before they died to provide for post-mortem repayment or collection of debts, either through executors or through other arrangements made on the deathbed.

By contrast, one may hypothesize that when a large number of current creditors and debtors died all at about the same time and with little warning, the amount of credit available to the surviving population would have shrunk dramatically, both in the very short term and over a number of years following. There are two main propositions that suggest this. First, although we have seen earlier that lending was fairly widely practised in village society, there is no doubt that particular individuals assumed unusual importance as

[36] Poos, 'Rural population', 521.

sources of credit. If most or all of a group of such persons were unlucky enough to die in famine or plague, then the negative impact on credit supply would have been considerable. The second proposition concerns the sudden death of a large number of debtors. Lending may have been curtailed during and immediately after episodes of excess mortality because of the difficulties in securing repayment from the estates of deceased debtors. If it was generally more difficult or time consuming to recover debts from a borrower's executors than from the borrower himself, then lenders' resources during months of high mortality would have become stretched. In this scenario, unusual difficulties in securing repayment of outstanding debts would have prevented lenders from extending new credit. Furthermore, such factors may also have made a lender less prepared to lend at periods of high mortality than at other times, owing to fear of getting embroiled in more post-mortem debt recovery if a borrower subsequently died. Such fears may have been exacerbated when large numbers of debtors were dying intestate, with no appointed person obviously responsible for their debts.[37]

These propositions are explored below. First, the extent of any sudden losses of major creditors is established. The first task is to examine the evidence for such a loss at Horwood and at Oakington, Cottenham, and Drayton in the Black Death, and, for the latter three villages, in the two plague outbreaks that followed. The lengthy reports of tenant deaths that fill the records of the spring and summer 1349 courts of Oakington and Horwood attest to the dramatic impact of the epidemic in the villages concerned.[38] At Horwood, tenant deaths in the first plague outbreak appear to have been exceptionally numerous, with a preliminary estimate putting plague mortality among villeins at around 68 per cent.[39] Yet was it the case that such deaths included groups of key active lenders, thereby depriving survivors of well-established sources of credit that might not be replaced for a number of years?

Answers to this question are necessarily impressionistic, because we cannot be certain that the deaths of all creditors appear in the court rolls. It is nonetheless possible to confirm that many of the most significant creditors operating at Horwood and in the village of Oakington in the years immediately prior to 1349 did in fact die in the Black Death. At Horwood, the 1340s saw few creditors of outstanding influence, in the sense that they lent relatively

[37] Schofield, 'Intestat', 217–18.

[38] For the surviving 1349 Oakington rolls, see CUL, Q 12, m.9d (26 May 1349), Q 4, m.17d (25 July 1349), Q 5, mm.1–1d (20 November 1349). For discussion of these, see also Page, *Estates*, 120–5; Ravensdale, 'Population changes', 198–200. The surviving 1349 Horwood rolls are located at NCA, 3914, mm.48–51d (25 February, ?29 April, 1 July, 29 August, 3 November, and 14 December 1349).

[39] This will be the subject of a future fuller investigation by myself and Matthew Tompkins.

large amounts or used the court many times to recover debts from different people. Early fourteenth-century Horwood certainly did feature creditors who, according to those measures, were exceptionally significant, in the shape of Walter Stevens and his brother William, vicar of Little Horwood. Yet these men did most of their lending between the 1310s and early 1330s, and both were dead by 1344.[40] In the 1340s, by contrast, no individual lender or group of lenders dominated the scene. Only three persons are recorded acting as creditor in more than one transaction in suits brought between 1340 and 1348. These were Peter le Taylor, John le Warrener, and Richard Cole, each of whom brought two successful actions.[41] Yet even though these three individuals do not appear to have formed a conduit for a disproportionate quantity of Horwood credit in the way that other local men did in earlier decades, it was nonetheless of potential significance for the credit supply that two of the three—Peter and John—were reported dead in the court of July 1349, almost certainly victims of the plague.

To judge by the Oakington debt litigation evidence, it was the credit market of Oakington itself, rather than that of Cottenham or Dry Drayton, which saw the most intensive activity in the 1340s.[42] Twenty-four of the seventy-seven recorded creditors of the years 1340–8 appeared in more than one action, and some twenty of those lived in Oakington. Investigating the twenty-four shows, if anything, rather stronger evidence than at Horwood of a substantial loss of key lenders in 1348–9. Only five of the twenty-four can be shown with confidence to have died in the Black Death.[43] However, the five included three of Oakington's most important creditors of the 1340s. John Gerard and John Noteman are recorded as creditors in more debt actions than any other individuals in this period, with seven and six actions respectively, and the third man who died in 1349, William Katelyne, was close behind with four.[44] In addition, Gerard and Noteman both appear once each among the lenders of the twenty largest recorded cash sums of the period, while Katelyne appears twice in that list. Furthermore, of the ten biggest grain debts recovered between 1340 and 1348, two were owed to Gerard and

[40] See Section 4.3.2.

[41] Taylor: NCA, 3914, mm.32d (27 July 1340), and 42d (4 February 1344); Warrener: NCA, 3914, mm.31d (1 March 1340), and 47 (15 July 1348); Cole: NCA, 3914, mm.33d (26 July 1341), and 42d (4 February 1344). Dates of first appearances of actions only.

[42] Briggs, 'Credit and the peasant household economy'.

[43] This is based on all legible death reports of the years 1349–50.

[44] Gerard: CUL, Q 3, mm.3 (17 October 1342), and 55 (26 January 1344); Q 4, mm.6 (20 May 1346), 10 (17 February 1347, two actions), 16 (7 November 1347), and 15d (5 December 1347). Noteman: Q 3, mm.43d (11 July 1341), 50d (26 November 1342, three actions); Q 4, mm.5d (14 January 1346), and 6 (20 May 1346). Katelyne: Q 3, mm.42 (25 May 1341), and 50d (16 November 1342); Q 4, mm.2 (16 February 1345), and 15d (5 December 1347). Dates of first appearances of actions only.

Katelyne. In other words, one effect of the Black Death was to remove at a stroke individuals to whom substantial numbers of Oakington residents had turned for credit over the previous few years.

What were the effects on creditors of the second and third plagues of 1361 and 1369? Here attention is restricted to the Oakington rolls, which show much less evidence of the death of key creditors than was the case in 1348–9. Recorded numbers of tenant deaths at the dates of the second and third pestilences are surprisingly low overall. No deaths appear for 1361, and for 1362–3 the rolls report just eight tenant deaths from the three manors. In 1369–70, only three such deaths are recorded. The reasons for this are not clear.[45] As known deaths are few, it is not surprising that there is little evidence of the demise of key creditors. In fact, the death of just one creditor appears among the tenant deaths of 1361–3 and 1369–70. This was Thomas Harger of Oakington, who brought debt actions in 1356 and 1360.[46]

A similar lack of positive evidence for the precipitate loss of key local creditors is also encountered when one turns from plague to consider the famine conditions of 1315–17. The Horwood debt plaints of 1304–17 reveal the existence of a total of twenty-seven creditors. Eighteen, or two-thirds, were recorded as still alive after 1317. Of the remainder, one creditor is last referred to in 1309, and perhaps died between that date and the Great Famine; a further three were alive in 1317 but there is no later reference to them; and four are recorded in just a single court roll entry, their dates of death being unknown. Only one of the twenty-seven, William de Boykote, definitely died in 1316. Yet William was not a creditor in the conventional sense of lending money or selling goods or services on credit. Rather, the debts he pursued through litigation were unusual in that they arose from a pre-existing obligation, namely an annual livery of items due to him under a maintenance agreement made when he had surrendered his holding to his son John in 1312.[47] These debts accordingly appear in row (b) of Table 2.3.[48] William, as far as we can tell, was not a major Horwood creditor of the years 1304–17. Indeed, the evidence we have, incomplete though it is, indicates that no such creditor died in the Great Famine.

The evidence for the Crowland villages tells a similar story. Fifty-four creditors are recorded in Oakington debt actions dated 1300–17, of whom twenty-one survived the years 1315–17, and six died before 1315. Nine

[45] See Ravensdale, 'Population changes', 208. The 1361 outbreak certainly affected this locality: see Page, *Estates*, 273, a reference to pestilence in the Oakington reeve's account of 1360–1 (incorrectly dated 1361–2 by Page).

[46] CUL, Q 5, m.17 (20 February 1356); Q 6, m.1d (18 June 1360).

[47] For these actions, see NCA, 3913, mm.17, 18, and 20 (12 August 1315, 4 May 1316, 7 August 1317).

[48] See Section 2.1.1 for debts in this category.

creditors are last mentioned before 1315, which in some cases is surely an indication that they died prior to that year. Four were definitely still living at dates between October 1316 and December 1317, but we do not know what happened to them after that. Thirteen creditors appear in a single court roll entry and their death dates are unrecorded. Only one creditor is known with certainty to have died during the Great Famine. This was Robert Aleyn of Drayton, who died some time between October 1316 and October 1317. He was not a major creditor. He is revealed as creditor by just a single debt case, which was the post-mortem action brought in 1317 by his executors, cited in the previous section. His only other involvement in debt litigation was three cases acting as defendant. The major lenders of the first decade and a half of the fourteenth century all survived the Great Famine, or died prior to it. There is hardly any sign that heightened mortality in 1315–17 removed key lenders from the scene, though this point is inevitably qualified by the fact that the death dates of many creditors are unknown.

The lack of famine mortality among creditors is perhaps unsurprising, given that few creditors came from the most vulnerable groups. As earlier chapters have shown, it was far from being the case that debtors were invariably poorer than creditors. Yet mortality rates during subsistence crises are if anything likely to have been higher among debtors than creditors, and it is to the effect of death among debtors, from famine as well as plague, that attention now turns.

Did lenders withhold credit at times of excess mortality because it was hard to recover debts from deceased debtors' estates? Probably not, since it appears that when a debtor died during a loan term, the executors or perhaps administrators who took over his estate usually repaid the debt without upset when it became due. This is reflected, for instance, in the unexceptional or low levels of debt litigation during and immediately following the 1348–9 epidemic. At Oakington in 1349, no lawsuits were begun in either the May or July courts, and only three were initiated in November. Admittedly there were twenty-one new Horwood debt actions in the year 1349, but one should not conclude that this high number reflects major upheaval as creditors sued the heirs of plague victims. Crucially, fourteen of the twenty-one actions were begun in February 1349, twelve of them brought by a single plaintiff, John Aschewy, and the relatively large total of suits is an anomaly reflecting one man's decision to recover outstanding obligations, rather than the more general impact of high mortality. Indeed, in Horwood deaths from plague had not begun by February,[49] as indicated by the mass reporting of deaths

[49] No tenant deaths are reported in Horwood's February 1349 court session. See Horrox (ed.), *Black Death*, 10, for evidence supporting this timing of the spread of plague.

which began only in the April court.[50] Overall, the information on new actions in 1349 indicates that the debts of deceased borrowers were largely repaid without problem.

Yet the key evidence for the smoothness of post-mortem debt repayment is the rarity of debt actions against the estates of deceased debtors. Of the 2,478 debt plaints initiated in the five case study courts, only 29 (1.2 per cent) were brought against deceased debtors' estates. Nor were these 29 concentrated in years of known high mortality. Only two, for example, date from 1349–50. Further, it is not even the case that the actions against executors were invariably generated by credit transactions in the true sense, since a few 'creditors' were simply seeking the fulfilment of testamentary legacies.[51] Also, in 1316 and 1317, in the only two Littleport cases against executors, the chaplain Thomas Tame claimed separate payments of 24*s*. 4*d*. and 50*s*. for anniversary masses performed for the souls of two dead villagers, rather than money or goods that those men had owed him in life.[52] It is conceivable that some debts from the villages studied were recovered from executors using the church courts, but the number of such cases was probably low. An indication is provided by testamentary suits appearing before the court of the bishop of Ely's official at Cambridge, of which there were just nineteen involving parties from across the entire diocese outside the Isle of Ely.[53] The very small number of manor court debt actions against the estates of debtors thus shows that executors were no less likely to repay a debtor's obligation than was the debtor himself. Consequently, even very high mortality affecting debtors was not a disincentive to lending.

With these considerations about the effects of high mortality upon creditors and debtors in mind, it is possible to return to Figures 6.1 and 6.2, which offer an indicator—albeit, of course, indirect—of changes in credit supply. Attention is focused in particular on quantities of litigation during the Black Death and the years immediately following, and, at Oakington, in subsequent plague years.

It is noticeable that totals of new Oakington suits between 1348–9 and 1354–5 were generally lower than they had been in the 1340s, and remained below the average for the years 1349–1400.[54] It is particularly significant that debt litigation in the period 1348–55 is low when compared with subsequent

[50] There were two new debt actions in April 1349, none in July or August, one in November, and four in December.

[51] See row (a) in Tables 2.2 and 2.3, above.

[52] CRO, R 93/96, mm.2 (8 December 1316), and 3 (3 December 1317). These masses are referred to as 'annuals'; compare Lock (ed.), *Walsham le Willows*, 135.

[53] CUL, EDR D/2/1, covering 1374–82.

[54] Oakington: average number of new debt actions per annum 1349–50 to 1399–1400: 10.4 (includes half 'unknowns'); national price index average: 119.4.

decades as well as with the previous one, since this reduces the likelihood that litigation, and hence total underlying credit, diminished simply because there were now fewer people around. These low litigation levels are especially telling given the high prices prevailing in the early 1350s which ought, if anything, to have both increased the rate of default and put pressure on creditors, leading to an upturn in lawsuits. Thus the debt litigation record, upon which we are forced to rely, clearly suggests that credit was scarce in the early 1350s. A picture of scarcity in this period accords well with our information about the demise of key lenders in 1349, and is probably also indicative of a withdrawal of credit during 1349–51, a notable run of dearth years.[55]

By continuing with the assumption that the total of debt suits in a particular year shows the amount of new credit created some eleven months previously, we can also use Oakington litigation in 1361–2 and 1369–70 to assess the impact of the plague outbreaks of 1361 and 1369. The year 1361–2 stands out as witnessing one of the lowest totals (three) of new plaints in the post-plague decades. To judge by prices in 1361–2, 1361 saw a reasonably good harvest, so one would not expect a vast proportion of outstanding debts to translate themselves into lawsuits in the year 1361–2. Nonetheless, the modest total of new actions in that year is suggestive of a greater plague-induced disruption to lending in 1360–1 than might be anticipated from the scant evidence for creditor deaths reviewed earlier. Finally, the exceptionally high price year 1369–70 ought to have seen a clear above-average total of debt plaints, provided that the credit relationships formed in the preceding year, and now at risk to generate litigation, were sufficiently numerous. The count of new actions in 1369–70—thirteen—was certainly above average, but not massively so, which may be a sign that lending in the plague year 1369 was down.[56] Overall, then, where plague mortality is concerned, the message of Figure 6.1 is essentially that, as with dearth conditions before 1331, the shocks of 1348–9 and later epidemic years certainly did reduce the flow of local credit. Yet the flow did not stop entirely, and it is equally important to stress this.

The Horwood evidence concerning the Black Death's impact on credit supply is harder to interpret, but perhaps suggests a greater resilience in lending activity than can be traced for the Crowland villages.[57] As noted above, the summer of 1349 experienced no great upsurge in lawsuits at Horwood of a kind one would expect had the exceptional mortality massively disrupted the business of debt repayment. Nonetheless, there was a healthy total of seven new debt actions in 1349–50, and in 1352–3, perhaps in response to

[55] For low yields in these years, see Campbell, *Three centuries*.

[56] But for this year, see also the discussion of prices, p. 206 below.

[57] Horwood: mean number of new debt actions per annum 1349–50 to 1359–60: 3.5.

high prices, there were eight new actions, which was a comparatively large total for this manor. Such evidence is a sign that lending did not greatly abate in the aftermath of the Black Death. By contrast, in other years—even high price years like 1350–1—litigation was scarcer, which suggests that comparatively little new credit had come on stream roughly eleven months previously. Horwood therefore offers a mixed picture of the effects of mortality on credit supply. The persistence of some lending and borrowing is clear, however, and is what one would expect given that on the eve of the Black Death the sources of credit in Horwood were widely dispersed in society, rather than being restricted to a handful of influential lenders.

In a system of rural lending where individuals, not institutions, were the credit providers, sudden death inevitably created disruption. Above-average mortality reduced the credit supply mainly by removing creditors, rather than by making surviving creditors less willing to lend for fear of their clients' futures. Even in the fourteenth century, however, the years of exceptionally high mortality were greatly outnumbered by 'normal' years in which, though individual creditors might die, it was unlikely that several key players would disappear at once. Furthermore, as already stressed, even during and immediately following periods of high mortality, lending was not entirely interrupted. A key reason for this is that lending and borrowing was not confined to particular small groups, but was engaged in by most people in local society whenever they had the capacity or the need. Credit ties still continued to be formed throughout the surviving population, even following episodes of very heavy mortality.

6.4 Money supply

All village credit, whatever its form, was extended in the expectation that it should be repaid at some stage. Debt litigation in manor courts reveals that most repayments were expressed in monetary terms, and that a transfer of coin was normally anticipated. In this, credit arrangements reflected the high degree of monetization of the rural economy evident by the close of the thirteenth century. On the face of it, therefore, access to coined money was a basic necessity for debtors in discharging their obligations, and lenders similarly gave credit on the basis that their debtors could obtain the coin with which to repay them. Yet the quantity of coinage circulating in the fourteenth-century English countryside was not constant. Instead, it was subject to substantial changes which were heavily influenced by factors governing the importation of precious metals, such as the level of their production in European mines and the balance of overseas trade in a period of frequent warfare, all of which were only partially within the control of the monarchs who issued the coins. This section asks whether the shifts in coin availability brought about corresponding changes in the extension of credit and, in particular, whether the credit supply always contracted when the money supply did so?

An affirmative answer to both questions has been voiced by some historians. Most notably, Nightingale has argued that although credit was widely used in a society where the amount of coin available was always too small for the work it had to do, the supply of credit was nonetheless constrained by the money supply, and expanded and contracted along with it. Nightingale has shown how creditors restricted their lending in periods of monetary scarcity, and expanded it when money supplies improved, a particularly significant signal to contemporaries being changes in mint output.[58] On this view, credit could never act in any sustained way as a substitute for coin, and it did not itself function as money. Thus in several fruitful applications of the Quantity Theory of Money to the medieval economy, credit is not placed under M (money) in the Fisher equation MV=PT.[59] Credit belongs rather under V, 'velocity of circulation', or, as Mayhew helpfully expresses it, 'the amount of times M has to turn over to accomplish the monetary work represented by PT to make the economy function'.[60] Credit was thus an expedient which could compensate for the inadequacies of the money supply, that is, of the supply of gold and silver coin, but it could only ever do so on a temporary basis. The key implication of this theory is as relevant and significant for a single village as it is for the kingdom as a whole: since in a fourteenth-century context V could not expand indefinitely to make up for a declining level of M, contraction in the number of transactions (T), and/or deflation as result of reduction in P, or the price level, was inevitable.[61]

Central to this thesis is the claim about the tendency for money supply and credit to expand and contract together. This is based primarily on work concerning largely mercantile credit in periods of recurrent currency famine at the end of the fourteenth century and during the fifteenth century.[62] In the present section, the focus is on village credit in an earlier phase of pronounced decline in the money supply, namely that occurring between about

[58] Nightingale, 'Monetary contraction and mercantile credit', 567–9; Nightingale, 'Money and credit', 60–7. See also Mayhew, 'Modelling', 67.

[59] For medieval credit to function as M it would need to consist of instruments that could be transferred or assigned. For the limited capacity of the available credit instruments to add to the effective money supply of this period, see Munro, 'Wage-stickiness', 216–17.

[60] Mayhew, 'Coinage and money', 80.

[61] Mayhew, 'Population, money supply, and the velocity of circulation', 253–4; Mayhew, 'Modelling', 67–8. T can also be expressed as GDP (Y).

[62] See, especially, Nightingale, 'Monetary contraction and mercantile credit', and Nightingale, 'Money and credit'.

1320 and the Black Death. There are signs that the relatively large, predominantly mercantile loans registered under the Statute Merchant system also fell in number in this earlier phase of monetary shrinkage. Statistics based on the entire dataset of Statute Merchant certificates of unpaid debt have not yet been published. Nightingale has, however, produced figures which show that the total of certificates registered at Norwich in 1300–9, when the money supply was nearing its medieval peak, was some 6 per cent higher than it was in the 1330s, and around 50 per cent higher than in the 1340s.[63] Numbers of certificates of debt extended nationally by parochial clergy, which averaged more than £20 in value, also fell, from 239 in 1300–9 to 122 in 1330–9, before recovering to 184 in 1340–9.[64] The intention here is to discover whether the village creditors responded in the same way to coin shortage as the creditors documented in the Statute Merchant data. The latter group very frequently included urban merchants who did not live in the same place as their debtors, and presumably had few or no other ties with them.

Attention is confined to the circulation of silver pence, halfpence, and farthings.[65] The most up-to-date estimates of the volume of the silver currency between 1300 and 1351, based on the evidence of coin hoards and mint figures, show a division into two clear phases. A total silver currency of approximately £1,100,000–£1,400,000 in 1299 grew to a high of approximately £1,900,000–£2,300,000 in 1319, before contracting from the 1320s to reach an estimated £480,000–£830,000 in 1351.[66] The most important causes of the contraction appear to have been the very low mint output of the 1320s, plus the marked impact, from 1337 especially, of war, which disrupted overseas trade and brought about the extraction of massive amounts of coin from the populace through taxation.[67] Although little is known about the varying local effects of this lack of money, few would doubt that its impact was felt by villages such as those studied, as much as it was in the larger towns.[68] Yet in the Crowland villages and at Horwood and Balsham, did the shortage result in a tendency to lend cash and to sell goods on credit less frequently in the second quarter of the century than in the first?

[63] Nightingale, 'Norwich, London, and the regional integration of Norfolk's economy', 86. My figures are approximate because based on a graph.
[64] Nightingale, 'English parochial clergy', 91.
[65] Gold coinage was introduced only in 1344.
[66] Allen, 'Volume and composition', 43, with a revised 1351 estimate from Allen, 'Fourteenth-century hoard', 71. For Mayhew's comments on Allen's revision of his earlier estimates, see Mayhew, 'Coinage and money', 86 n. 41.
[67] Prestwich, 'Currency and the economy'; Maddicott, 'English peasantry'.
[68] For reasons why it is reasonable to apply the monetarist thesis concerning money and credit to the rural as well as the urban and mercantile world, see Briggs, 'Availability of credit', 4. For the similarities between the peasant's money economy and that of the rest of society, see especially Dyer, 'Peasants and coins', 38–9.

In giving an answer, we face the usual difficulty that the total quantity of new credit is unknown. Only defaulted credit transactions, and not even all of those, have left a record. However, as in previous sections, the annual incidence of debt litigation can reveal something about quantities of new credit created just less than one year prior to the point at which the litigation is first observed. It is certainly possible to ask whether or not the supply of credit dwindled over a quarter-century of sustained contraction of coinage.

It is convenient to split that period into two shorter ones, 1325–37 and 1337–49. The Oakington and Horwood rolls reveal that some of the most marked concentrations of years with few or no new lawsuits occur in 1325–37, though there were years that plainly did not follow this pattern, such as 1328–9 (Figures 6.1 and 6.2).[69] Does this general rarity of debt litigation around 1330 indicate a withdrawal of credit consequent upon scarcity of coin? Not necessarily, since in years of relatively low prices the tendency for default, and litigation upon default, was low. This means that, in principle, there could have been a great deal of lending in the period 1325–37 without much litigation coming to court, because in most of these years most people were able to repay their debts. Only for 1330–2 do we gain a reliable indicator of the 'true' level of new credit, since these were the only years within this group when prices were well above average. These years saw largely depressed litigation levels, a feature that in the earlier discussion was taken as a sign of a contraction in the credit supply in anticipation of, and response to, harvest failure. There is a clear possibility, however, that this contraction also represents a reaction, in part, to the growing failure of the money supply.

Any monetary problems facing the peasantry probably intensified after 1337, largely as a result of the weight of wartime taxation which affected most lowland areas to some degree. The period from 1337 to the mid-1340s was perhaps the most likely to have seen a withdrawal of credit. It was during this period that one might expect creditors to have been most acutely aware of the shortage of coin available to potential borrowers. One might also expect that at this time creditors were also particularly disinclined to extend credit because they needed to preserve their own resources to meet the almost unprecedented state fiscal demands. After 1341, circumstances may have become more favourable to lending, following a sudden upturn in mint output in 1342–5 and the end of the heaviest phase of war taxation.[70]

[69] Balsham data for the period 1325–37 are too broken to be considered here.

[70] For mint output, see Challis, *New history*, 675–82. For the suggestion that 1340–1 marked the end of the heaviest wartime taxation demands, see Maddicott, 'English peasantry', 289, 351; Ormrod, 'The crown and the English economy', 158–9.

How in fact did the credit supply respond to coin shortage between 1337 and the mid-1340s? Any steady withdrawal of credit over this period ought to be shown by a falling-off in new debt actions during the six or seven years following 1336–7. Alternatively, where the annual counts of new plaints remained steady or went up over this period, one may argue that no withdrawal of credit occurred.

A falling-off in new debt actions is seen, broadly speaking, in the case of Horwood between 1336–7 and 1341–2, until in 1342–3 there was a slight rally in litigation which may be associated with increased lending in 1341–2. The Balsham evidence is difficult to interpret, since court records survive for only five years between 1336–7 and 1343–4. New suits, however, clearly did not decline but remained at a fairly constant level in this crucial period: 5 in 1336–7, 6.5 in 1337–8, 7 in 1338–9, and 7 in 1341–2, with the 5 suits of 1339–40, a year for which the records of just two court sessions survive, probably understating the true total. Yet the strongest evidence that the credit supply held up well comes from Oakington. The high debt plaint totals of 1337–8, 1339–41, and 1342–3 in particular indicate that credit continued to be extended even as coin was drained from the countryside with the opening of the French war. There are, to be sure, years between 1337 and the Black Death when the total of new suits dips some way below 1336–7 levels. Yet if the total of new plaints in a particular year can be taken as an indicator, albeit an imprecise one, of the quantity of credit extended some eleven months previously, then it is clear that the volume of credit transactions was as great on the eve of the Black Death as it was at the outbreak of the Hundred Years War. This evidence suggesting that the village credit supply did not falter in the late 1330s and 1340s in response to monetary constraints is surely of considerable significance.[71]

The impact of the money supply on the credit supply between 1325 and 1337 is hard to judge. Debt litigation in this period is strikingly rare, but, as explained above, this does not necessarily reflect a diminution in new credit. Generally more prolific litigation after 1337 gives a better opportunity to assess the flow of credit, which was surprisingly constant at Balsham and especially so at Oakington, if not at Horwood. As far as we can tell then, in some places there was no contraction of credit, at least between 1337 and 1349. But did credit 'come to the rescue', by expanding to fill the gap left by a declining money supply? It is impossible to know for sure. Numerous additional intervening factors prevent us from determining with the evidence at our disposal whether there was more credit in absolute terms in existence in the 1330s and 1340s than at the start of the fourteenth century. It would

[71] It is difficult to make firm observations on litigation levels at Horwood in 1346–8 and at Balsham in 1344–6 owing to the survival of such a small number of court session records.

certainly be very hard to argue that credit expanded between these two periods at Horwood and Balsham. On the other hand, it would be equally hard to maintain that it did not do so in the Crowland villages, when one compares the data on new debt suits from the decade 1301–10 with the peaks in such suits recorded in the decade or so preceding the first plague outbreak.

6.5 The credit supply, 1349–1400

Work on urban and mercantile credit in the second half of the fourteenth century seems to show that, at least up until the 1390s, the volume of credit expanded. As is discussed more fully below, historians disagree as to whether this expansion should be interpreted 'positively'—that is, as a sign of increased transactions in an era of commercial growth—or, alternatively, 'negatively', as a doomed attempt to compensate for the inadequacies of the coined money supply.[72] A similar overall post-Black Death increase in the quantity of credit extended is arguably discernible in the court rolls of Oakington, which is the only one of the five series to give near-continuous coverage of the whole century. The average number of new debt plaints per annum was 10.4 between 1349 and 1400, somewhere above the average of 6.6 of the years 1290–1349, in spite of population losses in 1349 and later. Tempting though such arguments are, however, they ignore the pitfalls of leaping to conclusions about absolute levels of new credit on the basis of debt litigation data. A safer course is to focus on the evidence for short- and medium-term shifts in the credit supply, and the impact of high prices and monetary conditions on such shifts.

6.5.1 Dearth and high prices

After 1349, there continued to be years of exceptionally high grain prices, which may be considered dearth years. Such episodes became generally rarer and less severe after the Black Death. However, as before 1349, they were primarily the consequence of smaller than average harvests.[73] After 1349, was there a change in the impact of such conditions on the propensity to extend credit? We have already seen that the succession of poor harvests of the early

[72] Compare Britnell, *Growth and decline*, 100–03, and Kowaleski, *Exeter*, 202, 348–9, with Nightingale, 'Monetary contraction and mercantile credit', 562–3.
[73] Farmer, 'Prices and wages, 1350–1500', 449–50; Farmer, 'Grain yields on the Winchester manors', 557–61. Prices could have been high because of labour shortages following second and subsequent plague outbreaks. Yet although low productivity may not necessarily have been responsible for such high prices, the situation was still one of a shortage of harvested grain available to consumers.

1350s, and the consequent upward leap in prices, coincided with a contraction in the extension of credit, which is especially evident at Oakington, Cottenham, and Drayton. Coming as it did in the aftermath of the demographic shock of the first plague outbreak, however, that contraction cannot be attributed solely to a run of high prices, but probably had much to do with the deaths of key lenders. Here, other years of unusually high prices—1363–4, 1369–70, and 1390–1—are examined in order to establish whether the anticipation or experience of dearth precipitated credit withdrawal at dates later in the second half of the century. However, as with the early 1350s, consideration of these years requires acknowledgement of the interconnected effects of plague mortality and harvest failure.

After 1349, the temporary shortfalls in food availability implied by high prices appear to have posed relatively little threat to access to credit in the villages studied. The continuous series of reeve's accounts of the manor of Oakington running from 1360 to 1399 provides valuable local evidence on the sale price of grain, confirming 1363–4, 1369–70, and 1390–1 as the years when prices rose furthest above the average for the period covered by the accounts.[74] The count of new Oakington debt plaints for 1363–4 (ten) is only marginally below average, which indicates that anticipation of cereal shortages had not produced a serious credit withdrawal in 1362–3. But did credit fail in 1363–4 itself? It is difficult to say for sure, since prices in 1364–5, although above average, were not exceptionally high, so, according to the methodology of this chapter, one is not able to treat the total of new debt plaints in that year as a reliable guide to the amount of credit created some eleven months previously.

One can do better, though, for 1369–70. An above-average total of new debt actions in that year (thirteen) reflects unabated credit provision some eleven months previously. Earlier, in discussing the effects of the 1369 plague outbreak, it was noted that since a total of thirteen new suits in 1369–70 was not markedly above average, this perhaps points to a slight contraction in credit following the epidemic of 1369, though not a complete collapse in its availability. However, this total of thirteen plaints now appears more impressive if one puts dearth into the equation, and notes that neither the plague mortality of 1369 nor the forewarnings of what turned out to be one of the worst dearths of the second half of the century was able to undermine the confidence of villagers enough to stop them extending credit. The credit supply's ability to weather such storms is further underlined by the total of Oakington debt suits of 1370–1. Like its predecessor, this was a year of exceptionally high prices locally, so the total of new debt actions in 1370–1

[74] The mean of the Crowland price index, 1360–1 to 1398–9, is 88.4.

can be treated as a reliable indicator of the scale of credit extension about eleven months previously. An above-average total (eleven plaints) reveals that the creation of credit ties continued unabated during the dearth year 1369–70, though as ever we can only identify trends in the creation of new credit, rather than provide exact indications of absolute quantities.

The exceptional two-year gap in the Oakington court rolls means that we rely here on those of Willingham for an assessment of the effects of the dearth of 1390–1 (see Figure 6.5).[75] Quite clearly, the above-average incidence of new debt actions there in 1390–2 shows that the anticipation or experience of food shortage in 1390–1 had no discernible tendency to constrain credit activity markedly. Indeed, it is quite possible that such activity expanded in 1390–1, since a healthy thirty-three new debt plaints were heard in the Willingham court in 1391–2, even though the Oakington price data demonstrate that this was a relatively cheap year locally.[76] It should also be remembered that this high level of credit extension was achieved in spite of any local deaths of major creditors that may have occurred in the plague outbreak of 1390.[77]

6.5.2 Money supply

After 1349, coin availability was probably a bigger influence on rural credit supply than were dearth and high prices. With respect to the quantity of coined money in circulation, historians agree that the period 1349–1400 should be divided roughly into two.[78] First, the years from the recoinage of 1351 to *c.*1375 probably witnessed an absolute and per capita increase in the money supply, largely as a result of high mint output in the 1350s. The second phase, beginning *c.*1375, involved a marked decline in money supply—the beginnings of the 'great bullion famine' of the later middle ages—consequent upon the return of heavy war taxation in the 1370s and falling mint output in the 1380s and 1390s.[79]

[75] The mean total of new Willingham debt actions per annum 1377–8 to 1399–1400 is 31.0.

[76] No weight should be attached to the low total of only five debt actions at Willingham in 1392–3, because records of only one court session survive for that year.

[77] The chronicler Walsingham states that plague ensued in Cambridge for an unspecified time following an incident of 1389, recounted by the writer as an *exemplum*, that occurred there during a procession on the feast of the Commemoration of St Paul (30 June). Presumably, this Cambridge plague was part of the great plague of 1390 that Walsingham goes on to describe as ravaging the whole country. In writing of this 1390 plague, Walsingham also observes that 'the epidemic was soon followed by a dearth of foodstuffs': Horrox (ed.), *Black Death*, 91.

[78] Mate, 'Gold coinage', 137–8; Munro, 'Wage-stickiness', 212–14; Farmer, 'Prices and wages, 1350–1500', 441.

[79] A decline by 1400 is accepted, though Allen's estimate of the size of the money supply in 1422 is about the same as that for 1351: Allen, 'Volume of the English currency', 607. This presumably reflects relatively high mint output in 1411–20.

As mentioned earlier, the dominant view regarding the effects of monetary conditions on medieval credit supply has been formulated largely in relation to the period after 1349. Crudely put, this states that increased use of credit may for a time allow economic activity and prices to be maintained at their former level in spite of a reduction in the quantity of coined money. However, such an effect can only ever be temporary, since credit will eventually contract in line with the dwindling money supply, just as it expands when the money supply expands. For Nightingale, this theory is borne out by evidence such as that pertaining to credit extended by London grocers in the course of their trade. Over the period between 1350 and 1389, decadal quantities of such credit more than doubled in value. This is seen as consonant with, first, the growth in the money supply in the 1350s and 1360s and, second, an effort to make up for the faltering monetary situation of the 1370s through increased credit use. Grocers' credit then declined in the 1390s as falling mint output sent a signal to members of the mercantile community to scale down their credit-based trade. Nightingale interprets other evidence within the same framework, most notably the picture of dramatic credit expansion in later fourteenth-century Colchester implied by the information on debt litigation culled from the town's courts. Whereas Britnell rejected the idea that Colchester's pattern of indebtedness reflected monetary movements, preferring instead to stress the growth of credit as a function of growing commercial activity, Nightingale pointed particularly to the decline in Colchester's debt litigation, and hence its credit activity, during the money supply crisis of the later 1390s, while at the same time arguing that the large numbers of credit transactions apparently entered into in the later 1370s and 1380s were an unsustainable expedient which failed to overcome the fundamental problem of a lack of coin.[80]

Does the Oakington and Willingham debt litigation evidence reveal the effects upon credit of the substantial monetary contraction that, by general consent, occurred between 1349 and 1400 in countryside as well as town? If anything, this crisis should, if the monetarist theory is correct, have hit ordinary villagers harder than those in the mercantile sector. Peasants are usually thought to have relied for their transactions largely on the low denomination silver coins, with gold coins, of which the standard coin was the noble worth 6*s*. 8*d*., being of too high a value to be used for any but the most exceptional peasant transactions.[81] However, with the exception of the 1350s, most of the new coinage minted after 1349 was gold rather than silver.

[80] Britnell, *Growth and decline*, 100–1, though see also Britnell, *Commercialisation*, 181; Nightingale, 'Monetary contraction and mercantile credit', 562–3, 574.

[81] Mayhew, 'Money in the late medieval countryside', 21–2; see, however, Dyer, 'Peasants and coins', 40.

Historians think that this factor contributed to a scarcity of silver currency throughout the second half of the fourteenth century which, in spite of the lower population after 1349, was perhaps becoming a problem even before *c.*1375.[82] The sums claimed in manorial debt actions confirm that villagers must have been primarily reliant upon silver in repaying debts. It is true that the median post-1348 debt claim exceeded the value of the smallest gold coin, which was the quarter-noble, worth 20*d.*[83] However, many obligations were of course for smaller amounts. Therefore, if rural creditors were prone to rein in credit because of fears about lack of coin, then there was perhaps more reason for them to have done so after 1349 than might be imagined when simply observing estimated trends in the total money stock.

With this in mind, one is better placed to interpret Figures 6.1 and 6.5. Particularly striking are the similarities in the movement between 1376 and 1383 of the two debt litigation series. This was a period of consistently low prices, and so, other things being equal, one would not expect above-average litigation levels. However, at Oakington new debt plaints rose from a slightly below-average nine plaints in 1377–8 to a substantially above-average twenty-one plaints 1379–80, before dropping slightly in 1380–1, and rising again to fifteen plaints in 1381–2. A very similar pattern of rising plaint totals in a phase of low prices is evident at Willingham in 1379–82, a period followed by the unparalleled high litigation peak of 1383–4, a year in which grain prices were only marginally above average. The point is that manorial debt litigation was increasing sharply at exactly the date when historical opinion suggests coin shortage was really beginning to bite. Given the price conditions of these years, the rising debt litigation almost certainly represents an increase in the amount of credit being extended in the later 1370s and early 1380s.

After that, however, there are strong signs of a contraction in credit, especially in the Oakington evidence. Little significance should be attached to the debt plaint peak of 1392–3, as there is a strong possibility that this reflects a build-up of suits following a break in court holding in 1391–2. More important is the total of just seven actions in 1397–8, a high price year locally. This total is indicative of only modest credit extension in 1396–7. It appears that whereas in the later 1370s the response of local creditors to a lack of money was to extend more credit than before, by the later 1390s this course had been abandoned. In other words, with respect to new credit creation, the

[82] Allen, 'Volume of the English currency', 607, estimates that per capita silver coin stocks declined from about 5–7*s.* in 1351 to about 1–2*s.* in 1422; see also especially Mate, 'Gold coinage', 135–8. Parliamentary petitions in 1379–1402 suggest a particular shortage of silver halfpence and farthings for retail trade: Allen, 'Proportions of the denominations', 192–4.

[83] Median money debt claims: 32*d.* at Willingham 1377–1400, 22*d.* in the Crowland villages 1351–1400.

Oakington material suggests much the same pattern for the last quarter of the century as the Colchester evidence and data on London grocers. At Willingham the picture is less clear, since although the new plaint total dropped below average in the high price year 1397–8, there were relatively high counts of new actions in the years immediately preceding and following. We therefore cannot rule out the possibility that in the 1390s there was local variation in the impact of coin availability on credit supply, with Willingham showing less contraction than Oakington, Cottenham, and Drayton.

6.6 Conclusion: local variation in the credit supply

At the start of this chapter it was argued that a central fact about credit was that it gave a villager flexibility about which payments he could make and when he would make them. Irrespective of the form of the credit given—whether it was a deferred payment on a sale or, less commonly, a loan of cash—its effect in this regard was the same. Yet credit would not necessarily be forthcoming at all times, especially in a system in which individuals, not institutions, were the lenders. The degree to which individuals were in fact ready to extend credit is what this chapter has defined as the credit supply.

Previous commentators have suggested that the fourteenth century was especially prone to conditions in which credit became largely or wholly unavailable to those who demanded it. The key conditions promoting this are seen as harvest failure and dearth, high mortality, and falls in the ratio of money supply to population. This chapter has indicated that the fourteenth century certainly witnessed periods of severe, if primarily short-term, crisis in the rural economy which included among other attributes a partial or total withdrawal of village credit. Looking at the century as a whole, however, there are also signs of surprising resilience in the credit supply. An equally important part of this conclusion, however, involves stressing the local and temporal variations in the extent to which the three 'factors'—dearth, crisis mortality, and coin shortage—brought about a large drop in the credit supply.

Many examples of such variations have emerged in the foregoing discussion, and a few may be reiterated here. Where the anticipation of and responses to harvest failure are concerned, the same year or years brought notably different effects in different villages. This is seen, to give just one example, in the apparent withdrawal of credit at Oakington, Cottenham, and Drayton in advance of the dearth year 1321–2, as reflected in the debt litigation figures for that year, which contrasts sharply with the picture from Balsham. The effects of poor harvests on credit supply also varied over time, as is indicated most generally and most obviously in the much more negligible effects on credit of such years after the Black Death than had been the case beforehand. Excess mortality also affected some places at some periods more than others. The 1349 plague contributed to a greater diminution in credit supply in the Crowland villages than it did at Horwood, for example, and plague mortality in 1390 at Willingham does not appear to have had a discernible effect on such supply. The drop in the Horwood credit supply in the later 1330s contrasts with the continuation of lending at Balsham and in the Crowland villages at the same date, thereby indicating variations in response to coin shortage. Finally, coin shortage influenced credit supply more in some periods than others, the evidence in the Oakington rolls for sustained lending between *c.*1337 and the Black Death offering a particularly significant contrast to that suggesting a fall in lending at the end of the 1390s.

Some of these contrasts are easily explained. It is not surprising that poor harvests did less to stop the credit flow after the Black Death than before, since potential borrowers had become generally wealthier, had greater access to non-cereal foodstuffs, and hence would be judged more likely to be able to repay debts than their counterparts of the early 1300s. It is also to be expected that the Black Death should have had a more disruptive effect on credit supply than other episodes of mortality. Other local variations in the effects of the three 'factors' on credit supply must simply reflect contrasts in the severity with which a factor affected the locality concerned, and it must also be remembered that dearth, excess mortality, and coin shortage never operated in isolation upon a rural community, but always in varying combinations.

It is particularly interesting to ask why the credit supply did not diminish substantially at times and in places where one might predict it to have done so, given the presence of dearth, high mortality, or lack of coin. One possibility is that the characteristics of the lenders and borrowers were such that the assumptions adopted here about behaviour in response to the three 'factors' are misconceived. In dearth years, for example, the prospect of selling surpluses at high prices might actually have made lenders with large landholdings decide to extend *more* credit than previously, rather than to withdraw it because forced to prioritize their own subsistence needs, as assumed here. Another possibility is that assumptions about creditor behaviour adopted from the mercantile sector are not applicable to rural credit. This applies particularly to coin shortage. For the village creditor, an inadequate supply of specie may not have formed the formidable obstacle to lending that it did for the town-dwelling mercantile creditor, since repayment in labour or kind was for the rural lender a practical alternative with some potential attractions. We should not necessarily assume that all debts described in monetary terms would be repaid in coin, even if the claim was for a repayment in this form and coin was the preferred medium.

Thus while one part of the explanation for the surprising success of the credit supply in apparently unfavourable circumstances lies in local and temporal variations in the impact of those circumstances, another undoubtedly concerns the attitudes and flexibility of the creditors. This chapter concludes with some reflections on a further factor which was probably influential in shaping the resilience or otherwise of the credit supply, namely the role of legal institutions in the countryside.

When would-be village creditors decided whether to extend credit, they deliberated mainly in reaction to objective conditions like the price and availability of food, mortality levels among debtors, and coin supply. However, they could not ignore the related question of what would happen if a debtor failed to repay. In practice, securing repayment after default meant harnessing the debt recovery machinery of the local courts, usually a nearby manor court. As tribunals in which to recover a debt, these courts did not all offer the same quality of service. Some were more efficient, operated more quickly, and offered more stringent measures against recalcitrant debtors than others.[84] While factors such as coin shortage would certainly have worked to restrict lending, one should probably add that such a tendency would have been even more pronounced in localities which lacked the effective and speedy legal jurisdictions necessary to recover private debts. Similarly, where such structures did exist, they encouraged the continued extension of credit in circumstances that might otherwise have been thought too risky.

The Oakington manor court underwent reforms in the second quarter of the fourteenth century which improved its performance as a tribunal in which to prosecute debt actions speedily and successfully. These procedural changes may have helped to prevent rupture in the local credit supply in the period of coin shortage of *c.*1337 to the Black Death.[85] Although we have no reason to doubt that at that time lack of coin was as much a problem in the Crowland villages as it was elsewhere, a restricted money supply was made to work harder in these villages because the changes in court procedure made individuals relatively willing to lend. In terms of the Quantity Theory equation MV=PT, V, in the shape of credit, was able to expand to a greater extent in the environs of Oakington than was the case in other places where legal institutions were less responsive to economic conditions.[86]

A full reconstruction of debt litigation procedures of the kind already undertaken for Oakington and Horwood is not repeated here for the remaining courts owing to the fact that the relevant rolls are not sufficiently continuous for the exercise, and also because it would take up too much space. It is therefore not practical to compare all the courts in an attempt to relate the

[84] Briggs, 'Manor court procedures'.
[85] Briggs, 'Manor court procedures', 552–3.
[86] On the relationship between rural legal institutions and the credit supply in the fifteenth century, see Briggs, 'Availability of credit'.

variations in credit supply to differences between the courts. There are hints, nonetheless, that an effort along those lines would reveal a correlation between, on the one hand, a court's ability to effect and enforce speedy judgments in large numbers of debt cases, and, on the other, the size of the local credit supply. At Littleport, for example, local people clearly had high expectations of what their local court should achieve in terms of the efficiency of its practices in the conduct of civil justice. These are shown in complaints against the hayward, the official primarily responsible for administering plaints, which first appear in the mid-1320s. Prior to that date, however, it appears from a lack of complaint that the Littleport court machinery was meeting the exacting demands of its litigants.[87] No doubt the attractions offered by the Littleport court around 1320 as a forum in which to sue partly explains the large quantities of debt litigation brought to the court at that time. Furthermore, it was argued earlier that those high levels of debt litigation are themselves a reflection of correspondingly high levels of new credit extension at Littleport before and during the high price year 1321–2. Quite probably, the perceived efficiency and dependability of the local court should be regarded as important in encouraging people to continue making loans and selling on credit at that time. At Littleport, as elsewhere, the credit supply depended upon individuals' assessments of the risks and opportunities entailed in the extension of credit. If we ignore the part played by formal legal institutions in that assessment, our picture remains incomplete.

[87] CRO, R 93/96, mm.21 (18 October 1324), 20 (1 March 1325; see *Court Baron*, 141), and 22 (22 September 1325). These complaints concerned the hayward's failings in making 'attachments', that is, in appointing pledges and seizing goods to secure the appearance of parties.

Conclusion

This book began by describing a shift that occurred in the 1990s in historians' attitudes to credit in the countryside. Through this change, investigators of medieval and early modern agrarian society in continental Europe, and of early modern England, began to stress the ubiquity and sophistication of rural credit mechanisms, and their positive effects within traditional economies.[1] Before this time, the consensus historical position had been very different, and rural indebtedness, when considered at all as a serious force, had generally been regarded as a marker of poverty and stagnation. Reference was also made to the puzzling fact that work on England prior to the fifteenth century appeared to constitute a notable exception to this wider rejection of the prevailing orthodoxy on rural credit. Clearly, it was not the case that historians of thirteenth- and fourteenth-century England were unaware that credit structures existed at village level, or that they considered them to be of only marginal importance. Instead, the interesting thing about most work on the pre-Black Death period in particular is that it tended to see credit almost entirely within the context of debates about agrarian crisis and falling peasant living standards. In general, credit relations were seen as a symptom of, and perhaps also as a factor contributing to, those phenomena. The position of existing work on medieval England, tentative and provisional as it is, was in fact quite close to the 'old' view of agrarian credit currently under critical scrutiny from historians of France and Italy in particular. The aim of this book has been to understand how far the current exclusion of medieval England from the wider shifts in scholarly attitudes to rural credit is justified by the evidence, rather than being largely a historiographical accident.

This book's overall conclusion, reached on the basis of the seven villages examined, is that there is no reason why the England of the period before 1400 should continue to be excluded from the 'new view' of agrarian credit in the pre-modern era. To be sure, it is in many ways perfectly understandable why credit in England has been considered primarily as a facet of crisis in the

[1] Holderness began this trend earlier for early modern England.

rural economy. If nothing else, manor court litigation shows that many people were indebted, and on one level, the most obvious way to treat that simple yet crucial fact is as an illustration of the complex bundle of problems that afflicted the countryside in the years between *c.*1290 and *c.*1375. Yet the tendency to view credit largely within the framework of crisis is also a function of the fact that previous work on the period has treated credit rather briefly and as an adjunct to other questions, and that until now there has been no study of any length which has concentrated directly on credit itself, and which furthermore uses what may be regarded as a substantial body of empirical data.[2] A change in perspective inevitably comes once one has brought detailed information to bear upon questions which previously have largely been matters of speculation. After this has been done, as in this book, it is impossible to avoid the conclusion that although many of the assumptions about rural credit adopted in work focused on crisis are borne out by a full examination of a sufficiently large corpus of debt material, others are simply not supported by such an enquiry. Thus, for example, it has been found that the credit supply did not always fail in problem periods; that debtors were not always markedly worse off than their lenders; and that the subletting of land by debtors was an effective strategy compatible with individual prosperity, not a marker of economic failure.

As part of its attempt to determine whether fourteenth-century England ought to continue to stand outside the 'new view' on rural credit, this study has assessed the strengths and weaknesses of the English credit system in the countryside, as measured by a number of criteria. In particular, the book has sought to establish how far England's rural credit networks were able to meet the demands placed upon them and to bring lasting benefits both to lenders and to borrowers. Wherever possible, verdicts have been reached on the English evidence by means of comparison with work on rural credit in other contemporary European settings. Had it been found that the organization of English credit was uniformly 'weaker' than that of its European counterpart, then this would have shown that previous work on England was probably correct to regard credit in much the same light as the proponents of the 'old' view of pre-modern credit had done. On the whole, however, a comparative investigation into strengths and weaknesses does not suggest that medieval England and medieval continental Europe were substantively different in terms of the organization and capacities of credit in the countryside, though it must be conceded that there were some key differences between European regions which meant that the strengths of the rural credit market were probably somewhat greater in certain continental areas than they were in the

[2] Schofield, 'Access', is a possible exception.

generality of English villages. In what follows, the book's findings concerning the strengths and weaknesses of village credit are summarized by reference to four general aspects that were indicated in the introduction, namely the availability, character, uses, and effects of credit.

How consistently was credit available to would-be borrowers when they wanted it, and in the forms that they wanted it? A major issue here was that in the English context the provision of credit to villagers was primarily a function distributed across a large number of neighbours. It was not as common in England as it was elsewhere in Europe to find that lending lay in the hands of relatively small groups of specialists. Another feature of those key sources of rural credit in regions outside England is that they were often non-resident and included townsfolk. Although the villages examined in this book were hardly unaffected by external credit links, they were perhaps not as important in those places as in certain zones of contemporary southern Europe. This in turn raises the question of intermediation, that is, of the means by which would-be creditors and would-be debtors hitherto unknown to one another found out about one another and were brought together. Obvious potential agents of intermediation in the Roman law regions of Europe were the notaries, who were responsible for creating and preserving the written record of many, if not all, debts. One possibility raised in this study is that the absence of rural notaries in England constrained the exchange of information that was key to the successful linking up of lenders and borrowers. In reviewing the sources of credit, it should also be noted that other potentially rich sources of capital, most notably the rural clergy, were not always as heavily involved as credit providers as one might have anticipated. In short, did credit in rural England struggle to meet demand, given that most of the relevant lenders were peasant neighbours rather than individuals who enjoyed, on the face of it at least, a superior capacity to extend credit even in unfavourable economic circumstances?

It is not clear that these weaknesses of credit availability were real rather than apparent. This book has confirmed that lending in the fourteenth-century countryside was, in Postan's phrase, 'disseminated', that is, it was practised by virtually everyone within a rural community who had the capacity or the opportunity, rather than being the preserve of a specialist few. As others have found, such disseminated lending was a persistent feature of the English rural world in all later centuries from the fifteenth to the eighteenth. It might appear on a priori grounds that a network dominated by local peasants would have been less capable of meeting demands for credit than one dominated by specialist usurers. However, the long-standing English preference over several centuries for 'disseminated' lending suggests an alternative, namely that the English and continental European systems, with their differing emphases in the major sources of credit, were nonetheless roughly equal in their capacity to provide credit at the times and in the forms required. In other words, it may in fact be correct to assume, as Holderness did, that the English 'diffusion of money-lending', as he termed it, 'obeyed a clearly defined and explicable logic within a well-developed and sophisticated credit system'.[3]

The best test of this hypothesis is to ask how well new credit supplies held up in the face of those short-term economic shocks for which the fourteenth century is well renowned. Chapter 6 showed that before the Black Death, creditors did not invariably curtail their lending activities in anticipation of periods of dearth and exceptionally high prices. Nor did they always dramatically reduce the quantities of credit they gave even in the midst of the worst conditions of harvest failure, though within the larger pre-plague period there were, to be sure, years in which a severe credit crunch could not be avoided in some places, the most obvious being the exceptional Great Famine years of 1315–17. After the Black Death, harvest failure tended to bring about a much more muted reduction in credit availability, though in the Crowland villages there was a marked fall in new credit creation in the early 1350s, which must have been driven by dearth, at least in part. The heavy mortality of 1349 among creditors certainly had a noticeable effect in those years as well, though above-average death rates can hardly be said to have substantially influenced credit availability across the century as a whole. Like harvest failure and high prices, shortage of coined money also had an effect upon credit availability which varied with time and place. However, it was only at the very end of the century, in the 1390s, that one begins to be able to observe a strong association between a significant downturn in the money supply and the sustained withdrawal of new credit.

Taken as a whole, therefore, the evidence shows that while the rural credit system all but collapsed in some settlements in response to the most marked economic and demographic reverses of the century, in general credit availability held up surprisingly well. But was credit always available to all, or just to a select few? A consistent theme of previous writing on the early fourteenth century was that the predicament of the increasingly vulnerable groups within village society who held inadequate quantities of land was often made worse by their contact with credit. In this book it had similarly been argued that the organization of credit in the case study villages was detrimental to the interests of those with little or no land, though not because their indebtedness compounded their other problems, but because they were largely excluded from significant participation in the credit network and its potential benefits. Although there are sound reasons for assuming that bor-

[3] Holderness, 'Credit in English rural society', 105.

rowing by smallholding families (primarily cottagers) and the landless should be revealed by the litigation evidence, there has nonetheless been a strong tendency to find that the majority of relationships entailed the extension of credit to people occupying 10 acres or more, holdings which in early fourteenth-century terms were not small. While households holding less land than this can certainly be traced as borrowers, one gains the impression that in the villages studied, with their 'midland' tenurial and landholding patterns, credit was mainly the preserve of the middling and upper peasantry only: the 10-acre tenants, the half-virgaters, and the virgaters. Thus if there were significant weaknesses with respect to the availability of credit, they lay primarily in restrictions on the social depth of credit's effects—in its 'horizontal' character, in fact—rather than in its temporal fluctuations.

What was the character of the credit transactions themselves; that is, what forms did credit arrangements take, and what were their conditions? In some aspects of the character of credit, England and continental areas do not appear to have differed that much. For instance, credit tended to be extended over roughly the same time periods both in the villages studied here and more generally, with terms of less than six months being the norm, and terms of more than one year being rare. Perhaps more often, however, as in the preceding discussion of the individuals who provided credit, there were contrasts between England and many areas of contemporary Europe with respect to the character of credit. Once again, however, these contrasts do not necessarily imply inequality between England and elsewhere in the overall balance of strengths and weaknesses.

For example, Chapter 3 confirmed that, apart from the possibility that a few short-term inter-peasant leases represent the pledging of small parcels at the outset of a credit relationship, customary land appears hardly ever to have been used as collateral in English village credit. This constitutes a contrast with southern Europe, where land was thus employed with some frequency. Did the limited use of customary land to secure debts serve to dissuade would-be lenders from making cash loans, and does it therefore represent a comparative weakness of the English credit network? This is possible, but the other side of the story is that the lack of any significant role for land as collateral meant that one potentially important route to the impoverishment of debtors was avoided in England. In the villages investigated, the outright loss of land by obviously overstretched borrowers was relatively rare, and one major reason for this must lie in the limited scope for foreclosure on lands pledged as security. In those settlements, possession of land was certainly an important requirement for obtaining credit. However, because debtors tended to sublet parts of their holdings on a temporary basis as a strategy for repaying debts, rather than to forfeit permanently lands pledged at the outset of a credit relationship, a strength of the situation in these English localities was that it did not tend to lead as inexorably as it might have to the expropriation of borrowers.

England and those continental localities studied to date also differed in other aspects of the character of rural credit, such as the numerical significance of the various transaction types. In England at this time, credit extended as part of a sale, especially the deferred payment, appears to have been much more significant than the straightforward loan than was the case in southern Europe. This feature is of course associated with the very minor role found in England for the use of land as security for loans: the rarity of loans went hand in hand with the rare use of land to secure loans, though the direction of causation here is unclear. At first glance, the contrast between England and the continent with respect to loans and sales credit might appear to represent a comparative weakness of the English situation, since a loan of cash was the most versatile form in which to receive credit. However, it would have been unnecessary to obtain a loan first if the items one wanted to buy were available on credit, as they so often were in the highly commercialized English countryside. Moreover, as Chapter 2 argued, the rarity of loans can easily be exaggerated. A close look at many of the simple debts of commodities—those of malt and sedge in particular—shows that they did not arise from consumption loans in kind, as one might at first assume, but were almost certainly the product of purchase price advances, in which the seller of the commodity concerned received a effective cash loan of a potentially substantial size.

One area of the character of credit transactions which may be thought to show quite clearly English rural credit's relative weakness concerns the use of written documents to record and authenticate credit deals. English peasant credit was almost entirely oral, whereas much of that created in other European settings was recorded in the notarial registers. It is therefore reasonable to assume that, in spite of the highly developed English system of personal pledges who were used to witness and guarantee credit acts, it remained harder in England than elsewhere to prove who owed what to whom, and that this tended to make the risks involved in lending in the English countryside comparatively great. However, it is just as important to remember that any proof showing that a particular debtor was obligated to a particular creditor was relatively worthless in the absence of a local institution which had both the authority and power to enforce that decision, and to collect the debt on the lender's behalf if need be. In this respect, English villages appear to have been at least as well served as most areas of continental Europe, if not better, thanks to the manor courts and their rights to enforce their decisions over conveniently small territories. This was something which, in many cases, they did with notable effectiveness.

When it comes to the uses of credit, comparison with regions outside England is more difficult, though as far as one can tell there appear to have been no significant contrasts between the villages focused on here and other documented areas of continental Europe. For instance, the evidence that credit was ever sought with the aim of acquiring landed property is comparatively scarce in both instances. Any claim that the English system of rural credit suffered weaknesses as a result of providing credit for consumption purposes only was strongly challenged by Chapter 2, which showed that the probable uses of credit were marked primarily by their diversity. Exigency credit obtained so that people could overcome temporary shortages in essentials co-existed with credit sought for purposes of investment.

The final general aspect of rural credit considered by this book was that of its effects upon individuals, households, and village society at large. Here, too, it is hard to argue that the negative consistently outweighed the positive. Among apparent negatives, it is possible, if somewhat anachronistic, to count the fact that neither married nor not-married women achieved any great independent or indeed significant role as providers or recipients of credit. Instead, married women obtained access to credit through membership of households. Here, women's role in determining the overall creditworthiness of their households should not be underestimated, though it is difficult to investigate empirically. More generally, one should emphasize again the finding that the effects of credit upon landless and labouring households were relatively limited, since their participation in credit networks as borrowers was only occasional.

What were the overall effects of credit upon those who obtained it more regularly? In some villages before the Black Death there was a marked polarization of credit network participants into serial creditors and serial debtors, with hardly any overlap. This does seem to suggest that in these contexts, credit helped to harden social divisions within the village, and conferred benefits upon a creditor class only. On the other hand, in pre-plague Littleport and Horwood, and in all post-1349 villages studied, there was no such clear separation into those who only lent frequently but did not borrow, and those who only borrowed frequently but did not lend. Close investigation of individual case histories also demonstrates that it is a mistake to assume that evidence of heavy borrowing is in itself proof that taking on numerous debts was destructive for livelihoods. In fact, sometimes it may show the opposite. It is only for the exceptionally difficult years of the century's second decade that the connection between debt and individual catastrophe shows up unequivocally in the evidence, and even in that period it is hard to claim definitively that the root of the problem lay in excessive borrowing.

As historians of other parts of pre-industrial Europe have been arguing for some time, indebtedness in rural England in the fourteenth century was not simply an inevitable consequence of peasants succumbing to economic changes which they were largely powerless to control. Instead, people also entered the records as debtors as a result of their involvement in arrangements that were designed to enhance the flexibility with which they could deploy the finite resources under their control, or even because they saw an opportunity for longer-term economic advancement for which a credit deal might be the starting point. This book's subject, at least in the way it has been approached and interpreted here, is thus a part of what Dyer has called a 'new middle ages', that is, an era in which the ordinary inhabitants of the countryside were not necessarily rendered completely helpless as a consequence of social subordination or technological constraint, as tended to be assumed by a previous generation of historians, but instead were adaptive, innovative, and surprisingly successful in tackling the difficulties they faced.[4]

How representative are this book's findings? The picture offered is based primarily on the records of just seven villages. All of them, very broadly speaking, were of the 'midland' type, in terms of their field systems, economic orientation, and landholding and social structure. Needless to say, the conclusions drawn on the basis of those locations cannot necessarily be applied to England as whole. It might further be objected that some of the villages investigated, especially Littleport and Willingham, featured exceptionally large quantities of both debt litigation and underlying credit activity, and that they were thus not even typical of the generality of 'midland' rural settlements. Certainly, there are numerous rural places both within the zone of 'midland' villages and outside it for which little or no debt litigation is extant in the surviving manorial records. With many of these, one is justified in assuming that the absence of litigation reflects the limited presence of credit structures. There are numerous possible reasons why credit did not flourish in particular localities. One is the complex matter of local variation in manor court procedures and practices, variations which in turn had the potential either to suppress or to encourage the provision of credit.[5] Yet, at least in the current state of our knowledge, it is not possible to go beyond these very local variations in the intensity of credit relations to argue for some clearly defined regional differences in the overall importance of rural credit. Places for which there are extensive records of debt litigation, and which hence appear to have witnessed a good deal of credit use, can be found in parts of the 'midland' village zone (broadly defined) which are a long distance away from the localities studied here. Examples are Halesowen (Worcestershire) and Gussage All Saints (Dorset).[6] Furthermore, evidence of

[4] Dyer, *Age of transition?*, 7–45.

[5] Briggs, 'Manor court procedures'.

[6] Worcestershire: Razi, *Life, marriage and death*, 37 (the extensive evidence of credit in Halesowen is confirmed by an ongoing analysis of debt cases in the Hales court rolls at Birmingham City Archives undertaken by myself and colleagues as part of the research project

extensive rural credit use exists for scattered parts of the north and west, rather than just the generally more prosperous midlands, south, and east of England. For instance, manorial records from specific localities in Yorkshire and the Welsh marches offer good evidence of flourishing village credit relationships.[7]

It cannot therefore be claimed that the marked variety and importance of credit argued for in this book holds good only for relatively prosperous Cambridgeshire and the Isle of Ely, and for its fenland and fen-edge zones in particular. However, while it is possible to argue that rural credit could be an important force in village economies in every part of England, one may also draw attention to the scope for significant regional contrasts in credit's operations and effects. The most important of these distinguished the midland zone of central and southern England from East Anglia proper, which consisted essentially of the counties of Norfolk, Suffolk, and Essex. As already noted, although the Cambridgeshire settlements which are the focus of this book were geographically close to the East Anglian heartland, they featured the tenurial and landholding system, and the related social structure, that was the hallmark of the 'midland' village. At various stages in this book it has been suggested that the character and effects of credit were not the same in the 'midland' village as they were in East Anglia, as part of more general contrasts in the distribution of land and in the intra-village economic hierarchy. As a rule, rural credit's impoverishing effects and tendency to promote differentiation in economic fortunes seem to have been more pronounced in East Anglia than in the localities studied here. Indeed, the heavy East Anglian focus of most previous work that mentions rural credit may offer a partial explanation of the broad correspondence between existing historical representations of medieval English credit and the 'old view' of agrarian credit that is so rapidly losing ground in the European literature.

What effect did village credit have on the broader development of the English economy in the fourteenth century? One short, crude answer to this difficult question is that although rural credit exerted little influence upon the overall contours of economic change, its presence shaped the way other more significant forces were felt. In the earlier part of the century, credit's main effect was to reinforce the wealth, influence, and separate identity of the more prosperous strata of village society, since, at least in the villages studied, these were the groups most fully immersed in lending and borrowing. If,

'Private law and medieval village society'); Dorset: Mayhew, 'Money in the late medieval countryside', 15–16 (the village of Gussage All Saints, the subject of an earlier and more detailed unpublished study by Mayhew).

[7] Yorkshire: Lister (ed.), *Court rolls*; Welsh marches (Dyffryn Clwyd lordship): Stevens, 'Race, gender and wealth', 255–73.

as has been powerfully argued, the agrarian problem affecting the mass of the population in this period was ultimately the result of the advantageous and unassailable tenurial position enjoyed by leading peasant tenants, rather than a consequence of the demands of lordship, then it should also be stressed that credit was another significant factor that tended to reinforce the dominance of those leading tenants.[8] In the second half of the century, many of the market opportunities associated with the rise in agricultural prices to *c.*1375 were exploited by peasants by means of credit mechanisms. However, when economic contraction took hold at the end of the century as a result of sustained demographic collapse and monetary difficulties, credit ultimately fell into abeyance also. At the local level, the nature and availability of credit could have a profound impact on, say, the market for livestock, as it did at Willingham in the 1380s. Yet at the same time it is very difficult to point to instances in which credit was obviously a prime mover precipitating changes in rural society's basic structures.

Assessing rural credit's place in the economy as a whole is a hazardous enterprise, and is in many ways beyond the scope of this book. What one can say with confidence, however, is that without the ubiquitous and often surprisingly resilient structure of credit that they developed for themselves in the later thirteenth and fourteenth centuries, medieval villagers would have been much less able to respond to change and emerging opportunities.

[8] Campbell, 'Agrarian problem'.

Appendix 1

Some manor court debt entries, with translations

Editorial conventions

[*text*]	denotes editorial comment or insertion
<text>^{i}	denotes interlineations in manuscript
<text>^{d}	denotes text struck through in manuscript
Text	denotes margination
text / text	denotes successive marginations pertaining to the same entry

1 Debt plaint at a preliminary stage:

misericordia iiii.d. Stephanus le Cartere querens optulit se versus Ricardum Annot in placito debiti. Et dictus Ricardus attachiatus fuit <per plegium Johannis Fraunk et Ricardi Margery>^{i} et non venit ideo <predicti plegii in misericordia quia ipsum non habent>^{i} preceptum est distringere dictum Ricardum ad respondendum dicto Stephano in predicto placito debiti ad proximam pleggii de prosequendo Johannes Fraunk et Ricardus Margery.[1]

Translation:

Amercement 4d. Stephen the Carter, plaintiff, appeared against Richard Annot in a plea of debt. And the said Richard was attached by John Fraunk and Richard Margery, pledges, and he does not come, therefore the aforesaid pledges are in mercy because they do not have him. Order is made to distrain the said Richard to respond to the said Stephen in the aforesaid plea of debt at the next court session, pledges to prosecute, John Fraunk and Richard Margery.

2 A plaint terminated by 'licence to agree':

misericordia vi.d. / preceptum est Adam de Tyd querens optulit se versus Wilelmum le Huxtere de placito debiti. Et ipse non venit et attachiatus fuit per Willelmum Havel et Johannem le Bolewere ideo ipsi in misericordia et preceptum est etc.[2]

[1] NCA, 3914, m.7d (Great Horwood, 18 February 1328).
[2] CRO, R 93/96, m.1d (Littleport, 21 June 1317).

Translation:

Amercement 6d. / order is made Adam de Tyd, plaintiff, appeared against William le Huxtere in a plea of debt. And he does not come, and was attached by William Havel and John le Bolewere, therefore they are in mercy, and order is made, etc.

misericordia iii.d. De Willelmo le Huxtere pro licencia concordandi <concordandi>[d] cum Adam de Tyd in placito debiti per plegium messoris.[3]

Translation:

Amercement 3d. From William le Huxtere for a licence to agree with Adam Tyd in a plea of debt, by pledge of the hayward.

3 A 'formal recognizance':

recognitio Willelmus Kille de Hokyton' recognouit hic in curia se debere Johanni Bate de Hokyt' capellano novem solidos soluendo eidem domino Johanni vel suo certo attornato apud Hok' in festo natiuitatis beate marie proximo sequenti per plegios Johannem Kate, Robertum Josep' etc. Et nisi fecerit concedit quod de bonis et catallis suis etc.[4]

Translation:

recognizance William Kille of Oakington, here in court, acknowledged himself to owe 9*s.* to John Bate, chaplain, to be paid to the same lord John or his certain attorney at Oakington on the feast of the Nativity of the Blessed Mary next following, by pledges John Kate and Robert Josep', etc. And if he does not do so, he grants that [the debt shall be levied] from his goods and chattels.

4 'Pleaded' cases terminated by inquest jury:

i.d. [*margin faded, possible further illegible words*] Compertum est per inquisitionem quod Willelmus Perchey debet et iniuste detinet Waltero le Smyth iiii.d. ob' ut idem Walterus versus eum queritur ideo preceptum est levare de predicto Willelmo predictos iiii.d. ob' ad opus predicti Walteri. Et nichilominus idem Willlemus pro iniusta detencione in misericordia per plegium Hugonis Laurenc'.[5]

Translation:

[*Amercement*] *1d.* It appears by the inquest jury that William Perchey owes and unjustly detains from Walter le Smyth 4½*d.*, as the same Walter complains against him. Therefore order is made to levy the aforesaid 4½*d.* from the aforesaid William to the use of the aforesaid Walter. And the same William is nonetheless in mercy for unjust detention, by pledge of Hugh Laurence.

misericordia ii.d. / preceptum est levare Compertum est per inquisitionem in quam se posuerunt Johannes Bonde querens et Robertus Smyth defendens in placito debiti

[3] CRO, R 93/96, m.4 (Littleport, 27 July 1317).
[4] CUL, Q 3, m.7d (Oakington, 28 May 1327).
[5] LMA, ACC/1876/MR/02/010, m.4 (Balsham, 11 June 1347).

quod idem Robertus debet sibi etc. xii.d. quos ei promisit soluere ad festum Pasche ultimo preterito ad dampna sua taxata ad ii.d. ideo consideratum etc. et predictus Robertus in misericordia et preceptum est levare.[6]

Translation:

Amercement 2d. / order is made to levy It appears by the inquest jury in which John Bonde plaintiff, and Robert Smyth, defendant, placed themselves that the same Robert owes to him 12*d.* which he promised to pay to him at Easter last past, to his damage taxed at 2*d.* Therefore it is considered, etc., and the aforesaid Robert is in mercy, and order is made to levy.

5 'Pleaded' case terminated by the defendant's acknowledgement of liability:

misericordia vi.d. Michael Kygel attachiatus fuit ad respondendum Roberto le Cartere de placito quod reddat ei duodecim solidos quos ei debet etc. Et predictus Michael venit et cognouit predictum debitum ideo consideratum est quod predictus Robertus recuperet versus eum dictos denarios una cum dampna taxantur ad vi.d. Et pro detencione in misericordia. Et preceptum est levare dictos denarios ad opus dicti Roberti.[7]

Translation:

Amercement 6d. Michael Kygel was attached to respond to Robert le Cartere in a plea that he should render to him 12*s.* which he owed to him. And the aforesaid Michael came and acknowledged the aforesaid debt, therefore it is considered that the aforesaid Robert shall recover against him the said money together with the damages, taxed at 6*d.* And for detention, [Michael] is in mercy. And order is made to levy the said money to the use of the said Robert.

6 Debt case against a pledge (personal surety) of the principal debtor:

misericordia iii.d. / preceptum est levare Nicholaus Soutere cognouit se debere Johanni Cake juniori xiiii.d. de quibus devenit plegius Thome Tredegold quos ei soluisse debuit et nondum soluit ideo etc. Et dampna remittuntur per querentem. Et preceptum est.[8]

Translation:

Amercement 3d. / order is made to levy Nicholas Soutere acknowledged himself to owe 14*d.* to John Cake junior, concerning which he became pledge of Thomas Tredegold, and which he ought to have paid but did not pay, therefore, etc. And the damages are remitted by the plaintiff. And order is made.

[6] CUL, Q 7, m.4 (Oakington, 15 October 1369).
[7] CRO, R 93/96, m.20 (Littleport, 1 March 1325).
[8] CRO, L1/177, m.41 (Willingham, 11 December 1391).

7 The enforcement of debt recovery through the manor court:

preceptum est levare / misericordia vi.d. Compertum est per Iuratam in quam se posuerunt Johannes le Gray querens et Willelmus le Warde <defendens>[i] in placito debiti quod predictus Willelmus in iuste detinet predicto Johanni iii.s. vii.d. ob' et dampna que taxantur ad ii.s. Ideo consideratum est per curiam quod predictus Johannes recuperet versus predictum Willelmum dictos iii.s. vii.d. ob' simul cum dampnis predictis. Et predictus Willelmus in misericordia pro in iusta detencione.[9]

Translation:

Order is made to levy / amercement 6d. It appears by the jury in which John le Gray, plaintiff, and William le Warde, defendant, placed themselves in a plea of debt that the aforesaid William unjustly detains from the aforesaid John 3*s.* 7½*d.*, and damages which are taxed at 2*s.* Therefore it is considered by the court that the aforesaid John shall recover the said 3*s.* 7½*d.* against the aforesaid William, together with the aforesaid damages. And the aforesaid William is in mercy for unjust detention.

Preceptum est / sine die Preceptum est sicut prius levare de Willelmo le Warde v.s. vii.d. ob' ad opus Johannis le Grey quos versus eum recuperauit ad curiam precedentem.[10]

Translation:

Order is made / [he goes] without a day Order is made as before to levy 5*s.* 7½*d.* from William le Warde to the use of John le Grey, which he recovered against him at the preceding court.

[9] CUL, Q 3, m.26d (Oakington, 12 May 1337).

[10] CUL, Q 3, m.25d (Oakington, 14 July 1337). It is not entirely clear why this entry includes the marginal note *sine die*. Possibly it was added to show that William had in fact repaid the outstanding sum since the previous court.

Appendix 2

Identifying individual creditors and debtors and their characteristics

Chapters 4 and 5 presented a detailed discussion of people: their numbers, their attributes, and their roles in the rural credit market. Of course, information of that kind cannot simply be harvested in a convenient form from the sources. Instead, in order to generate the tables and figures contained and discussed in those chapters, much sorting and analysis of the court roll data was required. To a certain extent, the nature of the findings discussed in those chapters is dependent upon the methodology used to sort and analyse the raw materials. Consequently, it is necessary to give a somewhat more extensive account of that methodology than the chapters themselves provide. The objective of this appendix is thus to describe in greater detail and to justify the techniques used both in the initial collection of the court roll information, and in the identification of individuals and their characteristics.[1]

Court roll data collection

The method of data collection applied to all five court roll series was selective. That is, no attempt was made to extract every single court roll entry and input it into the database.[2] Two different kinds of selective approach were used. The first was employed only in the 'core' court roll series, those of Oakington (to 1380) and Horwood. The second was used for Oakington between 1381 and 1400, and for the three remaining series of Balsham, Willingham, and Littleport.

In a preliminary trawl through the Horwood and pre-1381 Oakington rolls, every debt litigation entry was collected. Lists of all debt litigants were thereby produced for both courts. These lists formed the basis of the main data entry process, which involved inputting into a Microsoft Access database all the court roll entries of any kind that mention a name or names on the lists. Although selective, this method in effect makes machine readable the greater part of the contents of the court rolls. The result is a complete record of the citations of all the debt litigants' names, in whatever form they appear. If, for example, a man named 'Johannes Smygth' appeared in a debt case, all entries mentioning the name 'John Smith' (including all the various English and Latin spellings of the surname), plus any form such as 'John son of Roger Smith',

[1] For a fuller discussion of aspects of the methodology covered here, see Briggs, 'Rural credit', 321–33.

[2] The exceptions are the Oakington rolls of 1349–80 and the Horwood rolls of 1302–9, periods for which the records were made machine readable in their entirety.

or 'John Smith the Hayward', were inputted. Only later did the job begin of determining which of these citations referred to a single individual.

In certain specific aspects, of course, data collection from these Oakington and Horwood rolls needed to be exhaustive rather than selective. For example, every temporary lease of portions of customary land was collected.

From the rolls of Oakington after 1380, and from those of Balsham, Willingham, and Littleport, only the entries concerning debt litigation and interpersonal suits of 'unknown' type were extracted and entered in the databases. However, the court rolls of the three last-mentioned manors were trawled again following the analysis of the debt litigation in an effort to find relevant non-debt entries.

Identification of individual creditors and debtors

In identifying creditors and debtors, the processes used for Oakington (to 1380) and Horwood again differed from those used on the remaining court roll series. The aim in all cases, however, was to turn a list of debt litigants' names into a list of distinct individuals, each of whom would be given a unique 'Litigant Number'. For all manors, two lists of individuals were generated: the first consisting of the debt plaintiffs and defendants, the second consisting of the creditors and debtors. The composition of these two groups differs very slightly, for reasons given at the end of this section. Throughout, standardization of variously spelled names was used to aid the process of identifying individuals.[3]

The more exhaustive method was that applied to the Oakington (to 1380) and Horwood sources. This method constitutes an attempt to identify individuals without also undertaking a comprehensive reconstitution of the families to which they belonged.[4] The central task of the litigant identification process was to attach a Litigant Number to each citation of a personal name or names deemed to belong to an individual. For example, the plaintiff in the first debt case in the Horwood rolls was John Hildich. Therefore Litigant Number 1 was given to that particular citation of that John Hildich, and to a further forty-five out of the total of sixty citations of the name 'John Hildich'. Together, those forty-six citations, or entries, were all taken to refer to the same man, and collectively, the information in them comprises Hildich's court roll 'biography'.

Allocating Litigant Numbers to name citations was not always straightforward, however, owing to two well-known problems to do with surname instability. These are: (1) some individual villagers were referred to in the records by means of more than one surname; and (2) an identical name was often borne by more than one individual.

In neither case can it be claimed that any effects of these problems upon the correct identification of individuals have been entirely eliminated. On the other hand,

[3] In citing court roll entries and discussing individuals in this book, I have used either the most frequently occurring contemporary spelling of a person's surname or, where there is an obvious modern version of a surname, the standard modern spelling.

[4] For discussions of the interconnected processes of identifying individuals and reconstructing families from medieval manorial court rolls, and of the possibility of accomplishing the former without the latter, see Razi, *Life, marriage and death*, 15–24; Bennett, 'Spouses, siblings and surnames'; Bennett, *Women*, 199–205; Clarke, 'Peasant society', 31–40; Parkin, 'Courts and the community', 59–75; Phillips, 'Collaboration and litigation', 183–90.

errors have been minimized as far as is possible without undertaking the kind of exhaustive analysis of court roll data which would have drastically reduced the temporal span of the study and the number of communities covered. Problem (1) is the lesser of the two. One may concur with Bennett that the researcher is usually able to catch many instances of an individual having multiple surnames.[5] Where it was discovered that a debt litigant was known and recorded by more than one surname, all the relevant surnames were included on the list when searching for citations of known litigants. In some cases, the realization that a person was known by more than one surname occurred relatively late in the main data entry process, with the result that a secondary trawl of the court rolls was required.

Problem (2) formed a potentially greater obstacle to the correct allocation of Litigant Numbers. In dealing with this problem, the analysis proceeded on the assumption that the court clerks tried to distinguish between court suitors who shared the same name. Bennett gave great weight to this principle.[6] Numerous examples from Oakington and Horwood can be cited to support it, such as that of the four John Carpenters who regularly attended the Horwood court in the 1330s and 1340s, and whom the clerks distinguished by recording the men respectively as 'Johannes Carpenter', 'Johannes Carpenter junior', 'Johannes de Buk' carpentarius', and 'Johannes Carpenter' de Westbury'.[7] On the basis of such evidence, it was assumed that where two citations of the same basic name took differing forms—such as, for example, with and without a 'junior' added—this was because the citations referred to distinct individuals. This principle was most useful in sorting out different members of a family who shared the same forename. Thus the 'unmodified' form of a name, such as 'John Smith', was usually used to record a manorial tenant who owed suit of court. A 'John son of John Smith' active at the same time as a 'John Smith' was almost certainly a different individual, probably the son of the first man. When in time he inherited his father's holding, however, John son of John Smith would become plain John Smith. It is also clear the court clerks usually, if not invariably, distinguished between manorial tenants who shared a name. This is revealed by an analysis of the Oakington and Cottenham suitor lists, and the 1320 Horwood extent, which in any case strongly suggests that the simultaneous possession of the same name by multiple individuals was not widespread.[8]

In the case of Oakington, problem (2) was exacerbated somewhat by the fact that the court covered manors in three villages. This situation makes the likelihood of finding multiple individuals in the records sharing a name greater than it is when the court rolls cover just one manor. If, to take a hypothetical example, a debt case involved someone called John Smith, but it is clear that two different John Smiths—one of Oakington, and one of Cottenham—were alive at the same time, how does one know

[5] Bennett writes, 'although the incidence of . . . aliases is impossible to tabulate fully, the use of multiple surnames is relatively rare': 'Spouses, siblings and surnames', 38.

[6] 'The entire manorial record system was based upon the precise identification of the manor's residents in its account rolls and court rolls; how were lands to be administered and rents to be collected if several villagers shared an indistinguishable name?': 'Spouses, siblings and surnames', 38; see also *Women*, 201.

[7] Briggs, 'Rural credit', 324–5.

[8] Briggs, 'Rural credit', 326–7.

which of these was the man in the debt case, and furthermore, how is one to determine which of the numerous non-debt citations of 'John Smith' refer to the debt litigant? Fortunately, the medieval clerks made this job somewhat easier for the historian by routinely inserting the name, or initial letter, of each village—Oakington, Cottenham, and Drayton—in the margin of the roll as a heading, and then grouping the business involving residents or tenants of each place under the appropriate heading. Quite often, too, clerks distinguished, say, William Katelyne of Oakington from William Katelyne of Cottenham, by inserting 'of Oakington' in citations of the former's name. Sometimes, however, it was necessary to use slightly less reliable methods when determining which of two or more people from different places but with the same name one is looking at. For example, some such debt litigants were identified by inference from the place of residence of their opponent in the debt case.

For the Balsham, Willingham, Littleport, and post-1380 Oakington material, a simpler method of identifying individuals was used. Given the method of data collection adopted for those villages it was not possible, as it had been with pre-1381 Oakington and Horwood, to scrutinize every court roll citation of a particular name, and then to determine which citations referred to which debt litigant. Instead, the approach used for Balsham, Willingham, Littleport, and post-1380 Oakington was based on the simple principle that differently named litigants represent different individuals. As with the Horwood and pre-1381 Oakington rolls, it was assumed again that where both a 'modified' and an 'unmodified' form of the same basic name occurred, this was because the clerks wanted to know which one of several similarly named individuals they were referring to. Thus, for example, at Willingham, the citations 'John Prikke de le Esthonde', 'John Prikke in the Lane', 'John Prikke senior', and 'John Prikke junior' may all be taken to denote distinct persons, and were therefore given different Litigant Numbers. The system of distinguishing individual litigants adopted for post-1380 Oakington, Balsham, Willingham, and Littleport was necessarily cruder than that employed for the two 'core' case studies. However, it was deemed reliable enough, especially given the relatively short spans of time covered by the relevant rolls, to provide the basis for analysis included in Chapters 4 and 5.

As noted earlier, two slightly different groups of individuals plus their Litigant Numbers were produced for each village. The first group consisted of the plaintiffs and defendants, that is, the parties to the debt cases. However, the plaintiff in a debt case was not necessarily always the same person as the creditor in the disputed debt that formed the subject of that case. Similarly, the defendant in a debt action and the original debtor in the disputed debt could be two different people. Since Chapters 4 and 5 are about creditors and debtors, it was necessary to base them on listings of individuals which excluded people who appeared in court to prosecute a lawsuit, but had not themselves been involved in the transaction that was at issue.

Two main types of debt plaint required special treatment on these grounds: the post-mortem cases, and the cases involving personal sureties, or pledges. With the post-mortem cases, the decedent was always included in the analysis in the role of creditor or debtor, and the executors who appeared in court in connection with debts owed by or to him were excluded. With the pledge cases, the pledges who sued or were sued in the debt action were excluded. Instead, the principal creditor or debtor—the person for whom the pledge had stood surety—was incorporated into the investigations that underpin Chapters 4 and 5.

A final problem connected with the identification of creditors and debtors merits a mention. Sometimes, and especially in the Willingham rolls, a debt case was terminated via a 'licence to agree' without an explicit statement of which party was the plaintiff/creditor and which the defendant/debtor. In these cases, it has been assumed that the party who paid the court amercement for the 'licence to agree' was the defendant/debtor. This assumption is justified by the fact that in 'licence to agree' terminations in which the record does distinguish plaintiff and defendant, it was almost always the defendant who paid the amercement.

Attributing landholdings to creditors and debtors

Chapter 4 presented evidence on the landed holdings of creditors and debtors. Here, further details are added concerning the method by which a person's landholdings were established. Attention was restricted to property held within a 'debt period' during which, it is assumed, an individual's lending or borrowing took place. A 'debt period' was set for each of the creditors and debtors, and was intended to correspond roughly to the period of time in which the individual concerned carried out his or her lending or borrowing. Credit activity, of course, could occur many months prior to the debt plaint in which it is recorded. For this reason, the 'debt period' covers the ten years preceding an individual's appearance in a debt plaint as creditor or debtor. If the individual had several appearances in one capacity, the 'debt period' is dated from ten years before that individual's first appearance in a debt plaint, and runs until the date of the last such appearance. So, for example, if a man is recorded as creditor in 1320 and again in 1325, his 'debt period' runs from 1310 to 1325. A person who acted as both creditor and debtor at different times has two different 'debt periods': one as creditor, and one as debtor.[9]

The aim was to identify the holdings or combination of holdings that an individual enjoyed rights to and use of for all or part of the debt period. It was a requirement that there be no reason to doubt that the individual was able to cultivate freely or otherwise benefit from the property in question. Most of the land taken into account was held according to customary hereditable tenure, but villein land held according to custom for a specified term of years or for a life term was also included. Excluded from consideration were short-term inter-tenant leases of five years or less. Most of the information naturally comes from entries on land transfer in the court rolls, but the Oakington and Drayton rentals and Horwood extent were also used as a check on the picture provided by the court rolls.[10] Where freehold land was mentioned it was incorporated, if appropriate, into the landholding record of a particular creditor or debtor. In the case of Horwood, evidence about freehold land was taken not only from the court rolls but also from the surviving charters. Many of the personal names contained in the court rolls also appear in the charters, and it has been assumed that the same individuals were being referred to in each source. Tables 4.8 and 4.9 attempt to indicate the maximum combination of holdings held by an individual at any one time within the debt period. Unfortunately, it is not always possible

[9] For the 'debt period', see also Briggs, 'Rural credit', 230–2.

[10] Incidental court roll references to tenants' property, as well as details of its transfer, were also used.

to determine exactly how long particular properties were held for, but it was assumed that properties were in fact occupied within the 'debt period' unless there is a strong indication otherwise.

Usually, the task of building up a picture of an individual's landholdings—or at least those holdings revealed by the available records—was achieved in fairly straightforward manner by applying the criteria outlined above. However, certain types of entry caused particular difficulties. For example, some creditors and debtors acted as guardians of minors and held custody over the minor's land. Such property was excluded from consideration in compiling the landholding record of that individual. This is because it is uncertain how far the guardian was able to make use of the ward's land for his own economic benefit. Perhaps a more significant issue is raised by the fact that in the Oakington rolls marriage, especially the remarriage of widows with dower land, was a common mode of villein land transfer on the Crowland manors in the early fourteenth century. Quite a number of the deceased husbands of widows, and men who paid fines to marry widows in this way, were also creditors and debtors. For the purposes of making attributions of landholding, the deceased husband was treated as the sole tenant of the land prior to his death, just as the new husband was treated as enjoying the same status upon remarriage.[11] It is necessary to make it clear that the new husband, rather than the widow, has been regarded as the holder of the tenement the widow brought with her, especially since such remarriages were very common and a different interpretation would substantially affect the data presented.[12] Such marriages with land also occurred at Horwood, but are rare compared with those of Oakington, Cottenham, and Drayton. The Horwood custom was that the widow should receive a third of her deceased husband's holding as dower, whereas widows on the Crowland manors received the holding in its entirety.[13] Such dower lands are taken into account in Chapter 4, where any lands held by female creditors and debtors in their own right are included in Tables 4.8 and 4.9.

[11] Often no independent record is found of the first husband's death, and the only indicator of the land he held during his lifetime consists of the remarriage of his widow.

[12] A widow on the Crowland manors ought to have forfeited her husband's holding to the lord if she remarried: Page, 'Customary poor law', 126. In practice, however, the fine paid allowed the new husband entry to the property: Ravensdale, 'Population changes', 201–3; Smith, 'Some thoughts', 124. By contrast, as Bennett notes, on manors such as Brigstock, the widow held her free bench for life, and did not relinquish such properties at remarriage: Bennett, *Women*, 164.

[13] Poos and Bonfield (eds.), *Select cases*, 97, 101–2; Page, 'Customary poor law', 125–6.

Bibliography

Manuscripts

NB Most series of manorial documents listed below feature gaps within the date range.

Cambridge, Cambridgeshire Record Office

L1/177–9	Manorial court rolls of Willingham, Cambs., 1377–1458
619/M1–2	Manorial court rolls of Great Abington, Cambs., 1287–1400
R 93/96	Manorial court rolls of Littleport, Cambs., 1285 and 1316–27
Palmer/Barnard, Vol. I	Draft Cambridge borough court book, 1389–90

Cambridge, Corpus Christi College Archives

XXXV/121–2	Manorial court rolls of Landbeach, Cambs., 1327–98
XXXVII/1–2	Manorial court rolls of Barton, Cambs. (Lancaster manor), 1356–1400

Cambridge, King's College Archives

BAR/261, BAR/296	Manorial court rolls of Barton, Cambs. (Priory manor), 1326–47
GRA/284–5	Manorial court rolls of Grantchester, Cambs., 1398–1400

Cambridge, Pembroke College Archives

Framlingham rolls A1	Manorial court rolls of Framlingham, Suffolk, 1331–58

Cambridge, Trinity College Archives

Box 27, rolls 1–5	Manorial court rolls of Foxton, Cambs., 1276–1325

Cambridge University Library

Queens' College (Q) Boxes 1–2, 6	Thirteenth- and fourteenth-century account rolls of the manors of Oakington, Cottenham, and Dry Drayton, Cambs.
Q Boxes 3–4, rolls 1–10 and 12	Manorial court rolls of Oakington, Cambs., 1291–1400
Q Box 8	Account rolls of Oakington, Cottenham, and Dry Drayton, 1321–2; rentals of Oakington and Dry Drayton, 1344

Q Box 11	Manorial court rolls of Great Eversden, Cambs., 1382–99
EDC 7/13/2–5	Manorial court rolls of Swaffham Prior, Cambs., 1281–1377
EDR D/2/1	Register of the consistory court of the bishop of Ely's Official, 1374–82

London, British Library

Add. MS 5845	Extracts from a fourteenth-century 'leiger' of Crowland Abbey copied by William Cole, 1772
Add. Ch. 18521, 18523–5, 18530	Manorial court rolls of Harston, Cambs., 1313–1400

London Metropolitan Archives

ACC/1876/MR/02/001–011	Manorial court rolls of Balsham, Cambs., 1310–49
HO1/ST/E/079/1–18	Manorial court rolls of Meldreth, Cambs., 1316–95

London, The National Archives

E 179/81/7	County roll for Cambridgeshire and the Isle of Ely, lay subsidy of 1315
E 179/81/6	County roll for Cambridgeshire and the Isle of Ely, lay subsidy of 1327
E 179/242/86	Local assessment of Great Horwood, Bucks., lay subsidy of 1327
E 315/79	Manorial court rolls of Fulbourn, Cambs., 1361–1400
SC 2/155/47–52	Manorial court rolls of Bottisham, Cambs., 1320–72

London, Westminster Abbey Muniments

WAM 14544–14552	Manorial court rolls of West Halton, Lincs., 1313–42

Norwich, Norfolk Record Office

NRS 10115 2F6	Manorial court rolls of Blickling, Norfolk, 1311–25

Oxford, New College Archives

NCA 3912–3915	Manorial court rolls of Great Horwood, Bucks., 1302–98
NCA 4503	Extent of the manor of Great Horwood, Bucks., 1320
NCA 9744	Register of *c.*1530 (the *Liber Niger*)
NCA Horwood Charters	Fourteenth-century charters, nos. 15, 18, 22, 27, 28, 30–1, 33, 36, 39, 41–2, 44–52

Printed primary sources

Bailey, M. (ed.), *The English manor, c.1250–c.1500* (Manchester, 2002).

Beardwood, A. (ed.), *The Statute Merchant roll of Coventry, 1392–1416*, Dugdale Soc., Vol. XVII (London, 1939).

Brooke, C.N.L., and Postan, M.M. (eds.), *Carte nativorum. A Peterborough Abbey cartulary of the fourteenth century*, Northamptonshire Record Soc., Vol. XX (1960).

Cunningham, W. (ed.), *Common rights at Cottenham and Stretham in Cambridgeshire*, Camden Miscellany, Vol. XII (London, 1910).

Evelyn-White, C.H. (ed.), *Cambridgeshire and the Isle of Ely: lay subsidy for the year 1327*, *East Anglian*, new series 10–12 (1903–8).

Franklin, P. (ed.), *The taxpayers of medieval Gloucestershire: an analysis of the 1327 lay subsidy roll with a new edition of its text* (Stroud, 1993).

Horrox, R. (ed.), *The Black Death* (Manchester, 1994).

Index of Placita de Banco preserved in the Public Record Office. AD 1327–1328. Part I. Bedford to Norfolk, List and Index Soc., Vol. XXXII (London, 1909).

Lister, J. (ed.), *Court rolls of the manor of Wakefield, Vol. IV: 1315 to 1317*, Yorkshire Archaeological Soc. Record Series, Vol. LXXVIII (1930).

Lock, R. (ed.), *The court rolls of Walsham le Willows, 1303–50*, Suffolk Record Soc., Vol. XLI (1998).

Maitland, F.W., and Baildon, W.P. (eds.), *The Court Baron: being precedents for use in seignorial and other local courts, together with select pleas from the Bishop of Ely's court of Littleport*, Selden Soc., Vol. IV (London, 1890).

Mannyng, Robert, *Handlyng synne*, ed. I. Sullens, Medieval & Renaissance Texts and Studies (Binghamton, NY, 1983).

Poos, L.R., and Bonfield, L. (eds.), *Select cases in manorial courts 1250–1550: property and family law*, Selden Soc., Vol. CXIV (London, 1998).

Reyerson, K., and Salata, D.A. (eds.), *Medieval notaries and their acts: the 1327–1328 register of Jean Holanie*, Medieval Institute Publications (Kalamazoo, 2004).

Rotuli hundredorum temp. Hen. III & Edw. I, Record Commission (2 vols., London, 1812–18).

Salter, H.E. (ed.), *Newington Longville charters*, Oxford Record Soc., Vol. III (1921).

Thomas A.H. (ed.), *Calendar of plea and memoranda rolls preserved among the archives of the corporation of the City of London at the Guildhall, AD 1323– 1437* (4 vols., Cambridge, 1926–43).

Secondary sources

Allen, M., 'The fourteenth-century hoard from Chesterton Lane corner, Cambridge', *British Numismatic Journal*, 75 (2005), 63–90.

Allen, M., 'The proportions of the denominations in English mint outputs, 1351–1485', *British Numismatic Journal*, 77 (2007), 190–209.

Allen, M., 'The volume and composition of the silver currency, 1279–1351', *British Numismatic Journal*, 70 (2000), 38–44.

Allen, M., 'The volume of the English currency, 1158–1470', *Economic History Review*, 54 (2001), 595–611.

Ault, W.O., *Open-field farming in medieval England: a study of village by-laws* (London, 1972).

Ault, W.O., *Open-field husbandry and the village community: a study of agrarian by-laws in medieval England, Transactions of the American Philosophical Society*, new series, 55 (Philadelphia, 1965).

Bailey, M., 'Peasant welfare in England, 1290–1348', *Economic History Review*, 51 (1998), 223–51.

Bainbridge, V.R., *Gilds in the medieval countryside: social and religious change in Cambridgeshire, c.1350–1558* (Woodbridge, 1996).

Barton, J.L., 'The common law mortgage', *Law Quarterly Review*, 83 (1967), 229–39.

Béaur, G., 'Foncier et crédit dans les sociétés préindustrielles: des liens solides ou des chaînes fragiles', *Annales. Histoire, Sciences Sociales*, 49 (1994), 1411–28.

Beck, P., 'Historiographie du marché de la terre au Moyen Âge en France médiane (Lyonnais, Bourgogne, Orléanais, Vendômois, Maine, Anjou, Bretagne)', in Feller and Wickham (eds.), *Le marché de la terre*, 113–29.

Beckerman, J.S., 'Customary law in English manorial courts in the thirteenth and fourteenth centuries', Ph.D. thesis (London, 1972).

Beckerman, J.S., 'Procedural innovation and institutional change in medieval English manorial courts', *Law and History Review*, 10 (1992), 197–252.

Bell, A., Brooks, C., and Dryburgh, P.R., *The English wool market, c.1230–1327* (Cambridge, 2007).

Bennett, J.M., 'Spouses, siblings and surnames: reconstructing families from medieval village court rolls', *Journal of British Studies*, 23 (1983), 26–46.

Bennett, J.M., *Women in the medieval English countryside: gender and household in Brigstock before the plague* (Oxford, 1987).

Berthe, M., 'Marché de la terre et hiérarchie paysanne dans le Lauragais toulousain vers 1270–vers 1320', in E. Mornet (ed.), *Campagnes médiévales: l'homme et son espace. Etudes offertes à Robert Fossier* (Paris, 1995), 297–311.

Berthe, M. (ed.), *Endettement paysan et crédit rural dans l'Europe médiévale et moderne: Actes des XVIIes journées internationales d'histoire de l'abbaye de Flaran, Septembre 1995* (Toulouse, 1998).

Bocchi, F., 'I debiti dei contadini (1235). Note sulla piccola proprieta' terriera Bolognese nella crisi del feudalesimo', in *Studi in memoria di Luigi del Pane* (Bologna, 1982), 169–209.

Bottomley, A. 'Interest rate determination in underdeveloped rural areas', in J.D. von Pischke, D.W. Adams, and G. Donald (eds.), *Rural financial markets in developing countries: their use and abuse* (Baltimore, 1983), 243–50.

Bowers, R.H., 'From rolls to riches: king's clerks and moneylending in thirteenth-century England', *Speculum*, 58 (1983), 60–71.

Brand, P., 'Aspects of the law of debt, 1189–1307', in Schofield and Mayhew (eds.), *Credit and debt*, 19–41.

Brennan, T., 'Peasants and debt in eighteenth-century Champagne', *Journal of Interdisciplinary History*, 37 (2006), 175–200.

Briggs, C., 'The availability of credit in the English countryside, 1400–1480', *Agricultural History Review*, 56 (2008), 1–24.

Briggs, C., 'Credit and the freehold land market in England, 1200–1350: possibilities and problems for research', in T. Lambrecht and P.R. Schofield (eds.), *Credit and the rural economy in Europe, c.1100–1850* (Comparative Rural History of the North Sea Area (CORN) publications series), forthcoming.

Briggs, C., 'Credit and the peasant household economy in England before the Black Death: evidence from a Cambridgeshire manor', in C. Beattie, A. Maslakovic, and S. Rees Jones (eds.), *The medieval household in Christian Europe c.850–c.1550: managing power, wealth and the body* (Turnhout, 2003), 231–48.

Briggs, C., 'Creditors and debtors and their relationships at Oakington, Cottenham and Dry Drayton (Cambridgeshire), 1291–1350', in Schofield and Mayhew (eds.), *Credit and debt*, 127–48.

Briggs, C., 'Empowered or marginalized? Rural women and credit in later thirteenth- and fourteenth-century England', *Continuity and Change*, 19 (2004), 13–43.

Briggs, C., 'Manor court procedures, debt litigation levels, and rural credit provision in England, *c.*1290–*c.*1380', *Law and History Review*, 23 (2006), 519–58.

Briggs, C.D., 'Rural credit, debt litigation and manor courts in England, *c.*1290–*c.*1380', Ph.D. thesis (Cambridge, 2003).

Briggs, C., 'Seigniorial control of villagers' litigation beyond the manor in later medieval England', *Historical Research*, 81 (2008), 399–422.

Briggs, C., 'Taxation, warfare, and the early fourteenth century "crisis" in the north: Cumberland lay subsidies, 1332–1348', *Economic History Review*, 58 (2005), 639–72.

Briggs, C., 'Travelling in search of civil justice: English villagers and the law in England, 1275–1400', unpublished paper.

Briggs, C., 'What proportion of an English village's population was involved in credit networks *c.*1377?', in P. Maurice (ed.), *Le crédit au Moyen Âge*, forthcoming.

Britnell, R.H., 'Commercialisation and economic development in England, 1000–1300', in Britnell and Campbell (eds.), *A commercialising economy*, 7–26.

Britnell, R.H., *The commercialisation of English society, 1000–1500* (2nd edn., Manchester, 1996).

Britnell, R.H., *Growth and decline in Colchester, 1300–1525* (Cambridge, 1986).

Britnell, R.H., and Campbell, B.M.S. (eds.), *A commercialising economy: England, 1086 to c.1300* (Cambridge, 1995).

Campbell, B.M.S., 'The agrarian problem in the early fourteenth century', *Past & Present*, 188 (2005), 3–70.

Campbell, B.M.S., 'Population pressure, inheritance and the land market in a fourteenth-century peasant community', in Smith (ed.), *Land, kinship and life-cycle*, 87–134.

Campbell, B.M.S., *Three centuries of English crops yields, 1211–1491* (2007): http://www.cropyields.ac.uk (accessed on 27/02/2008).

Campbell, B.M.S., 'A unique estate and a unique source: the Winchester Pipe Rolls in perspective', in R. Britnell (ed.), *The Winchester Pipe Rolls and medieval English society* (Woodbridge, 2003), 21–43.

Campbell, B.M.S. (ed.), *Before the Black Death: studies in the 'crisis' of the early fourteenth century* (Manchester, 1991).

Campbell, B.M.S., and Bartley, K., *England on the eve of the Black Death: an atlas of lay lordship, land and wealth, 1300–49* (Manchester, 2006).

Cavaciocchi, S. (ed.), *Il mercato della terra secc. XIII–XVIII. Atti delle 'Trentacinquesima Settimana di Studi', 5–9 Maggio 2003* (Instituto Internazionale di Storia Economica 'F. Datini', Prato, 2004).

Challis, C.E. (ed.), *A new history of the Royal Mint* (Cambridge, 1992).

Cheney, C.R., *Notaries public in England in the thirteenth and fourteenth centuries* (Oxford, 1972).

Childs, W., '"To oure losse and hindraunce": English credit to alien merchants in the mid-fifteenth century', in J. Kermode (ed.), *Enterprise and individuals in fifteenth-century England* (Stroud, 1991), 68–98.

Clanchy, M.T., *From memory to written record: England, 1066–1307* (2nd edn., Oxford, 1993).

Clark, E., 'Debt litigation in a late medieval English vill', in J.A. Raftis (ed.), *Pathways to medieval peasants* (Toronto, 1981), 247–79.

Clark, E., 'Medieval debt litigation: Essex and Norfolk, 1270–1490', Ph.D. thesis (Michigan, 1977).

Clarke, C., 'Peasant society and land transactions in Chesterton, Cambridgeshire, 1277–1325', D.Phil. thesis (Oxford, 1983).

Coleman, M.C., *Downham-in-the-Isle: a study of an ecclesiastical manor in the thirteenth and fourteenth centuries* (Woodbridge, 1984).

Coulton, G.G., *The medieval village* (Cambridge, 1925).

Darby, H.C., *The medieval fenland* (2nd edn., Cambridge, 1974).

Dobson, R.B., 'The Jews of medieval Cambridge', *Jewish Historical Studies*, 32 (1990–2), 1–24.

Drendel, J., 'Commodities, credit and land on the local market and on the urban market; the role of secondary agglomerations in the economy: comparison of Anglo-Saxon and French historiography', in Cavaciocchi (ed.), *Il mercato della terra*, 685–702.

Drendel, J., 'Le crédit dans les archives notariales de Basse-Provence (haute vallée de l'Arc) au début du XIVe siècle', in Menant and Redon (eds.), *Notaires et crédit*, 279–305.

Drendel, J., 'Gens d'église et crédit dans la vallée de Trets au XIVe siècle', *Provence Historique*, 44 (1994), 77–88.

Drendel, J., 'Le marché de la terre dans la haute vallée de l'Arc au début du XIVe siècle', in Feller and Wickham (eds.), *Le marché de la terre*, 429–44.

Drendel, J., 'Notarial practice in rural Provence in the early fourteenth century', in Reyerson and Drendel (eds.), *Urban and rural communities*, 209–35.

Drendel, J., 'Society and economy in a medieval Provençal town: Trets, 1296–1347', Ph.D. thesis (Toronto, 1991).

Duby, G., *Rural economy and country life in the medieval West* (London, 1968).

Dyer, C., *An age of transition? Economy and society in England in the later middle ages* (Oxford, 2005).

Dyer, C., 'Market towns and the countryside in late medieval England', *Canadian Journal of History*, 31 (1996), 17–35.

Dyer, C., 'Peasants and coins: the uses of money in the middle ages', *British Numismatic Journal*, 67 (1997), 30–47.

Dyer, C., 'The political life of the fifteenth-century English village', *The Fifteenth Century*, 4 (2004), 135–57.

Dyer, C., 'Seigniorial profits on the landmarket in late medieval England', in Feller and Wickham (eds.), *Le marché de la terre*, 219–36.

Dyer, C., 'Small towns, 1270–1540', in Palliser (ed.), *Cambridge urban history*, 505–37.

Dyer, C., *Standards of living in the later middle ages: social change in England c.1200–1520* (revised edn., Cambridge, 1998).

Dyer, C., and Schofield, P.R., 'Recent works on the agrarian history of medieval Britain', in I. Alfonso (ed.), *The rural history of medieval European societies: trends and perspectives* (Turnhout, 2007), 21–55.

Engerman, S.L., Hoffman, P.T., Rosenthal, J.-L., and Sokoloff, K.L. (eds.), *Finance, intermediaries, and economic development* (Cambridge, 2003).

Farmer, D.L., 'Grain yields on the Winchester manors in the later middle ages', *Economic History Review*, 30 (1977), 555–66.

Farmer, D.L., 'Prices and wages', in H.E. Hallam (ed.), *The agrarian history of England and Wales, I: 1052–1350* (Cambridge, 1988), 715–817.

Farmer, D.L., 'Prices and wages, 1350–1500', in E. Miller (ed.), *The agrarian history of England and Wales, II: 1348–1500* (Cambridge, 1991), 431–525.

Feller, L., and Wickham, C. (eds.), *Le marché de la terre au Moyen Âge* (Rome, 2005).

Finucane, R.C., 'Two notaries and their records in England, 1282–1307', *Journal of Medieval History*, 13 (1987), 1–14.

French, H.R., and Hoyle, R.W., 'The land market of a Pennine manor: Slaidburn, 1650–1780', *Continuity and Change*, 14 (1999), 349–83.

Furió, A., 'Crédit, endettement et justice: prêteurs et débiteurs devant le juge dans le royaume de Valence (XIIIe–XVe siècles)', in J. Claustre (ed.), *La dette et le juge. Juridiction gracieuse et juridiction contentieuse du xiiie au xve siècle (France, Italie, Espagne, Angleterre, Empire)* (Paris, 2006), 19–53.

Furió, A., 'Le crédit dans les registres notariaux de la région de Valence au bas Moyen Âge', *Mélanges de l'École Française de Rome: Moyen Âge*, 117 (2005), 407–39.

Furió A., and Mira Jodar, A., 'Le marché de la terre dans le pays de Valence au bas Moyen Âge', in Feller and Wickham (eds.), *Le marché de la terre*, 573–623.

Galloway, J.A., 'Urban hinterlands in later medieval England', in K. Giles and C. Dyer (eds.), *Town and country in the middle ages: contrasts, contacts and interconnections, 1100–1500* (Leeds, 2005), 111–30.

Gaulin, J.-L., and Menant, F., 'Crédit rural et endettement paysan dans l'Italie communale', in Berthe (ed.), *Endettement paysan et crédit rural dans l'Europe médiévale et moderne*, 35–67.

Given-Wilson, C., 'Wealth and credit, public and private: the earls of Arundel, 1306–1397', *English Historical Review*, 106 (1991), 1–26.

Guinnane, T.W., 'Cooperatives as information machines: German credit cooperatives, 1883–1914', *Journal of Economic History*, 61 (2001), 366–89.

Hanawalt, B.A., *Crime and conflict in English communities, 1300–1349* (Cambridge, Mass., 1979).

Haren, M., *Sin and society in fourteenth-century England: a study of the* Memoriale Presbiterorum (Oxford, 2000).

Harvey, B., *Wesminster Abbey and its estates in the middle ages* (Oxford, 1977).

Helmholz, R.H., 'Usury and the English church courts', *Speculum*, 61 (1986), 364–80.

Herlihy, D., *Medieval and Renaissance Pistoia: the social history of an Italian town, 1200–1430* (New Haven and London, 1967).

Hoffman, P.T., Postel-Vinay, G., and Rosenthal, J.-L., *Priceless markets: the political economy of credit in Paris, 1660–1870* (Chicago, 2000).

Holderness, B.A., 'The clergy as moneylenders in England, 1550–1700', in R. O'Day and F. Heal (eds.), *Princes and paupers in the English church* (Leicester, 1981), 195–209.

Holderness, B.A., 'Credit in English rural society before the nineteenth century, with special reference to the period 1650–1720', *Agricultural History Review*, 24 (1976), 97–109.

Holderness, B.A., 'Credit in a rural community, 1660–1800', *Midland History*, 3 (1975), 94–116.

Jenks, S., 'The lay subsidies and the state of the English economy', *Vierteljahrschrift für Sozial- und Wirtschaftsgeschichte*, 85 (1998), 1–39.

Jones, G.P., 'Some sources of loans and credit in Cumbria before the use of banks', *Transactions of the Cumberland and Westmorland Antiquarian and Archaeological Society*, 75 (1975), 275–92.

Jordan, W.C., *The Great Famine: northern Europe in the early fourteenth century* (Princeton, N.J., 1996).

Kermode, J., *Medieval merchants: York, Beverley and Hull in the later middle ages* (Cambridge, 1998).

Kershaw, I., 'The Great Famine and agrarian crisis in England, 1315–1322', in R.H. Hilton (ed.), *Peasants, knights and heretics* (Cambridge, 1976), 85–132.

Kew, J.E., 'Mortgages in mid-Tudor Devonshire', *Report and Transactions of the Devonshire Association*, 99 (1967), 165–79.

Kitsikopoulos, H., 'Standards of living and capital formation in pre-plague England: a peasant budget model', *Economic History Review*, 53 (2000), 237–61.

Kowaleski, M., *Local markets and regional trade in medieval Exeter* (Cambridge, 1995).

Lambrecht, T., 'Money lending in rural Flanders, 1680–1800', paper presented at the CORN conference on Credit and the Rural Economy in Europe, *c.*1100–1800, Ghent, March 2003.

Laslett, P., *The world we have lost—further explored* (London, 1983).

Lee, J.S., *Cambridge and its economic region, 1450–1560* (Hatfield, 2005).

Lewin, M., *Russian peasants and Soviet power: a study of collectivization* (London, 1968).

McIntosh, M.K., *Autonomy and community: the royal manor of Havering, 1200–1500* (Cambridge, 1986).

McIntosh, M.K., 'The benefits and drawbacks of *femme sole* status in England, 1300–1630', *Journal of British Studies*, 44 (2005), 410–38.

McIntosh, M.K., 'Money-lending on the periphery of London, 1300–1600', *Albion*, 20 (1988), 557–71.

McIntosh, M.K., *Working women in English society, 1300–1620* (Cambridge, 2005).

McLaughlin, T.P, 'The teaching of the canonists on usury (XII, XIII and XIV centuries)', *Mediaeval Studies*, 1 (1939), 81–147.

McNall, C., 'The business of statutory debt registries, 1283–1307', in Schofield and Mayhew (eds.), *Credit and debt*, 68–88.

Maddicott, J.R., 'The English peasantry and the demands of the Crown, 1294–1341', in T.H. Aston (ed.), *Landlords, peasants and politics in medieval England* (Cambridge, 1987), 285–359

Marx, K., *Capital, Volume III* (Harmondsworth, 1981)

Masschaele, J., *Peasants, merchants and markets: inland trade in England, 1150–1350* (Basingstoke and London, 1997).

Mate, M., 'The indebtedness of Canterbury Cathedral Priory, 1215–1295', *Economic History Review*, 26 (1973), 183–97.

Mate, M., 'The role of gold coinage in the English economy, 1338–1400', *Numismatic Chronicle*, 18 (1978), 126–41.

Mayhew, N.J., 'Coinage and money in England, 1086–*c.*1500', in Wood (ed.), *Medieval money matters*, 72–86.

Mayhew, N.J., 'Modelling medieval monetisation', in Britnell and Campbell (eds.), *A commercialising economy*, 55–77.

Mayhew, N., 'Money in the late medieval countryside: Britain', in P. Delogu and S. Sorda (eds.), *La Moneta in ambiente rurale nell'Italia tardomedioevale. Atti dell'incontro di studio Roma 21–22 Settembre 2000*, Instituto Italiano di Numismatica (Rome, 2002), 5–26.

Mayhew, N.J., 'Population, money supply, and the velocity of circulation in England, 1300–1700', *Economic History Review*, 47 (1995), 238–57.

Menant, F., 'Niveaux et réseaux du crédit dans les campagnes de l'Italie communale, XIIe–XIIIe siècles', paper presented at the CORN conference on Credit and the Rural Economy in Europe, *c.*1100–1800, Ghent, March 2003.

Menant, F., 'Notaires et crédit à Bergame à l'époque communale', in Menant and Redon (eds.), *Notaires et crédit*, 31–54.

Menant, F., and Redon, O. (eds.), *Notaires et crédit dans l'occident méditerranéen médiéval* (Rome, 2004).

Miller, E., *The abbey and bishopric of Ely: the social history of an ecclesiastical estate from the tenth century to the early fourteenth century* (Cambridge, 1951).

Morduch, J., 'The microfinance promise', *Journal of Economic Literature*, 37 (1999), 1569–614.

Morduch, J., 'The microfinance schism', *World Development*, 28 (2000), 617–29.

Muldrew, C., *The economy of obligation: the culture of credit and social relations in early modern England* (Basingstoke and London, 1998).

Mundill, R.R., *England's Jewish solution: experiment and expulsion, 1262–1290* (Cambridge, 1998).

Munro, J.H., 'Wage-stickiness, monetary changes, and real incomes in late medieval England and the Low Countries, 1300–1500: did money matter?', *Research in Economic History*, 21 (2003), 185–297.

Nightingale, P., 'The English parochial clergy as investors and creditors in the first half of the fourteenth century', in Schofield and Mayhew (eds.), *Credit and debt*, 89–105.

Nightingale, P., 'Monetary contraction and mercantile credit in later medieval England', *Economic History Review*, 43 (1990), 560–75.

Nightingale, P., 'Money and credit in the economy of late medieval England', in Wood (ed.), *Medieval money matters*, 51–71.

Nightingale, P., 'Norwich, London, and the regional integration of Norfolk's economy in the first half of the fourteenth century', in J.A. Galloway (ed.), *Trade, urban hinterlands and market integration, c.1300–1600*, Centre for Metropolitan History Working Papers Series, No. 3 (London, 2000), 83–101.

Ormrod, W.M., 'The crown and the English economy, 1290–1348', in Campbell (ed.), *Before the Black Death*, 149–83.

Page, F.M., 'The customary poor law of three Cambridgeshire manors', *Cambridge Historical Journal*, 3 (1929), 225–33.

Page, F.M., *The estates of Crowland Abbey: a study in manorial organisation* (Cambridge, 1934).

Palliser, D.M. (ed.), *The Cambridge urban history of Britain, Volume I: 600–1540* (Cambridge, 2000).

Palmer, R.C., *English law in the age of the Black Death, 1348–1381: a transformation of governance and law* (Chapel Hill, 1993).

Parkin, K., 'Courts and the community: reconstructing the fourteenth-century peasant society of Wisbech Hundred, Cambridgeshire, from manor court rolls', Ph.D. thesis (Leicester, 1998).

Pelaquier, E., 'Les mutations foncières à Saint-Victor-de-la-Coste à travers la pratique notariale (1661–1799)', in J.-L. Laffont (ed.), *Le notaire, le paysan et la terre dans la France méridionale à l'époque moderne* (Toulouse, 1999), 131–59.

Phillips, J.L., 'Collaboration and litigation in two Suffolk manor courts, 1289–1364', Ph.D. thesis (Cambridge, 2005).

Pimsler, M., 'Solidarity in the medieval village? The evidence of personal pledging at Elton, Huntingdonshire', *Journal of British Studies*, 17 (1977), 1–11.

Poole, A., 'Debt in the Cranbrook region in the late seventeenth century', *Archaeologia Cantiana*, 123 (2003), 81–93.

Poos, L.R., 'The rural population of Essex in the later middle ages', *Economic History Review*, 38 (1985), 515–30.

Poos, L.R., Razi, Z., and Smith, R.M., 'The population history of medieval English villages: a debate on the use of manor court records', in Razi and Smith (eds.), *Medieval society and the manor court*, 298–367.

Postan, M.M., 'Credit in medieval trade', in Postan, *Medieval trade and finance*, 1–27.

Postan, M.M., 'Medieval agrarian society in its prime: England', in M.M. Postan (ed.), *The Cambridge economic history of Europe, Vol. I: the agrarian life of the middle ages* (2nd edn., Cambridge, 1966), 548–632.

Postan, M.M., *Medieval trade and finance* (Cambridge, 1973).

Postan, M.M., 'Private financial instruments in medieval England', in Postan, *Medieval trade and finance*, 28–64.

Postel-Vinay, G., 'Les relations de crédit dans les campagnes en France et en Angleterre, 1600–1800', in J. Marseille (ed.), *La terre et les paysans en France, 1600–1800* (Paris, 1998), 143–60.

Postles, D., 'An English small town in the later middle ages: Loughborough', *Urban History*, 20 (1993), 7–29.

Postles, D., 'Personal pledging in manorial courts in the later middle ages', *Bulletin of the John Rylands Library*, 75 (1993), 65–78.

Poulsen, B., 'Rural credit and land market in the Duchy of Schleswig *c.*1450–1660', in B.J.P. van Bavel and P. Hoppenbrouwers (eds.), *Landholding and land transfer in the North Sea area (late middle ages–19th century)* (Turnhout, 2004), 203–17.

Prestwich, M., 'Currency and the economy of early fourteenth-century England', in N.J. Mayhew (ed.), *Edwardian monetary affairs*, British Archaeological Reports, 35 (Oxford, 1977), 45–58.

Pugh, R.B., 'Some mediaeval moneylenders', *Speculum*, 43 (1968), 274–89.

Raftis, J.A., *Peasant economic development within the English manorial system* (Stroud, 1997).

Ravensdale, J., *Liable to floods: village landscape on the edge of the fens, AD 450–1850* (Cambridge, 1974).

Ravensdale, J., 'Population changes and the transfer of customary land on a Cambridgeshire manor in the fourteenth century', in Smith (ed.), *Land, kinship and life-cycle*, 197–225.

Razi, Z., 'Family, land and the village community in later medieval England', *Past & Present*, 93 (1981), 3–36.

Razi, Z., *Life, marriage and death in a medieval parish: economy, society and demography in Halesowen, 1270–1400* (Cambridge, 1980).

Razi, Z., 'The myth of the immutable English family', *Past & Present*, 140 (1993), 3–44.

Razi, Z., 'The Toronto school's reconstitution of medieval peasant society: a critical view', *Past and Present*, 85 (1979), 141–57.

Razi, Z., and Smith, R.M., 'The origins of the English manorial court rolls as a written record: a puzzle', in Razi and Smith (eds.), *Medieval society and the manor court*, 36–68.

Razi, Z., and Smith, R.M. (eds.), *Medieval society and the manor court* (Oxford, 1996).

Redon, O., 'Conclusions', in Menant and Redon (eds.), *Notaires et crédit*, 337–48.

Reed, M., 'Markets and fairs in medieval Buckinghamshire', *Records of Buckinghamshire*, 20 (1975–8), 563–85.

Reyerson, K., and Drendel, J. (eds.), *Urban and rural communities in medieval France: Provence and Languedoc, 1000–1500* (Leiden, 1998).

Richardson, H.G., 'The parish clergy of the thirteenth and fourteenth centuries', *Transactions of the Royal Historical Society*, 3rd series, 6 (1912), 89–128.

Rosenthal, J.-L., 'Rural credit markets and aggregate shocks: the experience of Nuits St George, 1756–1776', *Journal of Economic History*, 54 (1994), 288–306.

Rowell, T.A., 'Sedge (*Claudium mariscus*) in Cambridgeshire : its use and production since the seventeenth century', *Agricultural History Review*, 34 (1986), 140–8.

Salzman, L.F., *English trade in the Middle Ages* (Oxford, 1931; repr. 1964).

Schofield, P.R., 'Access to credit in the early fourteenth-century English countryside', in Schofield and Mayhew (eds.), *Credit and debt*, 106–26.

Schofield, P.R., 'Credit and the peasant land market in the medieval English countryside', in Cavaciocchi (ed.), *Il mercato della terra*, 785–96.

Schofield, P.R., 'Dearth, debt and the local land market in a late thirteenth-century village community', *Agricultural History Review*, 45 (1997), 1–17.

Schofield, P.R., 'L'endettement et le crédit dans la campagne anglaise au moyen âge', in Berthe (ed.), *Endettement paysan et crédit rural dans l'Europe médiévale et moderne*, 69–97.

Schofield, P.R., 'Intestat et pratique testamentaire des paysans en Angleterre et pays de Galles au XIIIe siècle et au début du XIVe siècle', in N. Vivier (ed.), *Ruralité française et britannique XIIIe–XXe siècles. Approches comparées* (Rennes, 2005), 207–18.

Schofield, P.R., 'Manorial court rolls and the peasant land market in eastern England, *c.*1250–*c.*1350: sources and issues', in Feller and Wickham (eds.), *Le marché de la terre*, 237–71.

Schofield, P.R., *Peasant and community in medieval England, 1200–1500* (Basingstoke, 2003).

Schofield, P.R., 'Peasants and contract in the thirteenth century: village elites and the land market in eastern England', forthcoming.

Schofield, P.R., 'Peasants and the manor court: gossip and litigation in a Suffolk village at the close of the thirteenth century', *Past & Present*, 159 (1998), 3–42.

Schofield, P.R., 'The social economy of the medieval village in the early fourteenth century', *Economic History Review*, 61 (2008), 38–63.

Schofield P.R., and Mayhew, N.J. (eds.), *Credit and debt in medieval England c.1180–c.1350* (Oxford, 2002).

Seabourne, G., *Royal regulation of loans and sales in medieval England: 'monkish superstition and civil tyranny'* (Woodbridge, 2003).

Shanin, T., *Russia as a 'developing society': the roots of otherness: Russia's turn of century, Volume I* (New Haven and London, 1985).

Smail, D.L., *The consumption of justice: emotions, publicity, and legal culture in Marseille, 1264–1423* (Ithaca, 2003).

Smail, D.L., 'Notaries, courts, and the legal culture of late medieval Marseille', in Reyerson and Drendel (eds.), *Urban and rural communities*, 23–50.

Smith, R.M., 'The English peasantry, 1250–1650', in T. Scott (ed.), *The peasantries of Europe from the fourteenth to the eighteenth centuries* (London and New York, 1998), 339–71.

Smith, R.M., 'Families and their land in an area of partible inheritance: Redgrave, Suffolk 1260–1320', in Smith (ed.), *Land, kinship and life-cycle*, 135–96.

Smith, R.M., 'A periodic market and its impact on a manorial community: Botesdale, Suffolk, and the manor of Redgrave, 1280–1300', in Razi and Smith (eds.), *Medieval society and the manor court*, 450–81.

Smith, R.M., 'Some thoughts on "hereditary" and "proprietary" rights in land under customary law in thirteenth and early fourteenth century England', *Law and History Review*, 1 (1983), 95–128.

Smith, R.M. (ed.), *Land, kinship and life-cycle* (Cambridge, 1984).

Soldevila Temporal, X., 'Credit and debt litigation in medieval Catalonia (ca. 1300)', paper presented at a conference on Banking, Credit and Finance in Late Medieval and Renaissance Europe, Queen Mary, University of London, 2004.

Spufford, M., *Contrasting communities: English villagers in the sixteenth and seventeenth centuries* (Cambridge, 1974).

Spufford, P., 'Credit in rural England before the advent of country banks', in *Banchi pubblici, banchi privati e monti di pietà nell'Europa preindustriale*, Atti della Società Ligure di Storia Patria, new series, Vol. XXXI (Genoa, 1991), 895–911.

Spufford, P., 'Long-term rural credit in sixteenth- and seventeenth-century England: the evidence of probate accounts', in T. Arkell, N. Evans, and N. Goose (eds.), *When death us do part: understanding and interpreting the probate records of early modern England*, Local Population Studies Supplement (Oxford, 2000), 213–28.

Sreenivasan, G.P., *The peasants of Ottobeuren, 1487–1726: a rural society in early modern Europe* (Cambridge, 2004).

Stacey, R.C. 'Jewish lending and the medieval English economy', in Britnell and Campbell (eds.), *A commercialising economy*, 78–101.

Stevens, M.F., 'Race, gender and wealth in a medieval Welsh borough: access to capital, market participation, and status in Ruthin, 1312–1322' Ph.D. thesis (Aberystwyth, 2005).

Stokes, H.P., *Studies in Anglo-Jewish history* (Edinburgh, 1913).

Stone, D.J., 'The consumption of field crops in late medieval England', in C.M. Woolgar, D. Serjeantson, and T. Waldron (eds.), *Food in medieval England: diet and nutrition* (Oxford, 2006), 11–26.

Swanson, R.N., *Church and society in late medieval England* (Oxford, 1989).

Swanson, R.N., 'Clergy and manorial society in late medieval Staffordshire', *Staffordshire Studies*, 5 (1993), 13–34.

Swanson, R.N., 'Profits, priests and people', in C. Burgess and E. Duffy (eds.), *The parish in late medieval England*, Harlaxton Medieval Studies XV (Donnington, 2006), 146–59.

Tawney, R.H., *The agrarian problem in the sixteenth century* (London, 1912).

Tompkins, M., 'Peasant society in a midlands manor, Great Horwood, 1400–1600', Ph.D. thesis (Leicester, 2006).

Toch, M., 'Geld und Kredit in einer spätmittelalterlichen Landschaft: zu einem unbeachteten hebräischen Schuldenregister aus Niederbayern (1329–1332)', *Deutsches Archiv für Erforchsung des Mittelalters*, 38 (1982), 499–550.

Tringham, N.J., 'The parochial visitation of Tarvin (Cheshire) in 1317', *Northern History*, 38 (2001), 197–220.

Udry, C., 'Credit markets in northern Nigeria: credit as insurance in a rural economy', *World Bank Economic Review*, 4 (1990), 251–69.

Unwin, G., 'London tradesmen and their creditors', in G. Unwin, *Finance and trade under Edward III* (Manchester, 1918), 19–34.

The Victoria history of the county of Buckingham, ed. W. Page (4 vols. to date; London, 1905–).

The Victoria history of the county of Cambridge and the Isle of Ely, ed. L.F. Salzman et al. (10 vols., London, 1938–2002).

Wernham, M., *La communauté juive de Salon-de-Provence d'apres les actes notaries, 1391–1435* (Toronto, 1987).

Whittle, J., *The development of agrarian capitalism: land and labour in Norfolk, 1440–1580* (Oxford, 2000).

Whittle, J., 'Individualism and the family–land bond: a reassessment of land transfer patterns among the English peasantry, *c.*1270–1580', *Past & Present*, 160 (1998), 25–63.

Whittle, J., and Yates, M., '"*Pays réel* or *pays légal*"? Contrasting patterns of land tenure and social structure in eastern Norfolk and western Berkshire, 1450–1600', *Agricultural History Review*, 48 (2000), 1–26.

Wood, D., *Medieval economic thought* (Cambridge, 2002).

Wood, D. (ed.), *Medieval money matters* (Oxford, 2004).

Zell, M., 'Credit in the pre-industrial English woollen industry', *Economic History Review*, 49 (1996), 667–91.

Zerner, M., 'Introduction', in Menant and Redon (eds.), *Notaires et crédit*, 3–5.

Index

Printed and bound by CPI Group (UK) Ltd, Croydon, CR0 4YY

16/09/2026

14963460-0002